Benito Mussolini teaches the stiff-legged goose step to high-ranking Fascist officers in Rome in January 1938. Obsessed with military trappings and determined to build an empire, Mussolini committed Italy to a "Pact of Steel" with Nazi Germany and in 1940 dragged his country into a war that it was fatally unprepared to fight.

ITALY AT WAR

TIME
LIFE ®
BOOKS

Other Publications:
PLANET EARTH
COLLECTOR'S LIBRARY OF THE CIVIL WAR
LIBRARY OF HEALTH
CLASSICS OF THE OLD WEST
THE EPIC OF FLIGHT
THE GOOD COOK
THE SEAFARERS
THE ENCYCLOPEDIA OF COLLECTIBLES
THE GREAT CITIES
HOME REPAIR AND IMPROVEMENT
THE WORLD'S WILD PLACES
THE TIME-LIFE LIBRARY OF BOATING
HUMAN BEHAVIOR
THE ART OF SEWING
THE OLD WEST
THE EMERGENCE OF MAN
THE AMERICAN WILDERNESS
THE TIME-LIFE ENCYCLOPEDIA OF GARDENING
LIFE LIBRARY OF PHOTOGRAPHY
THIS FABULOUS CENTURY
FOODS OF THE WORLD
TIME-LIFE LIBRARY OF AMERICA
TIME-LIFE LIBRARY OF ART
GREAT AGES OF MAN
LIFE SCIENCE LIBRARY
THE LIFE HISTORY OF THE UNITED STATES
TIME READING PROGRAM
LIFE NATURE LIBRARY
LIFE WORLD LIBRARY
FAMILY LIBRARY:
    HOW THINGS WORK IN YOUR HOME
    THE TIME-LIFE BOOK OF THE FAMILY CAR
    THE TIME-LIFE FAMILY LEGAL GUIDE
    THE TIME-LIFE BOOK OF FAMILY FINANCE

This volume is one of a series that chronicles
in full the events of the Second World War.
Previous books in the series include:

Prelude to War	The Resistance
Blitzkrieg	The Battle of the Bulge
The Battle of Britain	The Road to Tokyo
The Rising Sun	Red Army Resurgent
The Battle of the Atlantic	The Nazis
Russia Besieged	Across the Rhine
The War in the Desert	War under the Pacific
The Home Front: U.S.A.	War in the Outposts
China-Burma-India	The Soviet Juggernaut
Island Fighting	Japan at War
The Italian Campaign	The Mediterranean
Partisans and Guerrillas	Battles for Scandinavia
The Second Front	The Secret War
Liberation	Prisoners of War
Return to the Philippines	The Commandos
The Air War in Europe	The Home Front: Germany

WORLD WAR II · TIME-LIFE BOOKS · ALEXANDRIA, VIRGINIA

61150

BY HENRY ADAMS
AND THE EDITORS OF TIME-LIFE BOOKS

ITALY AT WAR

Time-Life Books Inc.
is a wholly owned subsidiary of
TIME INCORPORATED

Founder: Henry R. Luce 1898-1967

Editor-in-Chief: Henry Anatole Grunwald
President: J. Richard Munro
Chairman of the Board: Ralph P. Davidson
Executive Vice President: Clifford J. Grum
Chairman, Executive Committee: James R. Shepley
Editorial Director: Ralph Graves
Group Vice President, Books: Joan D. Manley
Vice Chairman: Arthur Temple

TIME-LIFE BOOKS INC.

Editor: George Constable
Executive Editor: George Daniels
Board of Editors: Dale M. Brown, Thomas H. Flaherty Jr.,
Martin Mann, Philip W. Payne, John Paul Porter,
Gerry Schremp, Gerald Simons, Nakanori Tashiro,
Kit van Tulleken
Planning Director: Edward Brash
Art Director: Tom Suzuki
   Assistant: Arnold C. Holeywell
Director of Administration: David L. Harrison
Director of Operations: Gennaro C. Esposito
Director of Research: Carolyn L. Sackett
   Assistant: Phyllis K. Wise
Director of Photography: Dolores Allen Littles

President: Carl G. Jaeger
Executive Vice Presidents: John Steven Maxwell,
David J. Walsh
Vice Presidents: George Artandi, Stephen L. Bair,
Peter G. Barnes, Nicholas Benton, John L. Canova,
Beatrice T. Dobie, Carol Flaumenhaft,
James L. Mercer, Herbert Sorkin, Paul R. Stewart

WORLD WAR II

Editor: Thomas H. Flaherty Jr.
Senior Editors: Anne Horan, Henry Woodhead
Designer: Herbert H. Quarmby
Chief Researcher: Philip Brandt George

Editorial Staff for *Italy at War*
Picture Editor: Peggy L. Sawyer
Text Editors: Paul N. Mathless, Robert Menaker,
Richard Murphy
Writers: Patricia C. Bangs, Donald Davison Cantlay,
Richard D. Kovar
Researchers: Reginald H. Dickerson, Margaret Gray,
Jane S. Hanna, Trudy W. Pearson, Marta Ann
Sanchez, Jayne T. Wise, Paula York-Soderlund
Copy Coordinators: Ann Bartunek, Allan Fallow,
Elizabeth Graham, Barbara F. Quarmby
Art Assistant: Mikio Togashi
Picture Coordinator: Betty Hughes Weatherley
Editorial Assistant: Andrea E. Reynolds

Special Contributor:
David Bridges (translations)

Editorial Operations
Production Director: Feliciano Madrid
   Assistants: Peter A. Inchauteguiz,
   Karen A. Meyerson
Copy Processing: Gordon E. Buck
Quality Control Director: Robert L. Young
   Assistant: James J. Cox
   Associates: Daniel J. McSweeney,
   Michael G. Wight
Art Coordinator: Anne B. Landry
Copy Room Director: Susan Galloway Goldberg
   Assistants: Celia Beattie, Ricki Tarlow

Correspondents: Elisabeth Kraemer (Bonn); Margot
Hapgood, Dorothy Bacon (London); Susan Jonas,
Lucy T. Voulgaris (New York); Maria Vincenza Aloisi,
Josephine du Brusle (Paris); Ann Natanson (Rome).
Valuable assistance was also provided by: Judy
Aspinall (London); Christina Lieberman (New York);
Mimi Murphy, June Taboroff, Ann Wise (Rome).

The Author: CAPTAIN HENRY H. ADAMS, USN (Ret.),
served aboard the destroyer U.S.S. *Owen* in the major
campaigns of the central Pacific. After the War he
taught naval history at the U.S. Naval Academy in An-
napolis, Maryland, and later chaired the English Department at Illinois State University. He has been a
consultant on seven previous volumes in the Time-
Life Books World War II series, including *The Battle of
the Atlantic* and *The Mediterranean.* He is the author
of *Harry Hopkins: A Biography* and a four-volume series on the War—*Years of Deadly Peril, 1942: The
Year That Doomed the Axis, Years of Expectation* and
Years to Victory.

The Consultants: COLONEL JOHN R. ELTING, USA (Ret.),
a military historian, is the author of *The Battle of
Bunker's Hill, The Battles of Saratoga, Military History
and Atlas of the Napoleonic Wars* and, for the Time-
Life Books World War II series, *Battles for Scandina-
via.* A former Associate Professor of Military Art and
Engineering at West Point, he was associate editor of
The West Point Atlas of American Wars.

EMILIANA NOETHER, Professor of History at the University of Connecticut, holds a doctorate in modern Italian history from Columbia University and has completed two Fulbright senior research fellowships in
Italy. A longtime editor of the Italian section of *The
American Historical Review,* she is an officer of the
Society for Italian Historical Studies. Her writings include numerous articles, a chapter on Italian intellec-
tuals in *Modern Italy: A Topical History Since 1861,*
and *Seeds of Italian Nationalism, 1700-1815.*

Library of Congress Cataloguing in Publication Data

Adams, Henry Hitch, 1917-
   Italy at war.

   (World War II)
   Bibliography: p.
   Includes index.
   1. World War, 1939-1945—Italy. 2. Mussolini,
Benito, 1883-1945. 3. Fascism—Italy. 4. Italy—
History—1922-1945.   I. Time-Life Books.
II. Title.   III. Series.
D763.I8A535   940.53'45   82-3182
ISBN 0-8094-3425-3
ISBN 0-8094-3424-5 (lib. bdg.)
ISBN 0-8094-3423-7 (retail ed.)

For information about any Time-Life book, please write:

Reader Information
Time-Life Books
541 North Fairbanks Court
Chicago, Illinois 60611

CHAPTERS

1: Vainglorious Bid for Empire 22
2: Cracks in the Grand Façade 52
3: Calamity on Foreign Fields 90
4: A Nation on the Brink 132
5: Surrender without Peace 154

PICTURE ESSAYS

Building a Fascist Nation 6
A Dictator's Private World 42
Flaws of a Proud Air Force 70
Mobilizing the Home Front 106
Eastward to the Don 118
Campaign of Fear 144
Trapped between Enemies 172
Fires of Insurrection 186

Bibliography 202
Picture Credits 203
Acknowledgments 204
Index 205

CONTENTS

BUILDING A FASCIST NATION

Civilian war volunteers and Fascist militiamen wearing berets and neckerchiefs mob a smiling Benito Mussolini and his police escort at a Rome rally in 1934.

THE TIMELY EMERGENCE OF A NEW CAESAR

In 1939 the conservative *Manchester Guardian* called him "the greatest statesman of our times." Winston Churchill, after a visit to Rome in 1927, declared that "anyone could see he thought of nothing but the lasting good of the Italian people." And a few years earlier, the fledgling German politician Adolf Hitler had written: "I have the keenest admiration for the great man who governs south of the Alps."

From a distance, at least, the man Italians called the Duce—the Leader—seemed to deserve such unrestrained praise. In the troubled 1920s and early 1930s, while other Europeans fiercely pursued the domestic and foreign quarrels that were the legacies of World War I, Prime Minister Benito Mussolini imposed social order at home and gave Italy a respected voice in the councils of Europe.

To revive the economy of his war-ravaged country, the muscular little man with the aggressively prominent chin squeezed surpluses out of deficits, created new towns and jobs with a public-works program unrivaled on the Continent, and put his own brawny back into a campaign to increase grain output. With one diplomatic stroke, the Lateran Accords of 1929, he restored to the Catholics of Italy the Church that previous governments had kept isolated for 60 years. And in ringing, Caesarian speeches he instilled in Italians a pride in their heritage and confidence in their future.

The people responded with zeal. They pasted Mussolini's picture next to their household Madonnas and prized as holy relics the spades and pickaxes he wielded in ceremonial labors all over the land. They commemorated his diplomatic victories by raising triumphal arches, and a leading churchman called him "a genius of government given to Italy by God."

Only a minority of Italians seemed to care that Mussolini and his Fascist Party had replaced democracy with dictatorship and imbued the nation with a mania for the trappings of war. Few of those who chanted "Duce! Duce!" at a National Rally of War Volunteers in June 1934 realized they were about to follow their leader down a path of foreign adventurism to world war and national ruin.

Rome's Piazza dell'Esedra is illuminated with a floodlit M for Mussolini to honor the Duce's good-will visit to Nazi Germany in September 1937.

Framed by ditchdiggers' spades, Mussolini in 1939 dedicates the tower of the new town of Pomezia, built on land reclaimed from the Pontine Marshes.

Bare-chested, and goggled against flying chaff, Mussolini stacks wheat to stimulate Italy's "Battle of the Grain."

The Duce ceremoniously sows grain in a newly plowed furrow to mark the completion of a reclamation project.

SETTING AN EXAMPLE OF TOIL AND SWEAT

Unemployment, rural poverty, a crushing national debt—these ills and more racked Italy when Mussolini took office on October 28, 1922. But the new Prime Minister promised, "Everything that is now wrong will be well," and gradually his driving energy and roughshod approach to bureaucratic inertia proved infectious.

"We shall succeed because we shall work," said Mussolini, and no one worked harder—or more visibly—than he did. He spent days touring the provinces, escorted by a claque of blackshirted Fascist Party functionaries, a small army of bodyguards and a train of journalists and photographers. Resplendent in an array of uniforms, he launched massive public-works projects, such as the draining of the Pontine Marshes near Rome to create 3,000 new farms and five agricultural towns.

Mussolini's favorite rural pose displayed him stripped to the waist, his muscles glistening with sweat as he joined farmers in self-help projects like the "Battle of the Grain," by which he sought to reduce Italy's dependence on imported wheat. And in 1932, a decade after he took office, he was able to announce that Italy's farmers, "working with the rhythm imposed by the Fascist regime," had reaped a record wheat crop, 50 per cent greater than those of the years before World War I.

Flanked by Fascist militiamen and driving a powerful Fiat tractor, Mussolini marks out the boundaries for the new village of Aprilia in April of 1936.

11

Standing on the roof of the Palazzo Sereni in Rome, Mussolini strikes the first blow in demolition to clear a route for the Via dell'Impero, the Imperial Way.

A ROMAN REVIVAL IN MARBLE AND CONCRETE

"We Fascists are the exaltation of all that is Roman," Mussolini declaimed, and to set off the ruins of Augustan Rome he destroyed many classical buildings dating from what he labeled the "centuries of decadence." Personally swinging a pick at the pediments of Renaissance palaces, he ordered new imperial parade routes bulldozed through antique alleys and decreed that all roads leading to and from Rome be paved for at least 50 kilometers.

An admirer of monumental architecture but no architect himself, the Duce commissioned the erection of "imperial testimonies" of marble and concrete—among them a new Roman Forum bearing not Caesar's name, but his own.

One of his creations was *Cinecittà*, or Cinema City, a Hollywood-inspired complex of movie sets, theaters and parkland in an architectural style termed Pharaonic. It was completed in 1937, only 15 months after Mussolini laid the cornerstone. Propaganda Minister Galeazzo Ciano dedicated Cinema City to "spreading the spirit and civilization" of Fascism, and all of Italy's propaganda films—as well as 120 comedies—were produced there until it was turned into a refugee camp in 1944.

Fascist leaders, including Mussolini in white suit and cap, admire a model swimming pool at the unfinished Foro Mussolini in 1934.

Mussolini tours the construction site of Cinema City, the modern motion-picture center that he commissioned on the outskirts of Rome.

MAKING PEACE WITH THE CHURCH

Their cassocks emblazoned with campaign medals, the chaplains of Italy's armed forces pass in review behind their Fascist-saluting Chaplain-General in January of 1938.

Nothing endeared Benito Mussolini to the people of Italy or swelled his reputation as a statesman more than his negotiation of the Lateran Accords, a series of treaties signed in the Lateran Palace on February 11, 1929, and ratified that June.

The pen strokes of the Prime Minister and the papal representative, Pietro Cardinal Gasparri, took only a few seconds, but they reversed six decades of hostility between the Roman Catholic Church and the modern Kingdom of Italy, years in which successive Popes had considered themselves prisoners of the state and their followers were barred from participating in national politics as Church members.

The accords recognized the Pope as sovereign of the Vatican City and restored the Church's right to teach religion in the schools and to administer laws governing marriage. In return, Mussolini's regime received worldwide recognition, plus support never before granted by the Church to an Italian government.

In diplomatic uniform and sash, Mussolini celebrates the signing of the Lateran Accords with Cardinal Gasparri (center). Pope Pius XI, who later countersigned the historic treaties, said that Mussolini "has given God back to Italy and Italy back to God."

Chins thrust forward, preschool boys of the Wolf Cubs, Fascist Italy's youngest uniformed militia, stand rigidly at attention during a weekly drill session.

16

NURTURING A CROP OF SCHOOLBOY SOLDIERS

One declared objective of the Fascist Party was "to develop in our citizens, from childhood on, an aptitude for combat and for sacrifice." To provide the blackshirted Fascist militia with trained zealots, members of the party put their sons into uniform, as part of the Fascist Youth, as early as the age of four, to undergo military and political indoctrination.

At the age of eight the youngest boys, or Wolf Cubs, became Ballilla (named for a boy hero of 18th Century Italy) and drilled with nonfiring miniatures of the Army's Model 91 rifle. At 14 they entered the Advance Guards for more training, and at 18 they received full-sized rifles. Finally at 21 those who qualified became party members and pledged their lives to the Duce.

Teenagers in summer uniform march past the tank-studded tower of the state-run Campo Mussolini.

Boys of the Fascist Youth learn how to operate the bolts of their scaled-down Model 91 infantry rifles during required manual-of-arms training in 1930.

THE BOLD UNVEILING OF IMPERIAL AMBITIONS

The year 1934 revealed Benito Mussolini as a modern Caesar bent on creating a new Roman Empire. Until then he had been satisfied to employ the Italian Army in its traditional role of protecting the nation's borders and garrisoning colonies in Africa. But in March of 1934 he made "Italy's natural expansion" the theme of a major address, asserting that Italians had a right and a duty to "civilize" backward nations. Then on the 1st of June he summoned 10,000 Fascist militants to Rome for a National Rally of War Volunteers.

Posturing at Julius Caesar's funeral altar (below), Mussolini spurred the volunteers to cheers by declaring grandiloquently that "Italy's historical objectives can be named in two words: Asia and Africa." Secretly the Duce had selected Ethiopia, located at the mouth of the Red Sea where the two continents meet, for his first imperial conquest. Early the next year he started shipping Army and militia divisions to East Africa.

Blackshirted Fascist militiamen brandish World War I banners and medals as their leader strikes a heroic pose at the 1934 rally in the Roman Forum.

With King Victor Emmanuel in uniform at his side, Mussolini admires a new light tank during maneuvers near the Austrian border in August 1935. The maneuvers served as a reminder, particularly to Germany, that Italy was pledged to defend Austria's independence.

Cheering troops line the rails of the liner Conte Biancamano as it sets sail for Africa in September 1935. To invade Ethiopia while simultaneously guarding the Austrian frontier, Mussolini called up reservists and militia, swelling his Army to almost one million men.

Jubilant Romans celebrate a historic victory by torchlight on the 6th of October, 1935, with signs proclaiming "Aduwa is ours." The Ethiopian town of Aduwa had been the scene of a humiliating defeat in 1896; many Italians considered its recapture a national vindication.

1

The education of a blacksmith's son
Blackshirted bullies with clubs and castor oil
The march that transformed Rome
A man to bring order from chaos
"The crowd is a terrible mistress"
An admiring visitor from Berlin
Erasing the shame of an old defeat
"I am not a collector of deserts"
Cold-shouldered into Hitler's arms
A chance to play power broker at Munich
Loopholes in the Pact of Steel
Watching Nazi victories from the sidelines
Italy thrusts the dagger

As the church bells of Rome pealed 6 o'clock on the evening of June 10, 1940, Benito Mussolini stepped out onto a balcony of the Palazzo Venezia and addressed the crowd in the square below. "An hour marked by destiny," he declared, "is striking in the sky of our country, the hour of irrevocable decisions. We are entering the lists against the plutocratic and reactionary democracies of the West, who have always hindered the advance and often plotted against the very existence of the Italian people."

Thus did Benito Mussolini inform his countrymen and the world that he was taking Italy into war on the side of Germany. Thirty-two Italian divisions were assembling along the French-Italian border from the Mediterranean Sea to the Swiss Alps, preparing to drive on France. Mussolini expected his dramatic pronouncement to evoke an enthusiastic roar of approval; nearly a dozen European nations were in one way or another already embroiled in the War, while for nine months Italy had only watched from the sidelines. But the crowd was curiously subdued. Shouts and cheers usually greeted any speech Mussolini made; this time he was answered with only perfunctory applause. Foreign Minister Galeazzo Ciano, Mussolini's son-in-law, reflected the general feeling when he wrote in his diary that night: "I am sad, very sad. The adventure begins. May God help Italy!"

Mussolini had dragged his country into a war that very few Italians wanted. The civilian population had little interest in the confrontation between Hitler's Germany and the Allies, and the military commanders knew that Italy's armed forces were in no shape to fight.

A few hours earlier, when Mussolini had broken the news to his ministers in the Palazzo Venezia, they had been aghast. Marshal Pietro Badoglio, Chief of the Armed Forces General Staff, spoke for them all when he said that to go to war now was suicide. "We have no arms, no tanks, no airplanes, not even shirts for our soldiers!" he sputtered. But Mussolini would entertain no differences of opinion. Scowling, his face red with anger, he rapped his subordinate in the chest with such force that Badoglio, who was half a head taller than Mussolini, nearly toppled over. "You, Marshal, are not calm enough to judge the situation," Mussolini shouted. "I can assure you that by September, everything will be over." In a quieter voice he continued, "All I need is

VAINGLORIOUS BID FOR EMPIRE

a few thousand dead so that I can sit at the peace conference as a belligerent."

That bald statement summed up Mussolini's real reason for going to war: He wanted prestige and a share in the spoils. At the same time it reflected how dimly he grasped the reality of the situation. Though on the surface it appeared otherwise, Mussolini had chosen a poor moment to open hostilities with Great Britain and France. To be sure, France was all but defeated. Even as Mussolini was haranguing his ministers, the French government and its military leaders were evacuating Paris and preparing to set up a temporary capital farther south. Facing the German Wehrmacht advancing from the northeast, the French nation had its back exposed to Italy.

But the gratuitousness of Mussolini's sudden declaration caused dismay and indignation all over the world. "It is a dagger thrust into a fallen man," said André François-Poncet, French Ambassador to Italy. U.S. President Franklin D. Roosevelt, delivering a commencement address at the University of Virginia a few hours after Mussolini's announcement, used a variation of the same metaphor. "The hand that held the dagger has struck it into the back of its neighbor," Roosevelt declared, his voice ringing with scorn.

Yet the wonder was that Mussolini had waited so long. He was belligerent by nature; and Fascism, the political movement through which he had fought his way to power, was born of the angry feeling that Italy, although it was on the winning side, had been denied its fair portion of the spoils of World War I. Only a nation that did battle, Mussolini believed, could win a place in the international sun. Not for him the pacifism of the League of Nations, that well-intentioned body conceived in the aftermath of World War I in the hope that disputes could be settled by arbitration and diplomacy rather than by force. "Words are beautiful things, but rifles, guns, ships and airplanes are still more beautiful," Mussolini had said early in the 1930s. "When tomorrow dawns, the spectacle of our armed forces will reveal to the world the calm and warlike countenance of Fascist Italy."

But Mussolini was also capricious, given to changing his mind when facing a crisis. His gambler's disposition impelled him, again and again, to place his bets on what he took to be the winning side, often in defiance of common

sense. In the present instance, unfortunately for himself and for the people he led, he had sorely underestimated the dimensions of the fight ahead. Worse, he had misjudged the German Führer, Adolf Hitler, the man whose alliance he had so earnestly sought. The result was to be tragic for Mussolini and for his nation. Far from gaining the rewards that Mussolini coveted, Italy was to be prostrated under the boot of the other belligerents before the conflict was done.

Because for two decades he held the country tightly in the grip of his personal dictatorship, the story of Italy at war is largely the story of Benito Mussolini and his miscalculated reach for empire.

For a man who was to occupy such a conspicuous place on the world stage, Benito Mussolini rose from unlikely beginnings. He was born in 1883 in Romagna, an ill-defined region abutting the Adriatic between Florence and Venice. Benito's father, a blacksmith, was a rarity among men of his station: He was literate. His reading had made him an ardent champion of the Socialist Party, which in Italy had organized labor leagues and strove to improve wages and working conditions through public ownership of industry. The elder Mussolini felt special contempt for the House of Savoy, the royal family that had reigned in Italy since 1861, when the nation's unification began. He railed against the successive elected governments that promised reform for Italy's poor yet did nothing to change the status quo. Benito himself parroted with youthful arrogance the ideas he heard voiced by his father. He fought incessantly with his classmates, and at the age of 11 he was expelled from school for stabbing an older boy.

Although in time he curbed his temper sufficiently to graduate with honors and a certificate entitling him to teach in elementary schools, Mussolini saw himself, at 18, facing a world fraught with injustices. He first came to public notice as the editor of *Avanti*, a Socialist daily in Milan. In 1914 he broke with his associates and lost his editor's job over the issue of Italy's role in World War I. Socialist dogma called for strict neutrality in "capitalist wars"; Mussolini advocated an armed neutrality tilted against Austria-Hungary, Italy's neighbor to the north. He soon founded his own newspaper, *Il Popolo d'Italia*, and by 1915 he was urging direct Italian intervention in the conflict. When Italy did go to war, Mussolini served in the Army and was wounded.

The Italy that Mussolini rejoined as a civilian was in a state of financial exhaustion, widespread popular disappointment and festering social unrest. Italians of all classes and regions had expected their nation to share in the spoils of Allied victory. Statesmen had anticipated that Italy would receive a substantial slice of the Habsburg Empire when it was carved up, and enlisted soldiers (who came largely from the peasant class) had gone into battle with vague ideas that they would be rewarded with land. Instead, Italy got slim pickings at the conference table—an outcome its statesmen and peasants alike considered unjust and humiliating. The nation entered the postwar years beset by swarms of problems: unemployment, a succession of ineffective governments, a cost of living that had risen more than 500 per cent since 1914, and a seemingly endless series of industrial, agricultural and municipal strikes.

Political parties sprouted like mushrooms. The Chamber of Deputies, Italy's parliamentary body, comprised representatives of at least a dozen parties—Socialists, Populists, Liberals, Republicans, Radicals and Nationalists, to name the most important. No party had a majority, and none could translate its views into effective policy. In March of

1919 Mussolini used the pages of his newspaper to announce the founding of yet another faction. He simply called a meeting, inviting all comers, and between 100 and 200 restive men turned up. They came from existing parties and from none. Many were discharged—and unemployed—veterans still wearing the uniforms of the Italian Army and lusting for a fight with almost anyone.

Mussolini dubbed his followers the *Fasci di Combattimento,* or "Combat Groups." The word *"fasci"*—which already had the connotation of seditious groups—was destined to stick, and it would come to mean government by dictatorship of the kind Mussolini instituted in Italy. Years later he took great pleasure in recounting that the word had a venerable ancestry that could be traced back to ancient Rome. Attendants, or lictors, had carried bundles of wooden rods called fasces as symbols of their office. Mussolini accordingly adopted the image of the bound rods as the emblem of Fascism and of the state of Italy, and took pleasure in the thought that he was presiding over a revival of the grandeur that was Rome.

At the outset, Mussolini endowed his newborn group with a vague platform that called for universal suffrage, proportional representation and a voice for labor at all levels of

government. There was no real plan for bringing about these reforms, but the men drank toasts and sang patriotic songs. "The important thing," Mussolini told them, "is to come into existence. Now we are a fact. From the fact we will proceed to deeds."

It is indicative of Italy's deeply unsettled condition that during the next three years Mussolini's movement, which formally became a party only in 1921, enrolled more than 300,000 members. Some of them became his personal bodyguards. Using clubs and the forced ingestion of castor oil to intimidate dissidents, they also kept order at unruly Fascist meetings and fomented disorder at the meetings of opposition parties. For those men, organized as *squadristi*, their black shirts became a uniform and a symbol of their muscle, both real and political. Some of them won seats in the Chamber of Deputies, and Mussolini himself laid plans to seize the government.

The year 1922 brought a series of crises that Mussolini was able to exploit. In July a governing coalition fell for the sixth time in three years, and on August 1 the Socialists called a general strike to underscore the government's paralysis. Mussolini gave the government an ultimatum: Either take action against the Socialists and their strike, or the Fascists would do it themselves. When the government remained inert, he was as good as his word. Squads of black-shirted Fascists moved in everywhere and kept vital services in operation; the trains ran, mail was delivered, fields were tilled and factories stayed open. The strike collapsed, a failure that discredited the Socialists—and led Italians by the thousands to look to Mussolini as the man who would bring order out of the nation's chaos.

Luigi Facta, the Prime Minister, considered offering some minor Cabinet posts to Fascists, but Mussolini was after a bigger prize. He told an audience in Naples on October 24, "Either they give us the government or we shall take it by marching on Rome." By the morning of October 28, Black Shirts by the thousands were assembling at four sites within 70 miles of the capital, waiting for orders from Mussolini to proceed.

The first reaction of King Victor Emmanuel III was to proclaim a state of siege, to which Prime Minister Facta strongly objected. By the following morning, the King had reversed his stand. Victor Emmanuel usually had so little to say about the running of the country that he was often overlooked when a crucial decision had to be made. But every now and then he made an unexpected show of authority, and he did so now. Undoubtedly the proclamation of martial law seemed to him to promise more trouble than safety; if the Army were unleashed on the marchers, blood would be shed—and even his throne might be in jeopardy. Victor Emmanuel therefore invited Mussolini to come to Rome and form a government. The March on Rome became a peaceful one. The Black Shirts entered the city, but with few exceptions they did so in orderly fashion, buoyed by the thought that their leader now stood at the head of the national government.

When the moment came to present himself to his monarch, Mussolini demonstrated a contrary independence. Convention dictated morning coat, striped pants and top hat; Mussolini presented himself to the King in the black shirt of the Fascists. He had not even bothered to shave. After the King conferred with his new Prime Minister, the two men appeared together on the royal balcony, where they were cheered by a crowd of 40,000 that had gathered in the piazza in front of the palace. The March on Rome was over, and at 39 Mussolini had become the youngest man in Italian history to hold the rank of Prime Minister. Simultaneously he was recognized as *Duce,* or Leader, a title that had first been bestowed on him years before in a newspaper article and that was his official designation as head of the Fascist Party.

Given the bold manner in which he had seized office, Mussolini seemed restrained as he grasped the instruments of power. Of the 14 ministers on his Cabinet he appointed only three Fascists in addition to himself. The other seats went, in the name of unity, to members of other parties.

Yet Mussolini kept for himself the key posts of Minister of Foreign Affairs and Minister of the Interior. And he was careful to find places for his loyal allies from the March on Rome. One, Cesare Maria De Vecchi, became Undersecretary for Military Pensions. Another, Italo Balbo, who had been an aviator in World War I, was given the job of building an Italian air force (*pages 70-89*). A third was General Emilio De Bono, a career Army officer, who took over the Black Shirts and was to oversee the discipline of the Fascist

Invading the South of France, Italian combat troops sprint past the shell-damaged store of a news vendor in Menton, a border town that was captured during the brief campaign of June 1940. Foreign Minister Galeazzo Ciano wrote in disappointment, "Our troops halted in front of the first French fortification that put up opposition."

25

Party. A fourth, Michele Bianchi, was a close personal friend whom Mussolini had already installed as Secretary General of the party.

These four men, who became known as the Quadrumvirate, were to be the Duce's closest political associates. With them, he set about revamping the internal structure of Italy. He began with a moderate approach to the Chamber of Deputies, giving every appearance that he intended to rule through the parliamentary system. In his maiden speech to the Chamber, he promised to work within the Constitution, to guard civil liberties, to restore domestic order and to put down strikes. He asked for—and received—emergency powers that gave him a free hand in bringing about administrative and fiscal reforms.

During the next few years Mussolini stilled the babel of voices in the Chamber by such measures as dissolving all political parties opposed to Fascism. He neutralized the press by repeatedly seizing editions of opposition newspapers and arresting uncooperative journalists. He formed a national Fascist militia outside the regular military establishment, and snuffed out civil disorder by decreeing capital punishment for attempts at insurrection. He enlisted the interest of youth in the state by requiring that boys aged six to 21 belong to Fascist groups, in which they were trained in the use of arms by militia officers. And in an attempt to create what Fascist theorists called "the corporate state," he brought all business and industry under the aegis of the central government; companies, trade unions and the professions were made responsible to a Minister of Corporations, who appointed executive officers and ruled on contracts, labor disputes and apprenticeship programs.

Mussolini was pleased with the early results of his rule. Speaking in 1926 at an anniversary celebration of the March on Rome, he congratulated "the Italian people, who thirsted to obey, who thirsted for discipline, who wanted to be governed."

It did not go unnoticed that these measures were despotic. University faculty members, recognizing that they had to pay at least lip service to Fascism if they wanted to continue teaching, joked sardonically among themselves that the letters *PNF* on the lapel buttons they wore stood not for *Partito Nazionale Fascista* but *per necessità familiare*—"driven by family need." But whether they liked Mussolini's policies or not, Italians generally agreed that they preferred him to chaos. And by and large the people loved him. He was surrounded by enthusiastic crowds whenever he ventured into the street. Once in Florence he had to flee an adoring mob for his own safety. "Give me a drink," he gasped when he had put himself out of reach. "The crowd is a terrible mistress."

The people, in turn, thought him so fit and strong that he acquired a legendary prowess. On one occasion, when he was visiting Sicily, a newspaper reported that a violent eruption of Mount Etna had miraculously stopped when Mussolini arrived on the scene. The journalist Margherita Sarfatti, one of his mistresses, read the account to him, thinking he would be amused. To her surprise, he found nothing out of the ordinary in the story. "He actually thought," she noted, "that he had helped stem the flow of lava." Farfetched though it was, Mussolini's interpretation of the episode had a certain justice, for he had certainly stemmed the flow of Italy's headlong rush to anarchy.

The Duce also geared the country for war by stepping up production of matériel for the armed forces. In 1933 he put himself in charge of the Ministries of War, Air and Navy. In full-dress uniform he appeared before 2,000 officers to

A squad of Black Shirts burns opposition publications in Rome in 1924. Fascist leaders used these squadristi to terrorize opponents, but the Black Shirts' excesses, which included beatings and murders, led Mussolini to curb their activities and organize them into a better-disciplined national Fascist militia.

Under an arch at Velletri commemorating the 10th anniversary of the 1922 March on Rome, Mussolini (left center) and other veteran Fascist leaders enjoy a moment in the sun.

tell them: "We are becoming, and we shall become still more, a military nation. And, since we are not afraid of the words, let us add: a militarist nation and in the end a warrior nation."

Eventually the Italian Army got a small amount of modern equipment. The Navy launched a program of replacing its obsolete tonnage with sleek, fast ships designed to dominate the Mediterranean. And Mussolini devoted particular attention to the newest branch of the armed services, the Air Force, which received new planes at a rate of 1,250 a year. In July 1933 Italo Balbo, who was now Minister for Air, led a formation of 24 seaplanes across the Atlantic to represent Italy at the Chicago World's Fair. The theme of that fair was "A Century of Progress"; Mussolini trumpeted Balbo's flight as a demonstration of the progress that Fascist Italy had made in a mere decade. At each stop along the way—Orbetello, Amsterdam, Reykjavik and Montreal—the flight received enthusiastic coverage in the press. After the fair in Chicago came a visit to New York City, where Balbo spoke at Madison Square Garden to a crowd composed largely of Italian-Americans. "Be proud that you are Italians," he told them. "Mussolini has ended the era of humiliations."

Indeed he had. By now the Italian leader was winning plaudits from every side. The American journalist Lincoln Steffens wrote that God had asked, "How can I, in a flash, clear up those poor humans?" and in answer had "formed Mussolini out of a rib of Italy." The Archbishop of Canterbury pronounced Mussolini "the only gigantic figure in Europe." British commentators spoke of the "Mussolini miracle." Winston Churchill, Chancellor of the Exchequer, told the Duce in an interview in the early 1930s: "If I were Italian, I am sure that I would have been with you from beginning to end in your victorious struggle." And from Adolf Hitler, who had recently come to power in Germany, Mussolini won that sincerest form of flattery: imitation. Beginning in January 1933, when he was installed as Chancellor, Hitler began to model the German state on Fascist Italy. The youth programs, the subsuming of industry under state control, the ceding of parliamentary power to the executive, even the stiff-armed Fascist salute—all these Adolf Hitler took from Benito Mussolini.

Mussolini's Grand Council, whose job was basically to approve decisions that had already been made, responded to Hitler by paying tribute to "the Fascist movement that is

developing beyond Italy's borders.'' Mussolini himself had vague misgivings. He liked to think the Italian state he had created was unique, and he looked down on Germans as ''dull Teutons'' who wore ''feathers in their hats and hobnailed shoes.'' But by the following year Hitler had attracted so much notice that Mussolini saw fit to receive the upstart leader on a state visit to Italy.

The Führer greeted the Duce at the Lido airport outside Venice on the morning of June 14, 1934, and for two men whose careers were to be so fatefully linked, they got off to a sorry start. Hitler, descending the steps of a Junkers plane, was dismayed to see his waiting host resplendent in a black uniform, with spurred boots, a dagger at his side, a fringed fez on his head and a blaze of gold braid and medals on his chest. Hitler, by contrast, was an unprepossessing sight in a belted yellow raincoat and a civilian suit. He scowled at Ulrich von Hassell, his Ambassador to Rome, and demanded, ''Why didn't you tell me to wear my uniform?''

As for Mussolini, although he played the hospitable host —the band at the airport welcomed Hitler with German marching songs—the contempt he held for his strange-looking guest was subtly manifest. Either by accident or design, as the two heads of government rode into Venice the crowds lining their way chanted ''Duce! Duce!'' and never breathed the name of Hitler.

Lunch at a villa outside Venice did nothing to improve the spirit of either man; Hitler's Foreign Minister, who had accompanied the Führer, reported that they ''barked at each other like two mastiffs.'' Mussolini, who could speak some German, insisted on talking without an interpreter—a show of braggadocio that did the conversation more harm than good, for his heavily accented and ungrammatical use of the langage was almost incomprehensible to his visitor. Listeners outside the room could hear them shouting, and the word ''Österreich'' was frequently repeated.

Österreich was Austria, and there was good reason for it to kindle the passions of both men. To Hitler, who was born in Austria, it represented a natural place to expand his Third Reich; to Mussolini it represented a buffer between his country and Germany. When Hitler wrote his famous book, *Mein Kampf,* in 1924, and countless times since, he had made it clear that he aimed at *Anschluss*—political union

In a grand prewar review, a battery of horse-drawn artillery parades smartly past the Victor Emmanuel monument in Rome. The tubes of the cannon, which dated from World War I, had been retracted for towing.

with Austria—claiming that common language and the will of the Austrians themselves warranted joining the two countries. For just as long a time, Mussolini had been publicly on the side of continued Austrian independence; in 1925 he asserted that "Italy would never tolerate such a patent violation" of the post-World War I treaties "as would be constituted by the annexation of Austria to Germany."

More recently Mussolini had given practical evidence of his sentiments; in 1933 he made available $350,000 to develop the Heimwehr, the Austrian Fascist Party. Moreover, he was in accord with France and Britain on the issue; in February of 1934 the three governments issued statements supporting independence for Austria.

Even two more mild-tempered men than Hitler and Mussolini would have been hard put to find a common ground on the Austrian question. As it was, when they left the room, both were visibly angry. Once Hitler had departed for home, Mussolini confided to his wife that the Führer was "a violent man with no self-control, and nothing positive came out of our talks."

Mussolini had badly underestimated his fellow leader. Less than six weeks later, on July 25, he was stunned, along with the rest of the world, to learn that Austrian Chancellor Engelbert Dollfuss had been shot to death in Vienna by a team of Nazis, wearing Austrian Army and police uniforms, who had stormed his office and seized the Chancellery.

For Mussolini the murder was a personal blow; Dollfuss' wife and children were at that moment his houseguests at Riccione, a resort on the Adriatic, and the Chancellor himself had been expected to join them shortly.

But the assassination had serious political implications as well. There could be no mistaking what was behind it, for Dollfuss was resolutely opposed to the *Anschluss* and had recently been imprisoning Nazi agitators for bomb scares and other terrorist tactics. Many Austrian Nazis were émigrés from Germany, and it was obvious that only orders from Hitler could have inspired the attempted *Putsch*.

The take-over failed; by nightfall Dollfuss' Cabinet and Austrian troops had overcome and jailed the plotters. But the episode sent shock waves around the world. Britain and France issued diplomatic protests, and Mussolini was even more emphatic. He announced that he had ordered Italian troops sent to the Austrian border. "We'll show these gentlemen they cannot trifle with Italy," he muttered.

The move was a bluff; all Mussolini actually had done was alert the border garrisons to be on guard. But the bluff paid off; Hitler ceased to speak of *Anschluss*, and he ordered the Austrian Nazis to lie low for a while. Germany, still under the constraints of the Treaty of Versailles, had no armed forces capable of taking on the Italian Army, and Hitler also had to consider that England and France might back up their censure with force. He was not yet prepared to fight.

All Europe breathed a sigh of relief when the Austrian crisis subsided, and Mussolini exulted at having flexed his muscle in the international arena. Now, however, he focused that sense of power on an expansion plan of his own.

The race for foreign territories had occupied most of the major European powers for 400 years. Italy, coming tardily to the race at the end of the 19th Century, had succeeded only in picking up some small holdings in Africa—Libya, Eritrea and Italian Somaliland. The last two were colonies located on the border of Ethiopia, the only African kingdom to have escaped European domination. In 1896, when Mussolini was a boy of 13 and Italy was making another grab for territory, Ethiopian troops had slaughtered 6,000 Italian soldiers at the town of Aduwa in northern Ethiopia and had driven thousands more back across the border into Eritrea. For years afterward "the shame of Aduwa," as it was known, smarted in Italian breasts—not least in Mussolini's. Ever since taking power, he had intended to avenge that national humiliation.

He took the first practical step toward doing so in 1932, when he appointed his old comrade General Emilio De Bono as Minister of Colonies, and dispatched him on a reconnoitering mission to Eritrea. The Duce wanted to know what needed to be done to turn Eritrea into a suitable base for launching an attack on Ethiopia. With De Bono's reports in hand, Mussolini mounted a program to make the Eritrean port of Massawa adequate for troopships, to construct roads that could carry tanks and trucks, to lay out airfields and to build a water supply sufficient to sustain an army.

Mussolini advertised these works as defense measures. And in December 1934, while he was still basking in the glow of having solved the summer's crisis in Austria, a border incident in East Africa played into his hands. Ethiopian tribesmen attacked Italian troops at Wal Wal, an oasis where Ethiopia converged with British Somaliland and Italian Somaliland, and where all travelers through the desert watered. Mussolini demanded a public apology from Ethiopian Emperor Haile Selassie, together with an indemnity of almost $100,000. Selassie, who was European-educated and whose nation in 1923 had won a seat in the League of Nations, was undaunted by Mussolini's bluster; he coolly suggested that their dispute be submitted to arbitration.

But Mussolini was spoiling for a fight; he refused to negotiate and began preparing for war. On February 1, 1935, Mussolini held a grand review of the Fascist militia in the main square of Siena. Later that month he began shipping troops to Eritrea. By the end of May, Italy had nearly one million men under arms.

Mussolini made no secret of what he was up to. The most practical route to Eritrea from Italy was via the British-held Suez Canal, and a million armed men could not pass through that narrow waterway unnoticed. But Britain and the rest of Europe were preoccupied during those months by a worrisome diversion closer to home. On March 16, Hitler summarily announced that Germany was conscripting an army of 36 divisions—in violation of the Versailles Treaty.

In the alarms that followed Hitler's statement, Britain made a heedless move that would influence Mussolini's attitude toward his European neighbors. Without consulting France (which shared with Britain what little strength existed in the League of Nations) or Italy (which at the time of the Dollfuss incident had shown a willingness to take a stand against Germany), Britain now opened negotiations with Hitler's government for a naval agreement to hold the Germans to a navy no larger than 35 per cent of Britain's.

The move was motivated by the fear that Germany might suddenly create a navy, as it was about to do with an army. But it proved a costly mistake. The British proposal in effect rewarded Germany for ignoring one treaty by offering up another. It therefore instilled doubt in the impressionable mind of Mussolini about Britain's resolve, and ultimately it contributed to the failure of England and France to enlist Mussolini as a counterpoise against Germany's designs.

Mussolini soon was too carried away with the excitement of his African venture to be dissuaded from it. That became clear in June, when Britain finally sent its Minister for League of Nations Affairs, Anthony Eden, to Rome to meet with Mussolini. In vain Eden implored the Duce to settle the dispute by diplomacy rather than force; he went so far as to offer to cede some territory in British Somaliland to Italy. Mussolini rejected the offer, scoffing: "I am not a collector of deserts." Eden returned from his mission with a melancholy assessment of the Italian dictator, saying there was "a gloomy fatality about his temper which I fear it may be beyond the power of reasoning to modify."

Through the summer of 1935, Mussolini went on pouring troops into Africa. By September, 12 divisions had been dispatched, and more were mobilizing at home. By then Mussolini was so primed for battle that he had only to wait out the rainy season before giving the order to attack. At the end of the month the rains ceased, and on October 2, Mussolini stood on the balcony of the Palazzo Venezia to announce that, as of the next morning, Italy and Ethiopia were at war.

In a radio broadcast, the Duce couched his declaration in terms that evoked Italian pride. "Here is not just an army marching toward a military objective, but a whole nation, 44 million souls, against whom the blackest injustice has been committed: that of denying them a place in the sun."

A Venetian gondolier and his woman passenger wear gas masks during a prewar air-raid drill. The Italians had used poison gas against Ethiopia, in violation of international law, and they feared retribution.

Bitterly alluding to the outcome of World War I, he cried: "When in 1915 Italy mixed her fate with that of the Allies, how much praise there was from them, how many promises! But after a common victory, these same Allies withheld from Italy all but a few crumbs of the rich colonial loot."

Then, turning to the unforgotten episode at Aduwa, the Duce said, "We have waited patiently with Ethiopia for 40 years." After vowing to pay no heed to whatever measures the rest of Europe might take in reaction, he concluded dramatically: "Fascist Italy, on your feet!" The crowd below him responded with cheers, and Italians across the land rejoiced as they heard his words over loudspeakers in city and village piazzas.

Over the next few days, Mussolini lived in a state of euphoria as he followed reports of his troops' progress. Under the leadership of General De Bono, the soldiers advanced swiftly. In three days they captured Aduwa. Within a week they had penetrated 45 miles into Ethiopian territory, by early November 80 miles. Then, at the city of Makale, General De Bono halted to regroup and secure his supply lines.

In his exhilaration, Mussolini had given little thought to the consequences of his action. Yet Italian guns in Ethiopia effectively sounded the opening shots of World War II. By any reckoning, they set in motion a grim chain of events. They constituted a violation of the League of Nations Covenant by a member nation. Though the League had failed to head off Mussolini's invasion, its members were treaty-bound to take some punitive action, and in doing so they inevitably put a distance between themselves and Italy. That gap widened irrevocably as one crisis generated another in the months and years that followed.

After lengthy diplomatic discussion and some tortuous maneuvering behind the scenes, the League settled on economic sanctions against Italy. The sanctions seemed mild; among them were an arms embargo and a prohibition on financial transactions between Italy and member nations. Significantly, there was no embargo on oil, without which Italy's engines of war could not run, and no closing of the Suez Canal, which would have blocked the passage of reinforcements and supplies to Ethiopia.

Nevertheless, the sanctions damaged an Italian economy already stretched thin by the African adventure. More immediately, the measures gave the Duce a rallying cry: "Italy against the world." He ignored the fact that the League had acted because the integrity of one of its members had been violated. He made it seem instead that the other nations had moved with the express purpose of suffocating Italy. Italians saw themselves as an isolated people; with everyone's hand seemingly against them, they united behind their Duce in his assault on Ethiopia.

Mussolini's only disappointment was De Bono's tactical halt at Makale in November. From his 60-foot-long office in the Palazzo Venezia, with its Renaissance mosaics and reliefs, Mussolini could see no reason for delay; he bombarded his general with orders to get on with the campaign. De Bono dragged his heels. His patience gone, Mussolini relieved De Bono and replaced him with Marshal Pietro Badoglio, Chief of the General Staff.

Badoglio launched a new offensive on January 12, 1936, and there was no stopping him. Using tanks, trucks and planes—matériel unavailable to the Ethiopians—and poison gas, which was outlawed by the Geneva Convention, the Italian forces rolled inexorably across Ethiopia. In four months they advanced 400 miles, and on May 5, Badoglio led them on a triumphant march into Addis Ababa, the capital. Three days earlier, Haile Selassie had fled with his family for England.

Once again the Duce had the exquisite pleasure of addressing an enthusiastic crowd from the balcony over the Piazza Venezia, this time to announce the victory and the establishment of a new Rome. "At last Italy has her empire," he exclaimed. "Raise high your insignia, your weapons and your hearts to salute, after 15 centuries, the reappearance of the Empire on the hills of Rome!" Then he demanded of his listeners: "Will you be worthy of it?" In affirmation the crowd roared: "Sì! Sì! Sì!"

Mussolini was tasting the greatest success of his life. He had defied the powers of Europe, had launched a war and won it. He could claim that, like the other major nations, Italy now had a foreign empire. In grateful acknowledgment, King Victor Emmanuel awarded him the Grand Cross of the Military Order of Savoy, Italy's highest decoration. And the people were behind him. The walls of Rome sprouted posters with such legends as "Mussolini has conquered" and "The tricolor sheds its rays over Addis Ababa."

However, Mussolini had drained Italy's coffers of $50 million and its armory of great quantities of arms and armaments. Moreover, he had put himself and his nation in jeopardy for the larger international crisis that was building.

Less than three months after he proclaimed victory in Ethiopia, Mussolini further strained the resources of his nation by thrusting it into another conflict, the Spanish Civil War, on the side of the right-wing insurgents led by Generalissimo Francisco Franco. Though Italy's participation in Spain was unofficial, it was nevertheless expensive: The Duce committed 70,000 troops, as well as large numbers of arms, aircraft and other equipment, in support of Franco's successful revolution. He asked for the Balearic Islands in the western Mediterranean as a reward, but in the end he received nothing.

Though he had no way of perceiving it, Mussolini had reached the crest of his career. He now began a precipitous slide into alliance with that "violent man with no self-control"—Adolf Hitler.

Hitler took advantage of Mussolini's Ethiopian victory to lionize the Italian hero. In the summer of 1937 he invited the Duce to visit Germany that September. Hitler had taken the measure of his fellow Fascist and recognized his susceptibility to flattery. He spared no expense and no detail to impress his guest—and this time Hitler too was in uniform.

The visit began in Munich, where Mussolini was treated to parades of the National Labor Service, the Hitler Youth and Nazi Party officials—all of them marching in goose step. Then followed a two-day sightseeing tour—to Mecklenburg for Army maneuvers, to Essen to visit the monumental Krupp arms works and inspect the tanks and artillery that German workers there were turning out at a staggering rate.

Next came a lavish visit to Berlin. For the 230-mile journey from Essen, two special trains were laid on—one for the Führer, one for the Duce. The trains ran side by side, their locomotives exactly even, to symbolize the parallelism of the revolutions the two men had effected in their respective lands. Just before reaching Berlin, Hitler's train sped up, and he was on the platform at the station to welcome the arriving Duce.

In Berlin, Mussolini was treated to a marvel of pomp and ceremony calculated to dazzle him. On the drive down the Unter den Linden, the broad avenue leading to the center of the city, the two dictators passed thousands of flags: The

GIFTS OF GOLD FOR THE FATHERLAND

By 1935, Mussolini was in need of both hard currency and a dramatic gesture to rally the nation behind his militarism. He solved the two needs simultaneously by asking Italians to donate gold possessions to the government, in a ceremony called the "Rite of the Wedding Rings."

Italy's Queen Elena was the first to make the sacrifice, followed by Mussolini's wife, Rachele. Soon millions of couples had exchanged their rings for steel bands inscribed "Gold for the Fatherland." Medals, jewelry, crucifixes and other valuables poured in until 73,969 pounds of gold had been collected. Most of it was melted down and deposited in the Bank of Italy.

But not all. On April 27, 1945, a fisherman on the Mera River near Milan noticed a glint on the riverbed. In the next few hours he excitedly dredged up almost 80 pounds of gold, including rings engraved with the names of people all over Italy. Perhaps the gold was stolen—by Mussolini, by the Germans, by partisans—then cast away; nobody knows. The mystery of how the glittering hoard came to be in the river has never been solved.

Rachele Mussolini donates her gold wedding ring and her husband's to the nation's cause.

symbol of the Fascist rods was as prevalent as the Nazi swastika. By state order, work ceased at 4 p.m., and laborers filled the streets to cheer the arrival of the Duce. Special trains had brought thousands more from the provinces to augment the crowd. Elaborate security precautions were evident everywhere; 60,000 SS men in black uniforms lined the parade route, supplemented by plainclothesmen and police dogs.

The climax of the visit was an appearance by Hitler and Mussolini the following day in the field adjoining the huge stadium built for the 1936 Olympics. As early as 4 a.m. crowds began to fill the grounds, carrying baskets of sausages and black bread to last them through a long wait. When late in the afternoon the two leaders approached the podium, the crowd roared its approval. Hitler introduced Mussolini, then turned the microphones over to his guest.

Here, as during Hitler's visit to Italy three years earlier, the Italian dictator made a determined effort to speak German. But as though the Teutonic gods were against him, the heavens opened, and lashing rains turned the pages of his manuscript into pulp and drowned out the sound of his words. All the crowd could distinguish were isolated phrases about "the Rome-Berlin Axis," "ever-closer association," "the greatest democracies—Italy and Germany," and how "I have a friend through thick and thin."

Such a storm might have dampened the spirits of a less ebullient man than Mussolini. But he was so pleased by the attention already paid him that the rain did nothing to quench his ardor, particularly when the Germans dutifully cheered him at the finish and attempted to overcome the noise of the downpour by singing patriotic anthems. When Mussolini left Germany the next day, he carried deep impressions of the might of the Third Reich and the conviction that Hitler could be a powerful ally. From that moment, the Duce was drawn into a net that was to bind his nation inextricably to Hitler's Germany. More than that, he was to slip into a posture of imitation. Until now, Hitler had followed the lead of Mussolini, fashioning Nazi Germany on the model of Fascist Italy. Henceforth, Mussolini would follow the lead of Hitler.

At first the shift was visible only in small ways. Shortly after his return to Italy, Mussolini decreed that Italian soldiers were to march in the rigid goose step he had seen in Germany—but, reluctant to give credit elsewhere, he dubbed the step the *passo romano*. "People say the goose step is Prussian," he said testily. "Nonsense! The goose is a Roman animal."

A more sinister instance of copying was Mussolini's espousal of anti-Semitism. Almost immediately after his visit to Germany, he asserted that "Jews will disintegrate civilization." In January of 1938 the government issued a document stating that Jewish influence in the nation's life must be limited to their proportion of the population. (At that time Italian Jews numbered only about 47,000, scarcely one in 900 of the total population.)

Before the end of the year a manifesto from the Ministry of Culture declared that Jews did not belong to the pure Italian race—an outright parroting of Nazi policy. Then came a series of repressive decrees giving teeth to the manifesto: One denied foreign Jews the privilege of studying in Italian schools, another forbade Italians to marry Jews. "I do not understand," said King Victor Emmanuel of Mussolini, "how a great man like him can import these racial ideas from Berlin to Italy." Pope Pius XI had harsher words. "You should be ashamed to go to school under Hitler," he ad-

Adolf Hitler, wearing an honorary Fascist shoulder patch above his swastika arm band, joins Benito Mussolini for a show of Italian military preparedness in May 1938. When the two men parted, Mussolini promised Hitler: "Henceforth, no force will be able to separate us."

monished. Both reproofs were lost on the Duce, who was now too mesmerized by the Führer to notice that he was drifting away from the sentiments of his countrymen.

Mussolini's newfound admiration for Hitler had other ominous implications. It diluted his opposition to a German take-over of Austria, the nation whose independence he had so often pledged to defend.

Hitler's interest in *Anschluss* had never flagged, and by March of 1938 he felt strong enough to move against his neighbor. This time he had no intention of yielding to Italian interference, but for diplomacy's sake he sent Prince Philip of Hesse, a Nazi Party leader and a son-in-law of King Victor Emmanuel, to Rome with a letter informing Mussolini that German troops were on the move. "Excellency, I am now determined to restore law and order in my native country," Hitler wrote disingenuously. "Consider my decision solely a legitimate defense step." Then, in a pointed reminder of Mussolini's invasion of Ethiopia, he went on: "At a critical time for Italy I gave you proof of the unshakable constancy of my attitude."

Both Italian national interest and Mussolini's personal honor required him to take a stand. But the Duce had been effectively seduced by the Führer, and he replied meekly to Hitler, through Hesse, that the fate of Austria did not matter to him. Hitler was lucky—and overjoyed. "I will never forget," he exclaimed, and told Hesse to inform Mussolini that "if he should need any help or be in any danger, he can be sure I shall stick by him whatever may happen, even if the whole world turns against him."

Without a fight, German troops entered Austria on the morning of March 12. Though Hitler had promised the troops would not advance beyond Innsbruck, they went as far as the Brenner Pass—the Alpine gateway to Italy.

Mussolini had been humiliated by the German coup and by his own acquiescence in it. Hard put to deny that he had been an outspoken guarantor of Austrian independence, he made an apologetic appearance before the Chamber of Deputies in which he rationalized lamely that the Austrians "had the comprehensible modesty not to ask for the use of force to defend their independence." He added that Italy and Germany could now "march forward together to give our tormented continent a new equilibrium." The nation was not fooled. Signs of fissure between Mussolini and his people began to appear; the Palazzo Venezia was inundated with anonymous letters protesting the *Anschluss*.

The following May, Hitler made a return visit to Rome and was treated to a scintillating festival of lights. He failed to share with Mussolini the fact that his next target was Czechoslovakia. As German troops gathered on the Czech border in late September, 1938, Britain's Prime Minister, Neville Chamberlain, asked Mussolini to intercede with his friend Hitler to save the peace. Mussolini, while making it clear he was on Hitler's side, jumped at the chance to play power broker. He telephoned Hitler and persuaded him to postpone hostilities long enough to sit down at a conference table in Munich with Chamberlain, Premier Édouard Daladier of France and Mussolini himself.

The fateful meeting took place on September 29, 1938, and the Duce was in his glory. He was the only one of the principals who could speak—if in a limited way—the four languages represented. But he was unable—indeed, unwilling—to save Czechoslovakia any more than he had been to help Austria.

The four-power discussions in Munich were disorderly in the extreme. No agenda had been drawn up to guide the proceedings. In the end, Hitler came away with exactly what he wanted: the incorporation into Germany of the Sudetenland, a border district of Czechoslovakia that was the home of many ethnic Germans.

A clash of military arms had been averted, and the participants went away taking satisfaction in that. Chamberlain, having bought the British another year to rearm, promised there would be "peace for our time." Mussolini's return to Rome was a triumphal procession down the Via Nazionale. The newspapers called it a welcome fit for Caesar. As Mussolini entered the palace at the Piazza Venezia, the crowds chanted "Duce! Duce! Duce!" When he strode onto his balcony to address them, the roar of the people could be heard for miles. One of the few sobering comments came from Pope Pius XI, who warned some visitors a few days later: "It is a fine peace that is patched together at the expense of the weakest party without even consulting him."

The peace was short-lived, for Hitler had never intended the Munich agreement to be anything more than a postponement. Six months later he occupied the rest of Czecho-

35

GABRIELE D'ANNUNZIO
D'Annunzio capped a successful career in literature by becoming an aviator in World War I at the age of 52. His wartime exploits expanded his renown but only partly satisfied his lust for action, and he threw himself into postwar Italian politics. He introduced the so-called Roman salute, adopted by Mussolini and later by Adolf Hitler.

CESARE MARIA DE VECCHI
De Vecchi was a Piedmont landowner and lawyer who backed Fascism as a bulwark for the throne. After World War I, he helped form the squadristi, or "action squads," that warred against Fascism's opponents. De Vecchi served as Governor of Somaliland and, after the Lateran Accords of 1929, he became Italy's first Ambassador to the Vatican.

EMILIO DE BONO
De Bono commanded an army corps in World War I. He later backed Mussolini and was rewarded with a series of posts, including commander of the Fascist militia and Minister of Colonies. His cautious leadership during the invasion of Ethiopia displeased Mussolini, but he was promoted to Marshal of Italy and remained on the Grand Council.

THE DUCE'S DURABLE LIEUTENANTS

Under Mussolini, the tenure of an Italian politician was often short. The power-jealous Duce fired or exiled his underlings almost routinely as a way to keep them from becoming competitors. Yet the coterie of lieutenants and advisers pictured here found ways to remain useful to Mussolini while carving out for themselves long if not always smooth careers, some of which spanned the entire Fascist era.

The career of the daring poet-soldier Gabriele d'Annunzio predated even Mussolini's. After World War I, many people—Mussolini included—thought d'Annunzio the best man to lead a reborn and militant Italy. Even after Mussolini took power he was careful to both assuage d'Annunzio and keep him under surveillance. D'Annunzio lived in honored domestic isolation, too popular to attack and too independent to employ in office, yet heeded and richly supported by Mussolini.

Others, such as monarchist Cesare Maria De Vecchi and aristocratic soldier Emilio De Bono, served as links to Italy's old

nobility, helping it—and the Crown—accept the bombastic new order. De Vecchi and De Bono joined with future Air Minister Italo Balbo to organize the March on Rome that established Mussolini's rule.

Balbo came nearer than any other aide to rivaling Mussolini—especially after the spectacular transatlantic flights he staged in the early 1930s. Mussolini embraced Balbo on his return, only to banish him from Rome as Governor of Libya, where in 1940 he was shot down—mysteriously—by Italian antiaircraft guns.

Roberto Farinacci was a political handyman who thrived on brutality, once boasting that "there's no man more hated than I." An arrogant super-Fascist, he made a career of dirty work, whether destroying reputations in his newspaper or burning houses with a gang of thugs.

Less bloodthirsty but equally ardent was Achille Starace, Party Secretary for most of the 1930s. Starace's campaigns against such bourgeois affectations as spats, top hats and handshakes eventually earned

him popular mockery, but he survived on the basis of his obsequious devotion to Mussolini. An aide once told the Duce that Starace was "a cretin." Replied Mussolini: "Yes, but he's an obedient cretin."

Ettore Muti managed devotion without sycophancy. The adventure-loving aviator adored Mussolini and never passed up a chance to fight for him, both in Italy and abroad. Between fights he held political offices, including a stint as Party Secretary.

Dino Grandi, by contrast, was a diplomat whose skill and popularity helped legitimize the Fascist regime in foreign eyes.

One of Grandi's successors as Foreign Minister, Galeazzo Ciano, although a politician in his own right, rose to the top with a little help from a powerful relative—his father-in-law, Benito Mussolini.

Yet even these men who managed to hold onto power—through brains, zeal or marriage—must have wondered if it was worth the effort. By the War's end all but De Vecchi and Grandi were dead—and only d'Annunzio of natural causes.

ITALO BALBO
A charismatic leader, Balbo went from organizing the brutal Ferrara squadristi during Fascism's early days to building the Italian Air Force, considered one of the world's best in the 1930s. Even Mussolini felt—and feared—the force of his personality, remarking after Balbo's death in 1940 that he was "the only one capable of killing me."

ROBERTO FARINACCI
From his earliest days as leader of the Cremona squadristi, Farinacci practiced the most truculent and extreme form of Fascism. He held office as both Party Secretary and Minister of State, and he edited the hardline newspaper Regime Fascista. Anticlerical and anti-Semitic, Farinacci advocated a close alliance between Italy and Nazi Germany.

ACHILLE STARACE
As Party Secretary in the 1930s, Starace strove to spread Fascism throughout Italian society. A humorless conformist who put teachers and other civil servants into uniform, he abolished Italy's New Year's Day holiday in favor of October 28—the day Mussolini took power—and attempted to purify the Italian language by ridding it of foreign words.

ETTORE MUTI
Muti flew hundreds of bombing missions in Ethiopia and Spain, and during World War II he served his country as both a pilot and a spy. For a time this courageous and hard-living Fascist was the official bodyguard for Mussolini's sons. Muti held the intellectual life in contempt, once boasting: "I stopped reading newspapers when I was 15."

DINO GRANDI
Grandi rose from being a provincial leader of the squadristi to become one of Italy's most accomplished diplomats. He served as Minister of Justice and as Foreign Minister (a position he assumed at the age of 34), and he spent seven prewar years as Italian Ambassador to Great Britain, where his social grace and his hostility toward Germany won respect.

GALEAZZO CIANO
Ciano, the son of a count, entered the diplomatic corps in 1925, married Mussolini's daughter Edda in 1930 and in 1936 found himself Foreign Minister, a post he held for the next seven tumultuous years. On the way up he served stints as chief of the press bureau, Minister of Press and Propaganda, and commander of a bomber squadron in Ethiopia.

slovakia—without notifying Italy in advance. By the time Mussolini learned of the coup, Hitler was on his way to Prague, the Czech capital.

Mussolini was stung. When Hitler belatedly sent a message, Mussolini forbade the Italian press to mention it. Poignantly he told his son-in-law, Ciano: "The Italians would laugh at me." They did anyway.

Mussolini's anger over the *fait accompli* in Czechoslovakia spurred him to stage an invasion of his own—without forewarning Hitler. His chosen victim was Albania, the little-developed kingdom across the Adriatic Sea whose natural resources could help Italy in its perennial struggle for self-sufficiency. To provide an excuse for the invasion, Count Ciano's hirelings in Albania trumped up a revolution; on the pretext of restoring order, Italian troops landed in Albanian harbors on April 7, 1939. Encountering only feeble resistance, Mussolini's forces quickly took over the country.

But the venture taught Mussolini a hard lesson; had the Albanians chosen to stand fast, the invasion could have been a disaster. It was launched with green troops mobilized at the last minute. Men who had never operated a motorcycle were assigned to motorcycle companies; some who did not even know Morse code were sent to signal

units. Many of the invading Italian infantrymen had never fired the weapons they carried into battle. As a result, the conquest of Albania was actually a showpiece of ineptitude. "If the Albanians had possessed one well-armed fire brigade," commented a member of Ciano's staff, "they could have driven us back into the Adriatic."

The Italian press presented a different picture to the world—that of a well-oiled Fascist war machine rolling smoothly over its opposition. But Mussolini took the Albanian affair seriously; pondering the poor showing in the spring of 1939, he came to the conclusion that his armed forces would need at least three more years to get ready for a real war.

Mussolini did not forget that timetable. In May, Hitler sent Foreign Minister Joachim von Ribbentrop to Italy with instructions to move the two countries from informal friendship to formal alliance. Mussolini obliged with reckless haste, but he cautioned his own Foreign Minister, son-in-law Ciano, to make it clear that Italy could not be ready for war for at least three years. Ribbentrop replied that Germany, too, wished for years of peace—concealing the information that Hitler had already ordered his armed forces to prepare to march on Poland no later than September 1. The formal alliance between Italy and Germany was signed

in Berlin on May 22, 1939. Mussolini, blissfully thinking he had acted as an equal with the strongest man in Europe, called the treaty the Pact of Steel.

Unwittingly, Italy's leader had taken another step toward his own doom. The Pact of Steel pledged both countries to stand together as allies in any war. Article III stipulated that should one of the contracting parties "become involved in warlike complications with another power or with other powers, the other contracting party will come to its aid as an ally and will support it with all its military forces on land, on sea and in the air." In effect, Hitler was free to make war as he chose, and Mussolini was bound to support him. No mention was made in the treaty of the three-year delay that Mussolini was counting on.

Hitler had no need of Italy. His visits to Venice and Rome had shown him all too clearly that his eager ally had nothing to match the arms of Germany. But the pact served Hitler's purpose in eliminating Italy as a possible opponent. And it further isolated Italy from England and France, which had recently made public their determination to come to the defense of Hitler's latest target, Poland, if need be.

For weeks after he entered into the Pact of Steel, Mussolini remained ignorant of Germany's intentions. Not until midsummer, when the Italian military attaché in Berlin reported a German troop build-up along the Polish border, did he begin to take alarm. In August he sent Ciano to Salzburg for a meeting with Ribbentrop, but got no comfort from the result. "We want war," Ribbentrop told Ciano unequivocally. The German diplomat would reveal no more than that. "Ribbentrop is evasive whenever I ask him for particulars about German policy," Ciano wrote in his diary. Nevertheless, Ciano was beginning to see—as his father-in-law did not—that his opposite number in Germany was not to be trusted. "He has lied too many times about German intentions toward Poland," Ciano wrote somberly.

The next day, Ciano visited Hitler, who was cordial but determined. "He has decided to strike, and strike he will," Ciano wrote. "His affirmation that the great war must be fought while he and the Duce are still young leads me to believe that once more he is acting in bad faith."

When Ciano carried that news home to his father-in-law a day or two later, Mussolini faced a bitter dilemma of his own making. To rescind his widely publicized alliance with Hitler would expose him to ridicule, if not to dishonor. But to honor the alliance would expose his nation to dire peril. Chief of Staff Badoglio, the hero of Ethiopia, had told him that his troops had barely a month's supply of ammunition. Their armor consisted of steel-clad vehicles that the soldiers referred to as "sardine cans" or "vanity cases." The Italian Air Force had 4,000 planes, including trainers, but only a fraction were in flying condition and there was no proper record of where they were all based. Industry was in no position to help build an arsenal; there was enough steel on hand for only two weeks of production, nickel for three weeks, iron ore for six months. Even the gold that had been collected from citizens during the Ethiopian venture (page 33) had long since been drained away.

Much as Mussolini wanted the prizes of conflict and the comfort of honoring an obligation, even more did he fear the prospect of immediate war. Clearly, a way out would have to be found. At length Hitler gave him one by asking what Italy would need in the way of arms and supplies, and how soon. Mussolini, on the advice of his armed forces chiefs, replied with a list that included seven million tons of oil, six million tons of coal, two million tons of steel and a million tons of lumber. Ciano drolly pronounced the list "long enough to kill a bull, if a bull could read it," and Hitler's Minister of Armaments, Albert Speer, observed that "granting such demands could have resulted in a disastrous weakening of the German armed forces."

In fact, the list enabled both leaders to save face, and Hitler, who knew that Germany could carry on perfectly well for now without Mussolini, wrote to let him off. "In my opinion, however," Hitler added, "the prerequisite is that, at least until the outbreak of the struggle, the world should have no idea of the attitude Italy intends to adopt. I therefore cordially beg you to support my struggle psychologically with your press or by other means. I would also ask you, Duce, if you possibly can, by demonstrative military measures, at least to compel Britain and France to tie down certain of their forces, or in any event to leave them in uncertainty." Clearly, if Britain and France were worried that Italy might join the War, they would have to deploy some of their forces in the Mediterranean and would therefore be unable to bring all their might to bear against Germany.

A bicycle platoon of elite Bersaglieri light infantry enters the Albanian city of Durazzo on April 7, 1939. Mussolini ordered the invasion as a show of strength; Albania was already an Italian satellite, its tiny army commanded partly by Italians and its economy subsidized from Rome.

On the morning of September 1, 1939, Mussolini learned along with the rest of the world that German forces had invaded Poland. Two days elapsed before France and Britain declared war on Germany, and by then the Duce had made one last effort to halt the War by proposing yet another peace conference among Italy, Britain and France. He was too late. His foreign ministry had already received word that London, expecting Italy to go to war on Germany's side, had cut communications with Rome. Mussolini realized with a jolt that he had alienated his nation from Britain and France—and that Italy now stood in peril of attack by either or both of them. On September 3, Hitler sent the Duce a message professing unaltered friendship but adding a warning that underscored the bitterness of Mussolini's plight. "Even if we now march down separate paths, destiny will yet bind us one to the other," Hitler wrote. "If National Socialist Germany is destroyed by the Western democracies, Fascist Italy will also face a hard future."

The nine months from September 1939 to June 1940 were frustrating ones for Mussolini. He watched grimly as his former junior partner smashed Poland in three weeks. He knew he was powerless to take part, but he felt ashamed to be sitting on the sidelines, for in his eyes Italy could not remain neutral for long without losing status in the family of nations.

This feeling intensified when Berlin began to pressure Italy to enter the War. In October, Hitler told Ciano, who was visiting Germany: "If Germany and Italy went into battle together, England and France would be so completely crushed that many of the still-unsettled problems would be solved once and for all." In February, Prince Philip of Hesse made a trip to Rome to suggest that the Duce meet with the Führer. In March, Ribbentrop arrived with an entourage of 35—including economic and legal advisers, two barbers and his gymnastics instructor—and a promise from Hitler to send shipments of coal overland, since Britain had moved to cut off shipments of the vital fuel to Italy by sea.

Then in March, Mussolini received peremptory notice that Hitler was coming as far as the Brenner Pass to meet him. "These Germans are unbearable," Mussolini huffed in exasperation; "They don't give us time to breathe or to think matters over." All the same, he did as Hitler bade him, and journeyed to the border in a raging snowstorm to greet the Führer.

The two men had not met since the conference at Munich in 1938, when the Duce had played the role of moderator in the Sudeten question. Now the Führer teased his vanity by pointing out that if Italy was content with a second-rate position in the Mediterranean, Mussolini should go home and forget all about the War. But if he wanted to achieve the status of a first-class power, he should join in the struggle against the Western democracies. Germany, for its part, was about to mount an attack on France, Hitler revealed.

This assault on Mussolini's pride was more than he could bear, and he now took the step from which there could be no retreat. He promised that Italy would indeed enter the War; the only safeguard he left himself and his nation was

Arm in arm, a helmeted Italian soldier and his bride celebrate their 1940 wedding at his antiaircraft emplacement near Rome. Such scenes implied both military readiness and a home front cheerfully adjusting to war.

that Italy's entry was contingent on the success of Hitler's advance into the north of France.

Hitler had no worries on that point, and he agreed to the Duce's condition. He left the Brenner Pass with what he wanted: a commitment from Mussolini. He could now distract the high commands of Britain and France with the prospect of having to fight on another front. And he still had no need of Italian military help.

Hitler had scored that gain without divulging some critical information. Three weeks later, on April 9, Mussolini received a 7 a.m. visit from the German Ambassador, who informed him that at dawn Germany had invaded Denmark and Norway. Mussolini gamely supported Hitler's move; that was the way, he said, to win wars. "I shall give orders to the press and to the Italian people unreservedly to applaud this German action," he told the Ambassador. Although Mussolini welcomed the news, he was stunned and resentful at having been kept in the dark yet again.

German troops occupied Denmark in a day, and thrust deep into Norway; on May 10 they struck west across Belgium and Holland en route to France. As the time drew near when Mussolini must keep his promise, he grew daily more fretful. When Victor Emmanuel ventured to urge caution, Mussolini scoffed: "The King would like us to enter only to pick up the broken dishes." And he snubbed a peace overture made by an old admirer, the new British Prime Minister, Winston Churchill, who asked in a letter, "Is it too late to stop a river of blood from flowing between the British and Italian peoples?"

It was indeed too late. The Duce was anxious for action, and on June 10 he announced his intention to his people and to the world.

In truth, the Italian declaration of war was at first little more than symbolic. On the second day of the formal hostilities, the Italian submarine *Bagnolini* sank the British light cruiser *Calypso* in the Mediterranean. But that was the only success the Italian armed forces scored in their first round of combat. The 32 Army divisions that Mussolini had dispatched to the French border were so poorly equipped that they could scarcely maneuver; some of their artillery batteries were dangerously outdated, and even their field kitchens lacked enough pots and pans to cook hot meals. Hitler's armies had in any event already overcome France, and seven days after the Italian declaration of war Marshal Philippe Pétain, the newly installed French Premier, asked Hitler for an armistice.

The French request threw Mussolini into a panic. Unless he acted swiftly, he would have no claim on the spoils that by his own admission were his reason for going to war. Taking Ciano with him, he hastened to Munich to discuss armistice terms with Hitler.

"I find Mussolini dissatisfied," Ciano noted in terse understatement of the confrontation between the two leaders. Mussolini learned to his dismay that the Führer had no intention of imposing terms so unacceptable that the French would, in desperation, resume the fight; Hitler saw that it was more to his advantage to have them quiescent. He curtly informed Mussolini—who had visions of helping himself to Nice, Corsica, Tunisia and French Somaliland—that neither France nor any of its possessions would be carved up for Italy. Hitler's only concession was to agree not to sign an armistice until the French had signed one with Italy. That gave Mussolini a few days' grace to press the French on his own for whatever territory his troops could seize by force of arms.

The grace period netted him little. In the Alps, Italian troops launched an attack through the Little Saint Bernard Pass, only to be stalled by a snowstorm. An assault along the Riviera toward Nice came to a halt on the outskirts of Menton, only five miles beyond the Italian border. By the time that trivial gain had been scored, the armistice was about to take effect. All that Italy had secured was a few acres of French soil.

Only then did Mussolini realize the bitter truth: He was scarcely needed by Hitler. The Germans had won the battle for France without him and, in fact, they now refused to take him into their confidence for the campaigns that lay ahead.

A DICTATOR'S PRIVATE WORLD

Finding brief escape from his government duties in 1927, a formally dressed Benito Mussolini strolls alone on the beach at Ostia, 15 miles from Rome.

THE SHADOWY SIDE OF A SELF-PROMOTER

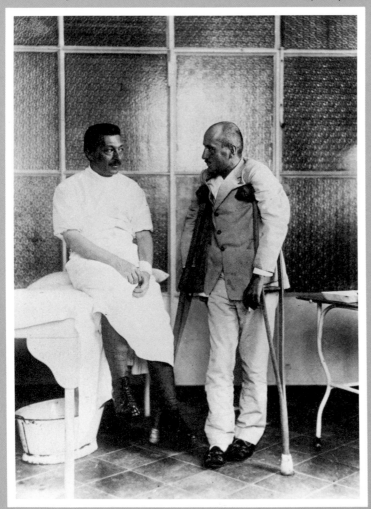

Convalescing from wounds that were caused by grenade fragments during World War I, Mussolini talks with a doctor at an Italian Army hospital.

As the leader of Fascist Italy, Benito Mussolini moved in a glare of self-generated publicity, leaving a trail of photographs that seemed to illuminate every minute of his waking life. The dictator personally censored the pictures that filled the pages of newspapers and magazines, approving only those that enhanced his public image. In interviews and in his own writings, he portrayed himself as one who had risen from humble laborer to become a college-educated teacher and writer, wounded war veteran, devoted family man, daring athlete and scholarly statesman.

The facts were somewhat different. During his vagabond youth, Mussolini had spent only a few hateful weeks at manual labor and a few months attending university lectures. During those early years he begged, borrowed or stole to support a life of wenching, brawling and fitful reading. A series of intellectual mistresses and admirers helped him acquire a high-school teaching certificate, which entitled him to be called "professor." But his war record was genuine. Called up for service in World War I, he fought gallantly until an accidental explosion peppered his legs with shrapnel.

Mussolini had trained himself as a journalist and public speaker, learning to highlight his virtues and obscure his shortcomings by sheer rhetoric and by such tricks as thrusting his jaw upward to make him appear taller than his actual 5 feet 5 inches. By memorizing statistics, foreign phrases and hastily skimmed facts, he managed to fool most people most of the time about his intellectual accomplishments.

Idealized portraits, busts and carefully posed photographs concealed as much as they revealed about the man for whom the Italian artistic term "chiaroscuro" might have been coined—a mixture of dazzling light and darkest shadows. Hidden within the public figure lurked an introverted megalomaniac who, according to his son Vittorio, felt toward other men "not only a psychological but a physical intolerance." His attitude toward women was typified by his remark that women "prefer brutality in a man to courtesy." Mussolini's public life was a performance, his private world one of mostly solitary pleasures.

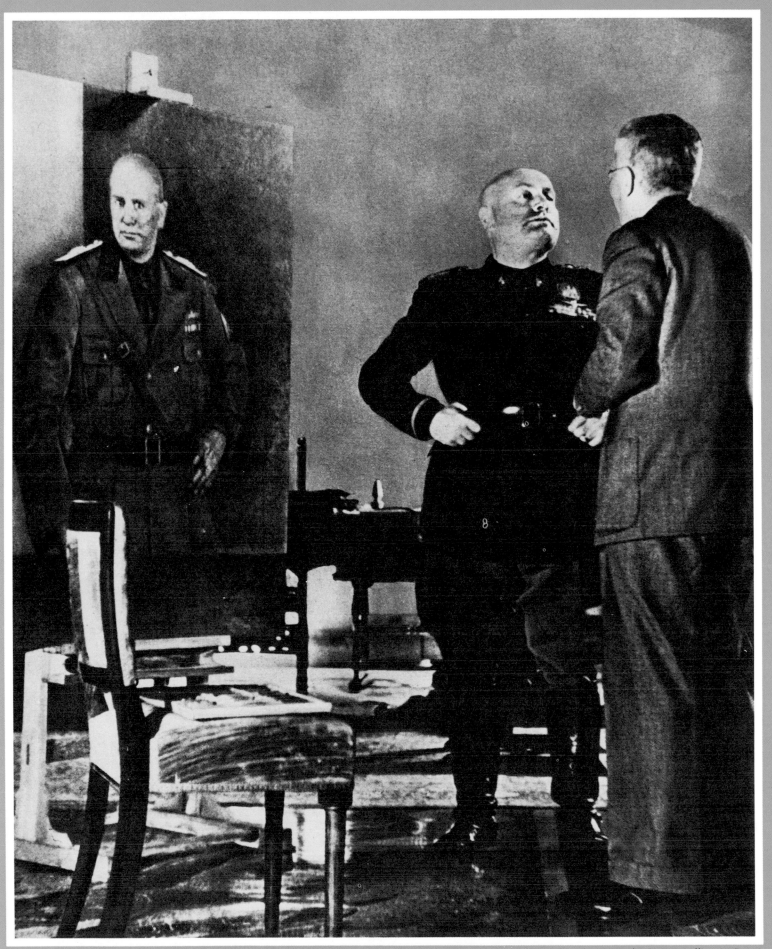

Assuming his favorite stance, Mussolini discusses a less aggressive portrait of himself with its painter, Pietro Gaudenzi, in the Duce's office in Rome.

PART-TIME DUTY AS HUSBAND AND FATHER

A 1930 family snapshot at their new home in Rome brings together wife Rachele with baby Annamaria, eldest son Vittorio, Romano in his father's arms, first-born Edda, and favorite son Bruno. Until they moved to Rome, the family saw Mussolini only on holidays.

Mussolini was a distant and erratically dutiful husband and father, though he paraded his family before the camera when it suited his career. He had lived with Rachele Guidi on and off for six years and had given her two children before he married her in 1915. The fiery peasant woman proudly bore three more children in rural homes while her political husband lived the unhindered bachelor's life in the city.

Not until late in 1929—the year he signed his acclaimed accord with the Vatican and launched a national campaign to encourage larger families—did Mussolini move his own family to a secluded villa in Rome. From that time on, Donna Rachele comforted herself, "my husband always slept at home."

Thin and pale after a stomach-ulcer attack in 1925, Mussolini reads government documents while he recuperates in his bachelor apartment. Here he entertained women friends and diplomatic visitors.

Smiling at her success, Rachele Mussolini shows off the hare she shot during a holiday in Romagna. The Duce's wife preferred the country life and shunned official society.

Mussolini appears on skis at Terminillo, a mountain resort near Rome. Detractors said he went there only to pose, not to ski.

The Premier prepares to leave home for his office astride a motorcycle. Crowds turned out each morning to watch Mussolini speed off, sometimes at the wheel of a sports car.

Mussolini displays his swimming form at Riccione, his favorite summer resort, where women often mobbed him. Some plunged fully clothed into the sea to get close to him.

A PASSION FOR FITNESS FIRED BY VANITY

The private and public lives of Mussolini merged in his passion for keeping his body fit and his mind alert. At home and among crowds of spectators he pursued such solo recreations as swimming, horseback riding, skiing, driving fast motorcycles, cars and airplanes—and playing the violin.

He began each day with brief calisthenics and a brisk ride, followed by a shower and a rubdown in eau de cologne. His wife ruefully recalled that when she teased him about this unfailing routine, "he replied that if he didn't keep his body in perfect condition, women would not like him any longer and he would be worthless."

Mussolini fingers his violin, which he played in order "to forget my preoccupations." One of his mistresses described his musical style as "dictatorial—he played everything his own way."

A qualified pilot, the Duce flies a seaplane in June 1939. Eighteen years earlier, following a serious training accident, anxious officials hid an instructor aboard the plane in which he took his solo examination.

Margherita Sarfatti pauses over a manuscript in the study of her Milan mansion. In 1934, after Mussolini had dismissed her from his newspaper and his life, she published Dux, an admiring biography of him.

LOVERS WHOSE LOYALTY SPANNED A LIFETIME

Though Mussolini's private life included hundreds of casual conquests, two women maintained lasting relationships with him outside of marriage.

Elegant, wealthy and intellectual, Margherita Sarfatti began writing in 1914 for the newspaper that launched the Duce's career. For years she polished his peasant manners and his political thinking, until Rachele Mussolini's jealousy ended the relationship in 1930. A few years later the middle-aged dictator took up with Clara Petacci, a vivacious 24-year-old whose simple ardor would sustain him until the moment of their death together.

Clara Petacci lounges in a feathered gown, right, and in the dim light of her chintz-and-satin bedroom suite, below, a kaleidoscope of kitsch paid for by seekers of political favors.

2

The dilemma of Italy's "blind" Navy
Mussolini's rule by midnight monologue
An air armada with clipped wings
Disaster in the mountains of Greece
"Don't say the Italian soldier is not brave"
Setback at Sidi Barrani
Making "a Nordic people out of the Neapolitans"
Prison for dissenters in cells without walls
Spies who spied upon spies
Plunder for the powerful few
A British trap closes in Libya
"Come down, Giuseppe; the Germans are here!"

The light cruisers *Giovanni delle Bande Nere* and *Bartolommeo Colleoni* cleared Tripoli on the afternoon of July 18, 1940, bound for Leros in the Dodecanese Islands. From there they were to prey upon British shipping on the crucial run from Gibraltar to Egypt and the Middle East. On the bridge of the *Bande Nere* stood Captain Franco Maugeri, at the age of 41 one of the Italian Navy's fastest rising and most respected line officers. To his intimates, Maugeri was known as a man of coolly analytic temper and great honesty who made no secret of his distaste for Mussolini's war.

Years later, Maugeri would remember the eerie sense of unreality he felt that afternoon as he sailed off to war beneath a serenely blue sky, with "the sleek *Colleoni* gracefully knifing through the water" behind him. A proud man, he was thinking with chagrin of Italy's only concerted fleet action thus far—a brief and inconclusive encounter with the British off the coast of Calabria nine days earlier, during which the Italian ships had mistakenly been attacked by land-based Italian planes. Captain Maugeri was determined that when he met the British he would show them something of the true seamanship and esprit de corps that animated the Italian fleet.

At 6 a.m. the next day the Italian ships were cruising through the Aegean Sea north of Crete when lookouts reported four British destroyers off the starboard bow. The Italians immediately gave chase, relying on their exceptional speed—37 knots—to catch up with the smaller British ships. During a running fight of nearly two hours, the *Bande Nere* and *Colleoni* fired salvo after salvo from their 6-inch guns. Just as they were coming within effective range, recalled Captain Maugeri, "Several shells suddenly crashed off our port bow." Steaming over the horizon were unexpected British reinforcements: the cruiser *Sydney,* accompanied by the destroyer *Havock.*

The lightly armored Italian cruisers now reversed course and made for the open sea, where they would have room for the kind of high-speed maneuvering at which they excelled. But before they could get clear, a shell from the *Sydney* smashed through the *Colleoni's* hull and exploded in her main engine room, leaving her dead in the water. Within minutes the British destroyers had closed in to fire their torpedoes, sending the *Colleoni* to the bottom.

The loss of a spanking-new cruiser was a bitter blow to

CRACKS IN THE GRAND FAÇADE

Maugeri, but what happened next he found inexcusable. As the British destroyers fanned out to pick up survivors from the *Colleoni,* a flight of Italian fighter-bombers came roaring in to strafe and bomb the British ships. The rescue attempt had to be abandoned, and hundreds of Italian sailors drowned because of the mistaken zeal of Italian airmen.

To Franco Maugeri, that comparatively insignificant action, which history recorded as the Battle of Cape Spada, was prophetic in a number of ways. It told him, first of all, that "the Italian Navy was a blind navy." Because of Benito Mussolini's misguided decision to place all of Italy's air power under the command of the Italian Air Force, the fleet was without an air arm. Deprived of aircraft carriers (the Italian peninsula itself was an unsinkable aircraft carrier, Mussolini had insisted), the Navy was dependent on the Air Force both for long-range reconnaissance and for air cover once contact was made with the enemy. When the Air Force failed in its functions, as it had in the actions off Calabria and Cape Spada, it left the Navy groping "hopelessly and perilously in the dark."

Maugeri was acutely aware that Italian fliers had not been trained in ship recognition and that they had never engaged in coordinated exercises with the fleet. He also knew that the Navy's problems went deeper than that: Like the Army and the Air Force, the Navy was suffering from the "dry rot" that Maugeri saw penetrating "every portion of the body politic," eroding the foundations of the Fascist state.

Although the decay had long been apparent to Maugeri and other insiders, it became obvious to the general public only in 1940, after Mussolini launched his country into the ill-conceived series of military campaigns that he dubbed "the parallel war." His avowed aim was to wage "a war parallel to that of Germany to obtain our objectives, which can be summed up in this phrase: Liberty on the seas, a window on the Atlantic Ocean." While Hitler concentrated on the "security of the north," the Duce intended to operate independently in the Mediterranean and the Balkans. But in fact Mussolini had only the vaguest military and diplomatic goals in mind. The real purpose of his parallel war was to provide a balm to his bruised ego by establishing Italy as an equal partner of the German Reich.

Throughout the summer of 1940, Mussolini fretted as he tried to decide which course his war would take. He talked grandiosely of an offensive by the Italian Tenth Army in Libya that would drive the badly outnumbered British from their positions in Egypt and capture the Suez Canal. The Italian Navy, meantime, would sweep the British from the inland seas, assuring Axis control of the Middle East and its vital oil supplies.

Under incessant prodding from the Duce, Marshal Rodolfo Graziani at last launched his Tenth Army in a leisurely offensive across the Egyptian frontier on September 13. After four days he stopped, pleading a lack of supplies and armor. He was 60 miles inside Egypt but still 80 miles short of the British defenses at Mersa Matruh. "Never has a military operation," noted Foreign Minister Ciano dryly, "been conducted so much against the will of its commanders."

Mussolini tried with a barrage of furious telegrams to get the Tenth Army moving again, but without success. He had no more luck exhorting the Navy. Bitterly the Duce dismissed all Italians as "too fond of drink and incapable of making decisions." But his commanders knew things about the malaise of Italy that Mussolini did not wish to know.

Within months of Italy's entry into the War, flaws in the structure of Fascism had become so evident that a classified police report spoke bluntly of "the progressive degeneration of the state." The mammoth party machinery was too unwieldy to respond to crisis, and too conformist to seek new solutions to problems the country had never before faced. Rivalries and jurisdictional disputes increasingly splintered the party hierarchy. Corruption was so widespread that, said one senior police official, the term *"gerarca"* ("Fascist leader") was used as a synonym for "thief." The Army, Navy and Air Force squabbled and plotted among themselves, going so far as to spy on one another's activities.

The underlying problem was that Mussolini had imposed on Italy such a highly personal style of government that he had, in effect, become the Fascist state itself. At the outbreak of war he bolstered his already far-flung authority by naming himself Commander in Chief of the Armed Forces, a title constitutionally reserved for the King. In areas where Mussolini was unable or unwilling to exert his personal power, there was no alternate authority to ensure the orderly conduct of government. And as the Duce's own judgment became increasingly erratic, so did the course steered by a party bureaucracy schooled in the dictum that was emblazoned on homes and public buildings all over Italy: "Mussolini is always right."

Although veteran Fascists occasionally complained to him about confusion and lack of direction in the ranks, Mussolini rejected all suggested reforms, believing that a certain amount of turmoil helped secure his own supreme authority. For the same reason, he was reluctant to delegate power to anybody of proven ability—or anyone too popular. "As soon as he sees too much light shining on us," remarked aviation hero Italo Balbo, "he turns off the switch." Another veteran of the March on Rome, Giuseppe Bottai, noted that Mussolini was so wary of any sign of concerted action on the part of his subordinates that he proceeded on the assumption, "If three ministers agree on a subject, it is a conspiracy." To an acquaintance the Duce once remarked: "If my sainted mother were to return to life, I should no longer trust even her."

By the time Italy went to war, the elected national legislature had been replaced by an appointed chamber heavily loaded with Fascists. This rubber-stamp legislature was largely ignored by Mussolini, as were the traditional Council of Ministers and the so-called Grand Council of Fascism, which had been set up in the 1920s as a kind of shadow cabinet to function as the highest governing body of the state. In practice, the Grand Council and the Council of Ministers were summoned only intermittently by Mussolini, who used them as sounding boards when he wanted to think out loud.

The Grand Council, which consisted of 20 of the Fascist elite, rarely convened before midnight and seldom adjourned before dawn. Mussolini conducted these nocturnal sessions as he would a high-school civics class. First the roll was called, with each member shouting "Present!" in a loud voice. Then the meeting was thrown open to discussion, which usually consisted of a harangue by Mussolini, sometimes lasting as long as three hours. When the Duce felt the need to pause he would rise abruptly and say, "This meeting is adjourned; go smoke a cigarette." At the buffet set up outside the meeting room, the Council members

54

would find the black-uniformed *moschettieri*, the Duce's personal bodyguards, each wearing a skull-and-crossbones insignia on his fez, a dagger at his belt and a carbine slung over his shoulder.

At Mussolini's insistence, no minutes were ever kept, nor any votes taken, at sessions of the Grand Council or the Council of Ministers. Thus the official records of their proceedings were incomplete and unreliable. Giusepp Gorla, who was Minister of Public Works at the outbreak of war, recalled a typical meeting of the Council of Ministers: "Suddenly the door of the President's study opened, and Mussolini appeared. Everyone was silent and saluted in the Roman fashion." In front of each minister was a list of drafted legislation to be approved. But Mussolini ignored the agenda and in his accustomed fashion started rambling over a wide range of topics as they came to mind.

Gorla surreptitiously began taking notes: "Mussolini noticed almost at once and asked what I was doing." When Gorla confessed that he was keeping a record for his own guidance, Mussolini snapped: "Do not do so. You can see that even the Secretary of the Council is keeping no records, on my orders, because I want to talk freely and I can do so only in this body, which alone can keep a secret."

The real business of government went on in the Duce's cavernous office in the Palazzo Venezia. This imposing structure, which was built in the 15th Century of massive stones transported from the Coliseum, appealed to Mussolini's love of the theatrical and to his yearning for tradition. The Palazzo had served as a residence for Pope Paul II and later for various ambassadors to the Vatican. Its four enormous entrances, its interior courtyard, its great halls, and its balconies jutting over the Piazza Venezia suggested a grandeur that Mussolini felt Fascism too often lacked.

He chose for his office the so-called Hall of the Globe, a gallery 60 feet long and 40 feet high. Two mosaics had been laid in the floor. One depicted Mussolini saving the Princess Europa from the bull of Bolshevism; the other portrayed Mussolini as the sea god Triton embracing a sea nymph symbolic of the Mediterranean. The Duce installed almost no furniture except two armchairs, a reading stand with an atlas, and a 13-foot desk in which he kept loose change to hand out to petitioners—as well as a pistol for self-defense.

Here Mussolini received visitors, starting at 9:30 every morning. His desk was situated at the far end of the room, and he established a psychological edge over his guests by remaining seated while they made the long walk to the desk under his penetrating gaze. Military officers, even admirals and generals, were required to run from door to desk before snapping to attention and giving the Fascist salute.

When he wished to, Mussolini could be highly impressive in these personal interviews. A fast reader with a good memory, he retained the habit developed in his youth of sprinkling his talk with quotations and statistics gleaned from desultory reading; as a result, he gave the impression of knowing far more than he did. On the other hand, he enjoyed playing the petty tyrant and disrupting an audience before it began. Often the hangers-on outside his office could hear his angry shouts as he dismissed some luckless official who had offended because his shoes squeaked on the stone floor, or because Mussolini did not care for the cut of his beard. He had a calculated way of scowling and of fixing a visitor with his famous "magnetic look," which intimidated even the most courageous of his colleagues and made balanced dialogue all but impossible.

Every morning Mussolini saw the chief of the *carabinieri*, or national military police, and the chiefs of the political and criminal police. He also met with Foreign Minister Ciano and the Ministers of the Interior and of Popular Culture (as the propaganda department was euphemistically called). He read war bulletins, Foreign Office telegrams, General Staff memoranda and reports from regional Fascist officials, initialing them with a blue letter "M." Much of the rest of his time he devoted to giving private audiences and reading secret-service reports that were spiced with telephone intercepts and dinner-table conversations supplied by bribed servants.

He read the daily newspapers with the eye of a professional journalist, issued instructions to editors, judged the covers of magazines submitted for his approval, and examined every official photograph he appeared in to determine which should be released to the press. He even wrote headlines, using words that had a resounding ring but that usually bore little relation to reality. Thus in July 1940, after the Action off Calabria in which Italian planes attacked Italian ships but left the British unscarred, Mussolini unabashedly

Grim and commanding, Mussolini presides over a meeting of the Chamber of Fasces and Corporations, an appointed body dominated by Fascists and by business and labor leaders. The legislative unit was formed in 1939 to replace the elected Chamber of Deputies.

composed a headline for release that read: "We Destroy 50 Per Cent of British Naval Potential in Three Days."

Although Mussolini spent long hours in his office, he did very little substantial administrative work while there. Part of the Duce's trouble was his fascination with trivia, over which he felt he could at least exert some measurable control. Thus in the early summer of 1940, when he should have been concerning himself with critical military matters, he worried instead about the date on which the Roman traffic police should switch to their white summer uniforms, and when the military band on the Lido at Venice should begin its schedule of summer concerts. Ciano complained bitterly that the Duce was so obsessed with detail that he could not, or would not, see the "disastrous" condition of Italy's armed forces: "What is the Duce doing? He concentrates on matters of form. There is hell to pay if the 'present arms' is not done right or if an officer does not know how to lift his legs in the *passo romano,* but he concerns himself only up to a certain point about the real weakness."

Mussolini reserved the late afternoon hours of his working day for his relations with women. Although he was extolled in Fascist propaganda as the faithful family man and the loving father of five children, he had always been a pursuer of women, becoming more active as his opportunities grew. A special secretarial staff at the Palazzo Venezia classified and filed the letters sent to him by adoring females. Those who sounded particularly interesting were first screened by the police and then sent a message inviting them to the Palazzo for a "private audience."

These casual encounters did not take much of the Duce's time. If a woman attracted him, he would throw himself on her without warning and assault her on the floor or on a window seat overlooking the Piazza Venezia. His tastes were eclectic, including women of different ages and backgrounds, although he confessed to a particular weakness for plump matrons of the middle class. Many women shown into the Hall of the Globe expected to conclude the interview on the carpet, but others were taken by surprise. A young woman painter recalled with wonder that she went to the Duce's office to make a few portrait sketches and came away "not only with a work of art, but with a child."

Most of Mussolini's visitors he never saw again. Others were kept in the active file for a brief time, until the Duce dismissed them by changing his private telephone number, so that they found themselves talking to a ministry official, or perhaps a party secretary, when they called.

But there were longer liaisons, notably the one with Clara Petacci, which began in 1936 and lasted to the end of both their lives. Mussolini was feeling his years when the affair began—he was 53, she was 24—and perhaps for this reason Clara took more of his time and distracted him from his duties more than any woman he had known. In the early years of their relationship the Duce phoned her constantly and ordered her to go to the opera or to military reviews, or other public functions he had to attend, so that he could see her and make secret gestures only she would understand.

At Mussolini's request, Clara went every afternoon at 3 o'clock to a private apartment in the Palazzo. There she would wait for him, passing the time reading, playing solitaire or listening to the phonograph. Often in those early days he would slip away to see her between audiences and meetings with his ministers.

When Clara became pregnant in 1940, Mussolini was pleased, despite the threat of scandal. Then she suffered a miscarriage and had to be operated on because of the danger of peritonitis. Terrified, Mussolini insisted on being present at the operation, dressed in a nurse's gown. Afterward he went daily to her family's home in Rome to sit at her bedside. Business at the Palazzo Venezia that critical summer was disrupted for more than a month.

During this period Mussolini became involved in the affairs of the Petacci family. Clara's father was a Vatican physician, her brother Marcello one of Mussolini's *moschettieri,* her sister Myriam an aspiring opera singer. Mussolini often dropped in on the family in the evening, and he interested himself in the activities of each one of them. He actively advanced Myriam's career, ordering the Italian radio to broadcast a slight Cherubini opera in which his "little sister-in-law," as he called her, made her debut.

Although Mussolini insisted that "women can have no influence on strong men," Clara probably exerted more influence on him than he was willing to acknowledge. Mostly she brought to his attention what she considered to be small injustices: One day she made him taste the soggy, unappetizing bread that was the staple food of the poor. On other occasions she pettily denounced people in his entourage whom she disliked, or championed the claims of her favorites, most notably an old family friend, Admiral Arturo Riccardi, who she believed should head the fleet.

Mussolini tired of Clara, as he did of all his women, and his visits to the apartment in the Palazzo became briefer and less frequent. Aware of the toll the affair was taking on his time and energy—and because, he said, their liaison was "the talk of Italy"—he tried several times to break off the relationship, without success. Because of the burdens of war, he told her plaintively, "I can't interest myself in your personal affairs at the moment; please leave me alone." But Clara's tears prevailed, and wearily Mussolini made up.

Complicating the Duce's tumultuous emotional life even more was the fact that he was unwilling to forgo other affairs

while involved with Clara. Often he slipped away to a villa in the Roman hills where he had installed a teen-age beauty from Brescia; eventually she bore him a son.

Harassed by these personal entanglements, unwilling to delegate authority, beguiled by his own propaganda and isolated from reality by the fear he inspired in his subordinates, the Duce governed Italy by impulse and improvisation. Much important state business he conducted either in private conversation or by telephone, neglecting to make any record of his decisions. The results were predictably chaotic. Because of his desire to appear omniscient, he was reluctant to ask questions of his ministers, and so was often led to write "Approved" on conflicting memoranda presented to him by different ministries. Officials urging rival policies on him always tried to see him late in the day because they knew his habit of deciding in favor of the last person who visited his office.

The Duce's inability to follow up on his decisions—and make them stick—endlessly complicated the business of government. When he decided to put General Sebastiano Visconti-Prasca at the head of the Eleventh Army in the summer of 1940, Marshal Pietro Badoglio publicly agreed; privately, however, Badoglio resented the fact that Visconti-Prasca was a political appointee who was leapfrogging a number of his seniors on the Army promotion list.

Badoglio sabotaged the Duce's order by giving Visconti-Prasca only an Army corps. Visconti-Prasca appealed to the Deputy Minister of War, who confirmed the original appointment. Badoglio then turned over the Eleventh Army to Visconti-Prasca, but he rendered the new command largely meaningless by depriving the Eleventh of most of its troops. Visconti-Prasca threatened to fly to Rome to see Mussolini. The skirmishing continued for three confused months before Visconti-Prasca was allowed to take over his command. Situations like these, Mussolini wearily confided to his old comrade-in-arms Giuseppe Bottai, made him think he was "the most disobeyed man of the 20th Century."

Perhaps Mussolini's greatest weakness as an administrator was that he was more adept at terrorizing his colleagues than at disciplining them. Anxious to avoid scenes, he sometimes responded to flagrant insubordination or inefficiency not by confronting the offenders but by completely overhauling the government—"changing the guard," he

Italian children of the mountain village of Capalbio, in Tuscany, stand at attention beneath a helmeted likeness of Benito Mussolini and his militant slogan: "Believe, obey, fight."

called it. The most extreme of these changes occurred in January 1941, when he rid himself of half a dozen ministers who displeased him by shipping them off to the war fronts. More customarily, he was content to call newspaper editors and inform them that such and such a minister was out.

This practice of Mussolini's became so commonplace that the verb "to resign" acquired a new usage in Fascist Italy; gossips wondered which minister was likely to be "resigned" next. The victims of such summary dismissals were usually the last to know. If they then left office without protest, Mussolini was duly grateful. "I do not forget," he said, "those who leave when the time comes and are careful not to slam the door."

Nothing in Mussolini's chaotic system of government was more damaging than the illusions it fostered in his own mind. Chief among these was the fallacy that Italy was ready to go to war. Fascist propaganda claimed that no nation in Europe was better prepared for battle, and even that Fascism had evolved a new and better way of fighting. Often Mussolini behaved as though he believed this.

Knowing his gullibility and afraid to disillusion him, his military commanders craftily produced the semblance of combat capability. Carmine Senise, the Italian Chief of Police, recalled how the Duce once was taken to an airport to see more than 1,000 military planes lined up: "Proudly, Mussolini admired that superb display of force and never knew that only a few of those planes could fly." Thus fooled, he talked of air armadas that would black out the sun. On other occasions, when the Duce wished to review the troops, the Army would borrow armored cars from the police, paint them a regulation gray-green, then restore them to their original color as soon as the parade was over.

To knowledgeable eyes, a coat of paint was not enough. The Army's Chief of Staff, Marshal Graziani, remarked in private that tactically the Italian Army had not advanced much beyond the level of "the Macedonian phalanx." Chief of Air Staff General Francesco Pricolo added that his own forces were "at the level of a Balkan state." Old-liner Roberto Farinacci had the courage to speak to Mussolini directly, telling him that Italy had a "toy army, without the least serious training." When faced with such unpalatable truths, Mussolini sometimes flew into a rage and vowed to punish those responsible. More often, he comforted himself that in war what really matters is morale. A German military attaché who observed him at a parade of Italian forces near the Yugoslav border was surprised to note that he was less interested in his troops' antiquated equipment than in how lustily they sang as they marched past the reviewing stand.

The Army's basic problems were both material and organizational, and these in turn had a devastating effect on morale. Before Italy went to war, Mussolini boasted of being able to mobilize "eight million bayonets"; the high command embroidered on this figure, envisioning an army of 10 million and, ultimately, 12 million men. In truth, the Army had equipment, uniforms and barracks to house no more than a million men, which was a primary reason why Italy never declared a general mobilization.

Moreover, the matériel furnished a few years earlier to Spain's General Franco—a quarter of a million rifles, 1,900 artillery pieces, more than 700 aircraft—had not yet been replaced. Much of the Army's remaining equipment was obsolescent—rifles of 1891 design, horse-drawn artillery dating to World War I. Unable to call more men to arms, Mussolini hit on the idea of reducing Army divisions from three regiments to two, which enabled him to claim 80 divisions. Later he forgot what he had done and badly overestimated his forces.

On paper, the Army had three armored divisions, which were said to include 25-ton tanks. In reality, it had two such divisions with no heavy tanks at all, only 70 medium tanks and 1,500 light tanks so thinly armored that machine-gun bullets could penetrate them. Mussolini defended them against heavier models by saying they were more "attuned to the quick reflexes of the Italian soldiers." Antiaircraft artillery was almost nonexistent, and motor transport was in such desperately short supply that only 24 vehicles were assigned to each division. Shortly after the War began, General Ugo Cavallero approached Count Ciano in all seriousness and said he had solved the problem of under-mechanization: From now on the infantry would be required to march 25 instead of 12 miles a day.

Some of the Army's matériel problems could have been solved or alleviated if Italian factories, in the years before the country entered the War, had not become arms suppliers to much of the world. In search of foreign exchange to bolster the economy, the government sent aircraft to both Finland and the Soviet Union during their Winter War, and arms to both sides in Japan's war on China. Weapons that the Italians themselves lacked went to Bulgaria, Rumania, Portugal, and to Brazil and other countries in South America. Even after September 1939, during the period of non-belligerency, Mussolini ignored the protests of the military and approved the export of large quantities of airplane engines, locomotives, torpedoes, mines, machine parts and even military boots and blankets. His two best customers were England and France.

The shortage of uniforms and equipment badly compromised the battle readiness of the Army, for it meant that recruits were usually trained for far less than the 18 months prescribed by law. In 1940, some officers at the battalion level were called back into service without any retraining since their demobilization after World War I.

Ill-equipped, ill-trained and skeptical of Fascism's bellicose propaganda, Italy's troops were probably less motivated than those of any other major combatant in World War II. Adding to their disillusionment was a command structure in which advancement came as often by political favoritism as by military skill. Mussolini not only stifled all debate—he fired one general on the spot for counseling him not to go to war—but judged his officers almost solely on the basis of their "Fascist merits."

At the outbreak of war the Duce announced that henceforth the Black Shirt militia would "fight with its legions incorporated in the great mobilized unity that is the Army." In practice, this meant that between every two regular regiments was sandwiched a regiment of Black Shirts. This merger of the Army with the so-called spiritual aristocracy of Fascism was bitterly resented by the regular officer corps. Stories were told of reserve officers who joined the Black Shirts and overnight leaped in rank from captain to general. These instant generals were accused by regular officers of having a "*squadristi* mentality" that led them to ignore strategic and material limitations and waste their time planning "grandiose offensives" that could not possibly come off. In cases where Black Shirt officers were actually given a top command—as when Party Secretary Achille Starace took over a column of 7,300 men in Ethiopia for two months—the situation quickly became so confused that regular Army

professionals had to be called in to save it. "The wearing of the uniform of a general does not make a general," Marshal Badoglio wrote caustically to Roberto Farinacci.

Almost as disruptive, said Army critics, was the effect of the Black Shirt presence on morale in the ranks. It was no secret that among the regular infantrymen, slogging along in threadbare uniforms and shoes with cardboard soles, the arrogant militiamen were often more cordially hated than the enemy across the line.

On those occasions when Mussolini acknowledged the defects of his army, he rationalized that air power was the way to win modern wars. Fascist propaganda insisted on the superiority of Italian aircraft, and on their ability to control the Mediterranean and neutralize the British fleet. Italy claimed 8,530 planes of all kinds in 1940, and Mussolini boasted of such marvels as a bomber that could fly nonstop to England without being heard. In fact, Italy had only 3,296 fighters and bombers, and these had neither the speed nor the armament to match the best Allied planes.

Of the three services, Italy's Navy was the best prepared. It was better equipped and better commanded than the other branches, and it had more successfully resisted political meddling—what Captain Maugeri called the "lascivious ogling" of the Fascists. Morale and discipline were good. When the American correspondent Eleanor Packard visited the Navy bases at Naples and Messina, she was struck by the contrast with the other armed forces: "Everything both above and below decks was clean and orderly. The crews' uniforms were spick-and-span, and the sailors saluted smartly, avoiding both the shambling indifference of the Italian soldiers and the exaggerated ostentation of the Fascist fliers. The kitchens were as well scrubbed as the decks."

For sheer tonnage, the fleet was impressive. Its special pride was its force of six handsome battleships, with two more nearing completion. There were also 19 light and heavy cruisers, 59 destroyers, 67 torpedo boats and a larger fleet of submarines—115 of them—than any other nation yet possessed. Italian naval designers had sacrificed weight of armor and cruising range to speed and firepower, but in theory, at least, this was no disadvantage. The Admiralty reasoned that its ships would be operating in a closed sea, in surprise raids against enemy convoys, where the ability to

ECHOING THE NAZIS' RACIAL HATRED

A thrusting sword separates the classical Italian from both Jew and African in this publication entitled "Defense of the Race."

Modern Italy had never experienced a serious problem with anti-Semitism—until Mussolini invented one to solidify his alliance with Germany and create the "clear-cut racial consciousness" he thought necessary to build a new Roman Empire.

By November of 1938 the Duce had pushed through laws that banned marriages between Christians and Jews, excluded Jews from military service and top government jobs, and ordered the confiscation of the most valuable Jewish-owned businesses and land. One edict demanded the expulsion of any Jew who had come to Italy since 1919—a hard blow to those who had sought refuge there from Nazism.

Special exemptions were made for Jews who had distinguished themselves in Italy's wars or in the "Fascist cause," or who had otherwise "earned exceptional recognition"—usually by paying extortion to Fascist officials. And the laws were ignored by many citizens, who considered such racism "un-Italian."

Nevertheless, the campaign encouraged vandalizing raids on Jewish homes and temples. It cost Italy's universities the services of many scholars who were Jewish and at least one who was not—physicist Enrico Fermi, who left Italy because his wife was Jewish, and transferred his genius for nuclear research to the United States.

A synagogue in Ferrara lies wrecked by Fascist thugs in 1941. Some Fascist officials enriched themselves by appropriating confiscated Jewish property.

hit hard and run was more important than the ability to remain under way for long periods.

In practice, however, the Navy had such grave problems that after a few early actions it rarely put to sea. Italian submarines had only limited range and firepower. And they submerged too slowly—with the result that a tenth of the force was sunk in the first three weeks of war. The vaunted speed of the capital ships was largely nullified by the lack of air reconnaissance, which allowed the British to approach undetected and pound the lightly armored Italians almost at will. Maugeri, who soon rose to Rear Admiral, and others in the Navy command believed that the war at sea was lost on the day Mussolini decided carriers were obsolete and that land-based planes could cover the entire Mediterranean.

Yet even the lack of reconnaissance might not have proved fatal had the Italian ships been equipped with radar. Without it, they were virtually helpless against the British, who were first to employ the radio-detecting and ranging device. The Italians had no idea such an invention was being used against them, and they were baffled, as Maugeri observed, when the British showed disquieting signs of being able "to see our ships in the darkness of night."

Ironically, Italian scientists had begun before the War to experiment with short-wave direction-finding equipment for ships but had abandoned their expensive research because it promised no immediate rewards. The Fascists had a strangely ambivalent attitude toward all such research. They desired the military advantages that new technology would bring but distrusted the "inconsistent and antagonistic results" that could be expected if experimentation became too free. Although the ideal was a new "Fascist science" dedicated to serving the state, the practical result was to stifle research and deprive the armed forces of the technology they desperately needed. Mussolini said—and may have believed—that he was a champion of technology, but his imagination ran to miracle weapons that would help him win the War at a stroke. He talked wistfully of a death ray that, he claimed, radio pioneer Guglielmo Marconi had invented but refused to explain before he died in 1937.

In addition to its technical limitations, the Italian fleet was plagued by a persistent shortage of oil and a lack of spare parts. Under normal conditions, Italy received much of its oil from Rumania. But with Suez and Gibraltar closed to Italian shipping after 1940, and the Rumanian fields taken over by the Germans, the Italians found themselves dependent on their northern ally for all their oil—and were soon reduced to one fifth of their peacetime consumption. The shortage became so serious that training cruises were canceled and recruits were taught the rudiments of seamanship aboard imitation ships on dry land. For the conduct of the War, the Navy was allotted no more than 30,000 tons of fuel a month, most of which went to the submarines. Rarely able to put to sea even if they wanted to, Italian sailors listened bitterly to a gibe often made on British radio broadcasts: "While the United States Navy drinks whiskey and the British Navy prefers rum, the Italian Navy sticks to port."

Compounding all other problems, the armed forces suffered from an almost total lack of liaison among the services. Not only did they have no plans for joint operations, but they vied with one another to obtain scarce supplies and pursue their own tactical projects. Mussolini tried to resolve these rivalries when he took over the Supreme Command, but he was too far removed from the daily conduct of the War and too immersed in his own concerns and delusions.

The Duce had been warned in advance that there was not enough oil to fight a war and that other raw materials also were in chronically short supply. Mussolini chose to ignore the warnings, believing instead that the British would be defeated before the shortages became critical. From the beginning, Italy lacked cotton, wool and iron. Many industries geared up for war production with only a few days' supply of coal on hand. Although the Fascists liked to boast that by winning the "Battle of the Grain" they had made the country self-sufficient in food, they suppressed the fact that Italy imported three quarters of its fertilizers, making its food supply highly vulnerable to a blockade.

After the declaration of war, Italian industry came to depend on the Germans for more than oil. Certain key factories in Milan and Turin reported losing one out of every six hours of work because they lacked one strategic material or another. The situation would not have been so critical if the government had allocated its limited resources wisely. But until well into the War great quantities of steel and cement continued to be diverted to the construction of stadiums, highways, canals, bridges, public housing and a projected tunnel under the Strait of Messina. Reasoning that it was important to retain public confidence in the regime, Mussolini instructed his Minister of Public Works to proceed "as though the War did not exist." He even ordered that construction continue on a World's Fair project slated to open in 1942 in celebration of 20 years of Fascist rule.

Many Italian industries never did go on a genuine wartime footing. Partly this was inadvertent—the result of shortages and misallocation of raw materials—but partly it was by design. Counting on a short war, some industrialists with powerful political ties had reserved part of their productive capacity for a quick return to the manufacture of civilian goods in the predicted postwar boom. One result was that the percentage of production devoted to armaments was lower than in other belligerent nations, and even less than it had been in Italy during World War I.

None of these crippling problems daunted Mussolini. In the early autumn of 1940 he looked around for another theater in which to pursue his parallel war. If the offensive in Egypt was stalled, he would show Hitler that he could strike in other directions with speed and audacity. His eye settled on Greece. Grinning with joy, Mussolini greeted Hitler in Florence on October 28 with the words: "Victorious Italian troops crossed the Greco-Albanian frontier at dawn today."

Mussolini's generals had learned of the planned invasion of Greece only two weeks earlier, and they had been appalled. The Duce had explained to them as his private rationale for attacking Greece that he wanted to settle a long history of border and territorial disputes—although his public reason was that the Greeks were giving aid and safe anchorage to the British fleet.

Rarely has a major military campaign been launched so haphazardly. Many of the invading troops were raw recruits, for 600,000 trained soldiers had been demobilized temporarily to help with the fall harvest. According to makeshift strategic plans that the General Staff hastily threw together, the bulk of the expeditionary force was to disembark at the Albanian port of Durazzo, which turned out to be clogged with vessels unloading marble for Fascist buildings under construction in Albania. Nine divisions of the Ninth and Eleventh Armies were committed. Two of these divisions remained in Albania to guard against revolt there,

leaving only seven to carry the attack. Although the troops had to be transported across the Adriatic Sea, and the invasion would require air cover, no one had thought to include either the Navy or the Air Force in the initial discussion of the plan. Nor was any thought given to the fact that in mountainous northern Greece the rainy season had begun, and temperatures soon dropped below freezing.

Mussolini assured the senior officers of the departing invasion force that the Greek Army could muster only 30,000 men, and Ciano predicted that the Greeks would not fight at all because their leaders had been well bribed in advance. Even if he should suffer unexpected losses, Mussolini told his hand-picked Eleventh Army commander, General Visconti-Prasca, he was always to advance. "I have given orders," the general gallantly replied, "that the battalions are always to attack, even against divisions."

Within hours of crossing the frontier, the Italian infantrymen learned that they were up against a tenacious foe. Whereas the Greek troops were completely at home in the chill climate and difficult terrain, the Italians found their advance elements in alarming disarray. During the chaotic disembarkment at Durazzo, some 30,000 tons of supplies had been left stacked on the piers for lack of transport, and many a soldier marched into the mountains without his winter boots.

The Italians advanced in a four-pronged drive as far as the Kalamos River, five miles inside the Greek border, and one column probed 20 miles beyond the river. Every pass and defile seemed to conceal an ambush. American correspondent Reynolds Packard reached the front close behind the invading army. As he moved up over muddy mountain roads, he saw in the ravines below him overturned Italian trucks that had slithered off the road, and the bodies of soldiers that had spilled out of the trucks.

Packard's first real intimation that the campaign was going badly for the invaders came when he and a group of Italian correspondents met General Visconti-Prasca on a muddy road behind the front. "We are going much faster, now that the rain has cleared up," the general told them. "We were delayed by the Greeks' blowing up their bridges and roads, but we have repaired all the damage. Naturally, there is still much to be done. I am confident there is nothing to cause worry."

The Italian journalists were disconcerted, for they were sufficiently familiar with Fascist rhetoric to recognize that Visconti-Prasca's failure to claim smashing victories might well mean the campaign was lost. As the party moved within range of Greek artillery fire, Packard saw three infantrymen shouting as they raced toward the rear. "They're crazy," said an Italian correspondent at his side. "They say the Greeks are coming."

Indeed they were. Attacking three divisions strong, the Greeks maneuvered skillfully through the hills to pummel the Italian flanks. After sustaining heavy casualties, the Italians fell back across the frontier and deep into Albania, with the Greeks on their heels. Mussolini began desperately sending reinforcements while the Italian infantry tried to make a stand in the bitter cold. Most of the soldiers either had no winter clothing or had been issued overcoats made of a synthetic called Lanital that gave virtually no protection. With few medical supplies and scant provisions, thousands of men suffered frostbite or died of cold and hunger in the alien land.

With timely aid from the Royal Air Force, whose planes struck Italian airfields and ports in Albania, the Greeks occupied nearly a third of southern and eastern Albania. Even Fascist censors could not conceal the disaster. On the home front a story went around that the French were putting up signs in the Alps reading, "Greeks! Stop here! This is the French border!"

By the middle of December the Italians had stemmed the Greek advance, but they were unable to mount a counteroffensive. "Whatever you write," an Italian officer told American correspondent Richard Massock, "don't say the Italian soldier is not brave." In fact, the Italian infantrymen were fighting well under appalling conditions. It was not their fault that their leaders had grossly underestimated the ferocity of the Greeks.

On December 4, 1940, Mussolini had summoned to the Palazzo Venezia his Ambassador to Germany, Dino Alfieri. The Duce's eyes were swollen and his face was drawn and unshaven. He told Alfieri to fly to Berlin at once and appeal for German help to drive the Greeks out of Albania and end the fighting there. Alfieri's mission was ultimately successful—Hitler decided he had no option but to rescue his ally—but Fascist pride had suffered a blow from which it never recovered.

Germany rushed powerful forces to Greece, and the months that followed saw a sharp reversal in the fortunes of war there. In April of 1941, Greece surrendered to an overwhelming Axis force. Fascist propaganda tried to claim the victory was Italian, without success. The fiasco in Greece in fact marked the end of public confidence in Mussolini and his regime. The Duce himself now became the butt of jokes. It was said that during Hitler's momentary absence from the room at a summit conference, Mussolini tried to open a

In Athens at last, two Italian soldiers patrol the Acropolis while a third in the background sketches the ancient ruins. After their independent invasion in 1940 was repulsed, the Italians rolled into Greece in April of 1941 on the coattails of 13 German divisions.

bottle of champagne and was hit in the eye with the cork. The Führer returned, saw the black eye, and exclaimed reproachfully: "Duce, Duce, if I leave you alone one minute you get beaten up!"

The news from Italy's other fronts was no better. While Marshal Graziani was debating when to resume his offensive in Egypt, the British launched an attack that, according to Foreign Minister Ciano, struck the Italians "like a thunderbolt." The first blow fell on the 10th of December at the seven linked camps that Graziani had constructed at Sidi Barrani. Taken by surprise as they were cooking their breakfasts, the Italians fought back desperately. They were hampered by poor communication and by a lack of coordination all along the line. Rallied by their officers, Graziani's men flung themselves in hopeless machine-gun and grenade attacks against British tanks. In one instance of courage, General Pietro Maletti sprang from his tent still wearing his pajamas and manned a machine gun until he was killed. But such heroics were not enough. "One cannot break steel armor with fingernails alone," Marshal Graziani later wrote in a letter to his wife.

Forced to retreat, the Italians made a stand at Bardia, a Libyan port that Mussolini ordered them to hold at all costs. But here too they lacked either the equipment or the firepower to stand up to British armor. The retreat became a rout as the Tenth Army fled west to Tobruk. Soon the roads behind them were choked with columns of Italian prisoners moving to the British rear. Then Tobruk fell, and Mussolini noted bitterly that one general had been killed and five had been captured. One to five, he raged to Ciano, was "the ratio between Italians who have some military ability and those who have none." At a cost of 476 killed, the British had advanced 200 miles in a month, taking 130,000 Italian prisoners and 700 guns.

The Italians were no more successful on the sea. On November 11 a British task force centered around the carrier *Illustrious* approached the southernmost Italian Navy base at Taranto without being detected and launched its aircraft in a daring torpedo attack on the Italian fleet anchored there. The battleships *Conte di Cavour*, *Littorio* and *Duilio* were sunk, and the heavy cruiser *Trento* was damaged. One day later the surviving ships were moved to less-exposed bases, notably Naples. The raid not only shifted the balance of naval power in the Mediterranean but confirmed Admiral Maugeri's gloomy prediction that in the absence of adequate aerial reconnaissance the Italian fleet would be disastrously vulnerable.

The successive military disasters bred a climate at home that was both cynical and despairing. After the fall of France, Italians reminded themselves of the difference between the First and Second World Wars: "In the first war, we prepared, then we fought, and then we made the armistice; in this one, we made the armistice, then we fought, and now we must prepare." The government conceded privately that 85 per cent of Italians already were against continuing the War. Weary of government propaganda, people were turning to forbidden broadcasts from London to learn the fate of their friends and relatives fighting overseas—and the truth about conditions in their own country.

In the cafés, people talked most about the British air raids. The first bombs had fallen on the Piedmont city of Turin the day after war was declared, killing 30 civilians. Throughout the summer of 1940 the Royal Air Force bombers concentrated on the industrial cities of the north—Genoa, Milan, and Turin again—because they were the only Italian targets within reach of bases in southern England. Then in the autumn a squadron of long-range Wellingtons arrived on British Malta, in the central Mediterranean, and Naples came under attack.

With exceptions, the raids had greater psychological than material effect. Although Italian antiaircraft defenses were minimal—some units relied on old Saint-Étienne machine guns from World War I—the British lacked the planes and the bomb capacity to mount a major air offensive. In those early months a few hundred houses were destroyed, but important factories remained intact and the flow of goods at Italian ports was not interrupted. Among the 200 civilian casualties were a considerable number hit by Italian antiaircraft shells that had exploded prematurely or not at all.

The most ominous raid by far was the one launched against Naples on December 15. Eighty civilians died, and fires raged through the centuries-old Spanish quarter near the waterfront, burying victims under the collapsing rubble. The experts in England's Psychological Warfare Branch watched that raid with particular interest, for they reasoned that southern Italians were highly emotional and would panic under fire. As it turned out, the Neapolitans proved admirably cool through years of adversity.

Fascist propaganda felt compelled to extol "the clear virtues of the Italian and Fascist people in resisting enemy air attacks." Mussolini declared that continued bombing would "make a Nordic people out of the Neapolitans." Anxious that the population of Rome not forget that they too were at war, the Duce ordered that sirens be sounded in Rome whenever there was an alert in Naples. An air-raid shelter was established in the ancient catacombs, where early Christians had found refuge. And in the streets of the Holy City appeared huge banners of green, white and red proclaiming "We are at war."

Few Italians needed reminding. Already the use of private automobiles was prohibited. Even taxis were banned after 10 p.m., and people urgently needing one had to argue their case with the police. Cafés, restaurants and places of amusement closed early. In the blacked-out cities the supply of flashlight batteries was soon exhausted—and never replenished, for Italy lacked the materials to make them. Pedestrians took to wearing luminous buttons in their lapels to avoid running into one another in the dark.

Prices rose steadily, and in some places so did unemployment. Just before the October invasion of Greece, 8 per cent of the work force in Milan and 10 per cent in Genoa were without work. The cost of living had doubled in four years. Demonstrators in both rural and urban areas protested a wage freeze imposed by the government. Even the movie extras at Cinema City outside Rome marched to demand more money, and had to be dispersed by the police.

The rationing of food and clothing came comparatively slowly to Italy, because Mussolini expected a short war and because he was determined to give the impression that Italy was strong enough to fight without disrupting its civilian economy. While Italian troops in Albania were suffering frostbite for lack of boots, shop windows in Rome abounded with unrationed leather shoes. Bread was not rationed until late in 1941. But other shortages were felt long before then, as commodities disappeared from the stores. Laundry soap and sugar were among the first to go, followed by milk and potatoes. The Ministry of Agriculture requisitioned 30 per cent of the nation's beef cattle for shipment to Germany in exchange for raw materials, and Italians were urged to observe four meatless days a week.

Fascist district leaders reported a civil restiveness, which Ciano diagnosed in his diary. "The name of the uneasiness that disturbs our people," he wrote, "is lack of bread, fats and eggs." Shrewd though he was, Ciano only partly guessed at the truth, for he failed to see how quickly faith in the Fascist Party was eroding. The party emblem worn in the buttonhole was being referred to as "The Bedbug," only in part because of its shape, and people joked bitterly that by now everybody was anti-Fascist—including the Fascists. One story had it that the last Fascist left in Italy was a very small minnow caught one day in the Tiber River. The fisherman, reflecting aloud that he lacked olive oil, butter and flour for cooking his catch, threw back the minnow, which then swam to the surface, raised a fin in the Roman salute and cried gratefully, *"Viva il Duce!"*

Disillusioned though the public was, there were as yet few signs of organized resistance. Most people were still referred to as "sleepers"—potential fighters against the regime who for the moment kept their views to themselves. To detect and control its enemies, dormant or otherwise, the government had at its disposal an elaborate police apparatus augmented by a highly sensitive network of informers. Any criticism of the regime—whether written or oral—was outlawed; every citizen lived in fear that some negative remark might be overheard and reported to the authorities. By law, porters in apartment buildings were required to report regularly to the police on their tenants and the visitors they received. Every office had its *fiduciàrio,* a stool pigeon who listened for hostile talk. Even in their homes people developed the habit, when they wanted to discuss politics, of turning on the radio or phonograph in order to cover their conversation.

Snooping was so universal that English-speaking journalists in Rome learned to refer to Mussolini as "Mr. Smith" or "the Duke" when they met in public places. Correspondent Richard Massock assumed that his home telephone was tapped, but he had no proof until one day when his wife called a Spanish friend and started talking to her in French, their only common language. A woman's voice broke in on the line and said, "Quit speaking French, speak Italian."

The Spanish woman protested that she knew no Italian. "Then you shouldn't be in Italy," snapped the voice. The line went dead.

Massock discovered that all calls from his office were channeled through the Ministry of the Interior and were subject to immediate termination. After the German intervention in Greece, Mussolini became obsessively sensitive about suggestions that he was now operating under orders from Hitler. He banned any reference to his own or Ciano's frequent trips to Germany. Correspondents phoning their stories to Switzerland for cable relay overseas found that the line almost always clicked dead on the words "Mussolini" or "Ciano." If correspondents persisted and tried to argue their case with the invisible censor, they received no reply. The effect, recalled Massock wryly, was somewhat like "talking to God."

In countless ways small and large, people were reminded that their lives belonged to the state. Anyone abroad in the city after 9 p.m. could be stopped by the police for an identity check and asked about his intentions. Strikes and protest demonstrations of any kind were forbidden. It became dangerous to listen to American jazz, or to read books by English or American authors, which consistently had been best-sellers in Italy. Saturdays were reserved for party activities: "There is only one Saturday," the propagandists declared, "the Fascist Saturday." At rallies and meetings of all kinds, citizens were exhorted to live in the Fascist style. The true Fascist, according to party doctrine, cultivated a terse manner of speaking, never let his hair grow too long, was careful not to be too deferential, and refrained from such decadent habits as drinking excessive amounts of coffee or going for holidays in the country.

Above all, the true Fascist was instructed not to fraternize with Jews. As discontent with the regime grew, various party leaders urged that a more vigorous anti-Semitic campaign be launched as a means of diverting attention from the failings of the government *(page 60)*. In schoolbooks, reading lessons appeared with titles such as "Little Carl, the Vengeful Jew," "We Are Not Jews!" and "Get After the Jews!"

The responsibility for protecting the state against its own citizens was in the hands of various police forces, the most effective of which was the secret organization known as OVRA. Details of OVRA's operations were so carefully guarded that the unit never appeared in any official document, and even the origin of its name was a riddle. Some said the initials stood for *"Opera Vigilanza Repressione Antifascista"* ("Anti-Fascist Repression Force"), but others believed that the initials had been chosen at random by Mussolini, simply because he thought they sounded mysterious. No records were kept of OVRA's size or the disposition of its forces, but insiders estimated it numbered as many as 50,000 agents.

In theory, OVRA was charged with suppressing anti-Fascist activity in the workers' syndicates, government offices, party organizations and among foreign populations—particularly the Slovene community in the area near the Yugoslav border.

In practice, OVRA involved itself in every aspect of life on the Italian home front. Although it was not as systematically brutal as the SS and Gestapo were in Germany, more than one instance was reported of prisoners dying or being driven insane under OVRA interrogation. OVRA's favored techniques included beating prisoners, subjecting them to mock executions and forcing them to drink iodine. Interrogators also succeeded in eliciting "confessions" by the skillful administration of drugs.

Those considered enemies of the regime generally were summoned before the Special Tribunal for the Defense of the State. The tribunal was composed of five Black Shirt officers, none of whom was required to have a law degree. Established by Mussolini as a means of circumventing the regular judiciary, the tribunal could order suspects held indefinitely without trial, since in Fascist Italy there was no right of habeas corpus. The tribunal's verdict, from which there was no appeal, was frequently decided in advance, and in many cases the defense was a farce. The lawyer assigned to defend a group of Slovenes accused of bombing a Fascist newspaper began by declaring that "death would be the proper thing" for his clients.

Those accused who somehow escaped judgment at the hands of the tribunal were automatically remanded to one of the *commissioni del confino*—courts charged with sentencing anti-Fascists to exile in remote villages or on the Lipari Islands off Sicily *(opposite)*. Most of those who experienced banishment found it a maddeningly unconstrained

INTERNAL EXILE FOR DISSIDENTS

If a convicted dissident escaped the death penalty, he might still be sentenced to internal exile, or *confino*. Any small sin was cause for banishment: A slip of the tongue or a bit of casual grousing—if overheard by an informant—could bring a sentence of up to five years. As Italy and the United States went to war in December 1941, one group of Roman aristocrats was banished for attending a farewell party for the American Ambassador.

In two decades of Fascism, more than 10,000 Italians were exiled. The luckier ones were sent to isolated villages, where boredom and malaria were their worst problems. These exiles (some of them Fascists who had fallen from favor) had the run of their villages so long as they signed a register every day.

Dissidents thought to be more dangerous were shipped in chains to penal islands off Sicily and incarcerated in wretched dormitories run by the Fascist militia. They slept on plank beds alongside hardened criminals—thieves and roughnecks who robbed and beat and informed on them. The militia subjected the exiles to torture and to isolation on bread and water.

Through it all, the dissidents kept alive their spirit of resistance. They formed secret branches of their political parties and organized classes to benefit from the prodigious intellects of some of the prisoners. A number of them even escaped, usually in motorboats supplied by friends who spirited them across the open sea to Africa—and from there to lands beyond Fascism's reach.

Internal exiles sit on their wooden dormitory beds on Favignana Island, off Sicily, just before being freed by the Allies in October 1943.

form of imprisonment. "The *confino*," wrote convicted anti-Fascist Carlo Rosselli, "is a large cell without walls, a cell composed entirely of sky and sea." Among those exiled were some of Italy's leading thinkers, including the writers Carlo Levi, Cesare Pavese and Curzio Malaparte. Levi later wrote a classic account of his exile in the book *Christ Stopped at Eboli.*

In the intrigue-laden atmosphere of wartime Italy, spies were assigned to keep watch on spies, and no one was safe from denunciation or arrest. Since all members of the police forces were required to belong to the party, they were subject to constant surveillance by the party apparatus. At the same time, one of the important missions of the police was to check on party members themselves, watching for signs of disloyalty. In addition, informers were at work in the armed forces and the civil service and inside every ministry. When Italy's battered troops returned from Greece they were forced to surrender their arms—on the advice of spies within their ranks, who had warned that they were on the verge of rebellion.

This internecine surveillance worked all too efficiently, as party members sometimes learned to their sorrow. Mussolini's old comrade Giuseppe Bottai was denounced as pro-Jewish by a Roman noblewoman, the Contessa Giulia Brambilla-Carminati, who turned out to be an OVRA informer. Even Foreign Minister Ciano was not immune. One day Achille Starace came to him and said he had received an intelligence report that Ciano had been personally critical of the Duce. Ciano shrugged off the report as a fabrication, and Starace promised he would not bring the matter to Mussolini's attention. But Ciano was left with a feeling of uneasiness—as Starace had undoubtedly intended.

Mussolini himself was spied upon. The head of the Italian counterintelligence service was in the pay of the Germans. He supplied Berlin useful background about Mussolini's moods and opinions, which often were the opposite of his public statements.

Italy had been at war only a few months when fault lines began to appear in the rock of Fascist unity. The new Party Secretary, Adelchi Serena, got into a fistfight with the Minister of Agriculture, Giuseppe Tassinari, while the two were waiting to see Mussolini—even though footmen at the Palazzo Venezia had been instructed to usher rival min-

isters into different rooms to avoid such confrontations.

The old feud between party and civil authorities flared again. The police and local party leaders, the so-called *federali,* accused each other of plundering scarce rationed goods before they could be released to the public. Factional disputes within the party grew sharper—none more visibly than the silent warfare between the so-called Petacci faction and the coterie around Galeazzo Ciano.

Without Mussolini's knowledge, Marcello Petacci was using his sister's intimacy with the Duce to advance and enrich himself. He acquired a medical degree by appearing for a hasty examination before a specially convened board of

Sightseeing in Rome, German aviators of Fliegerkorps X visit the Coliseum in March of 1941. Their experienced, 300-plane outfit had been transferred from Norway to the Mediterranean in December 1940 to help the Italians defend Axis convoys steaming for North Africa.

examiners. He was said to have made a fortune by dealing in illicit foreign exchange and black-market liquor. Petitioners came to him, cash in hand, hoping that he would help them secure profitable government contracts.

Clara Petacci herself was also wooed by businessmen who attributed to her even more influence than she had. She was kept well supplied with furs, and a Lombardy banker presented her a 12-carat diamond ring because he believed she had helped him close a deal. The Minister of the Interior, Guido Buffarini-Guidi, discreetly sent her $10,000 a month, which he accounted for as "charitable contributions." In some circles Clara became known, exaggeratedly, as "the Madame Pompadour of the 20th Century."

The Petacci faction's influence, real or imagined, was bitterly resented by Ciano, the ambitious son-in-law who aspired to be chief dispenser of favors in the entourage around Mussolini. Since marrying Mussolini's daughter Edda and becoming the Duce's chief lieutenant, Ciano had grown enormously wealthy. His preferred method of operation was to artificially depress the stock of a strong company by exerting his official influence, then buy a controlling interest in the company at a price far below its value. He owned a newspaper and other enterprises and had vast farmlands in Tuscany, including three properties near Florence valued at $4 million. The coral doorknobs and tortoise-shell window frames alone at his Florentine villa were said to be worth $40,000.

At the height of his power, Ciano shuffled his friends in and out of ministries or installed them at the head of corporations almost at will. With the emergence of the Petacci faction to challenge this system of patronage, a kind of internal warfare broke out that disrupted the functioning of government and at times involved even Mussolini.

The Duce accepted a certain amount of freebootery among his subordinates. Within limits, he welcomed it as a means of blackmailing them and keeping them in line. His main interest was to prevent such corruption from becoming public. This became increasingly difficult as the behavior of many prominent figures grew more and more brazen. There was a saying that if a plutocrat was a man who gained power through wealth, then the Fascist leaders were "cratoplutes," or men who gained wealth through power.

One of those whispered about was General Ugo Caval-
lero, Chief of the General Staff, who attempted to seize for himself 2,750 acres of land in Albania. Earlier he had bought a run-down castle in Piedmont for a few lire. By arranging for the King and the Army high command to stay at the castle during Army maneuvers, Cavallero managed to have an access road built and to have the castle repaired and furnished at government expense.

Equally enterprising was Osvaldo Sebastiani, Mussolini's private secretary, who bought up marble quarries in Carrara, then used his influence to have a law passed requiring at least 10 per cent of the façades of all new buildings to be covered with marble. Even the stern and dedicated Fascist Roberto Farinacci had been notorious for years for lining his pockets: As a lawyer (he had qualified for the bar by copying someone else's thesis), he charged outrageously high fees for assisting at court actions in which his influence was sure to result in a favorable verdict.

Fascist officials worried, with good reason, about the effect of such scandals on public morale. Everybody knew that the bribe—popularly known as the bustarèlla, or "envelope"—had become almost a way of life in wartime Italy. The well-to-do depended on it to obtain everything from a choice restaurant table to a defense contract.

In this atmosphere of intrigue and petty corruption, reports from the battlefront provided no relief. Even as the Italians appealed for German assistance in Greece, news came that the British had broken loose again in North Africa. On the 5th of February, 1941, a stunned Rome learned that the British had struck in Libya south of Gebel el Akhdar in a brilliant encircling maneuver that closed the trap on what remained of the Italian Tenth Army. A week later, Lieut. General Erwin Rommel alighted from a German aircraft at Tripoli with orders to turn the situation around in North Africa.

At the same time, German troops began moving through the Brenner Pass into Italy itself. Nobody needed to be told that Mussolini's parallel war was over—and that from now on, at home and abroad, Italy would pursue the War as a virtual prisoner of the Reich. In Rome, someone scrawled a plaintive message beneath a statue of Giuseppe Garibaldi, the 19th Century patriot who had led Italy's drive for independence. "Come down, Giuseppe," read the message. "The Germans are here!"

FLAWS OF A PROUD AIR FORCE

a prewar spectacle of the kind that made Italy's air force world-famous, a formation of Ansaldo C-3 fighters spreads simulated toxic gas over La Spezia.

A FAILURE ROOTED IN MISLEADING SUCCESS

Italy's Regia Aeronautica entered the War as one of the best-tested and proudest air forces in the world. For nearly two decades Italian airmen had been setting distance and speed records and winning international competitions. During the 1930s, Italian planes had bombed and strafed a valiant but ill-equipped Ethiopia into submission, and they had helped tip the balance for Franco in Spain. Yet by 1940 the Italian Air Force was bedeviled by problems—some of them traceable to the successes of the past.

Italian aviators saw themselves less as soldiers than as audacious acrobats of the air who could fly circles around any rivals. That cocky pride prompted fighter pilots to disdain the less flashy bomber pilots and encouraged bomber pilots to emulate the risky maneuvers of the fighter pilots. In a similar vein, the Italian engineers who had built a superb 2,500-horsepower engine for racing never succeeded in producing a satisfactory fighter engine half its size.

One-sided victories in Ethiopia and Spain spoiled the Regia Aeronautica for the reality of doing battle against larger powers with the ability to fight back. As a consequence, both designers and pilots were slow to appreciate the value of adequate armament: Italian fighters typically had just two machine guns, whereas the Allied planes they fought against often carried cannon.

Italy boasted 3,300 planes when it entered the War, but only half of them were ready for combat. The little wars of the 1930s had used up spare parts and had left the nation no time to restock. (Italy never did build enough parts; it preferred to invest its production capacity in finished planes that looked good on display but were often grounded for want of spares.) Success had also tempted Italian designers to rest on their laurels. In 1940 more than half of Italy's fighters were Fiat CR.42 Falcon biplanes, solid but obsolete craft that had little chance against British Spitfires and Hurricanes. The Falcon was so slow, in fact, that it sometimes surprised enemy fliers; on one occasion a Spitfire overtook a Falcon and, unintentionally, rammed it out of the sky.

Italy eventually developed some of the War's best planes, including the powerful and innovative P.108B strategic bomber pictured below. But its fragmented aircraft industry wasted immense amounts of money and experience dreaming up new designs rather than refining the best of the old ones. Thus Italy produced more than twice as many kinds of bombers and fighters as did Germany, whose simpler air force enjoyed far greater success. In any case, material shortages and Allied bombing raids prevented Italy from building enough of any model, old or new. All told, the Italians manufactured only 12,000 planes during the War, fewer than 40 per cent of which survived to the armistice.

Looking much like an American B-17, Italy's P.108B long-range bomber stands ready in 1943. It arrived too late and in numbers too small to be effective.

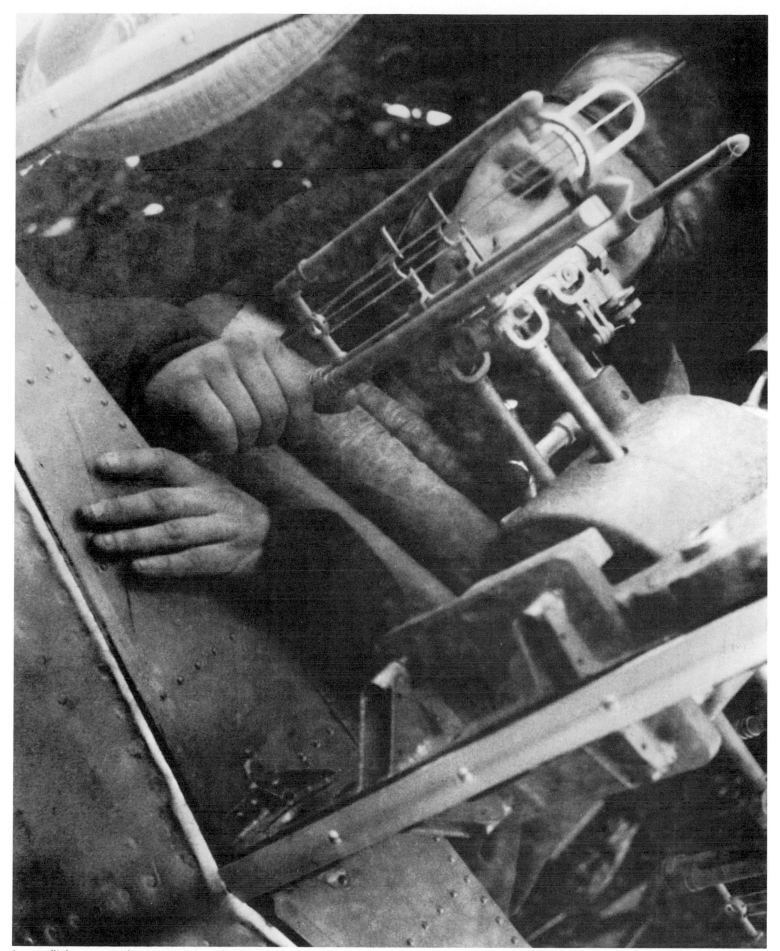

In a preflight test, an Italian airman adjusts his bombsight in the gondola on the underside of an SM.79 Sparrowhawk, the backbone of Italy's bomber fleet.

LAST HURRAH FOR AN AGILE BIPLANE

The Fiat CR.42 Falcon was the best—and the last—of the biplane fighter aircraft that had dominated aerial combat since World War I. The single-seater had an open cockpit; it was made of the finest light metal and had fabric covering aft and on the wings to reduce its weight and increase its maneuverability. "I dived to attack," recalled a British Spitfire pilot of his first encounter with a Falcon. "As I opened fire he half-rolled very tightly and I was completely unable to hold him, so rapid were his maneuvers."

Unfortunately the Falcon was as slow as it was agile; its top speed of 270 miles per hour was about 80 miles per hour less than that of the Spitfire. And its lightness of weight had been achieved at the expense of protective armor. Worst of all, Falcons lacked radar—and, frequently, radios as well. The last drawback struck the Italian aviators as particularly ironic: "After all," complained one pilot, "Marconi was an Italian."

Dressed for combat in cold northern skies, Falcon pilots stand beside their open-cockpit planes at an Italian air base in occupied Belgium in late 1940.

Belgian-based CR.42 Falcons fly escort for Italian bombers during the Battle of Britain. In addition to escort duty, the Falcon flew reconnaissance and nightfighter missions, and for the North Africa campaign it was modified to carry two 220-pound bombs.

As a Falcon's engine warms up, a ground crewman helps an Italian pilot into the cockpit for a nighttime mission over England. The Falcon was the only biplane to attack Great Britain during World War II.

75

A Fiat G.50 Arrow (foreground) provides fighter cover for a torpedo-laden German Me-110 bomber on a mission off the North African coast in 1941. Some 800 of the 294-mph Arrows were built.

A RELIANCE ON OVERMATCHED FIGHTERS

Italy's early monoplane fighters were little better than the biplane Falcon. The Fiat G.50 Arrow and the Macchi MC.200 Thunderbolt were slower than the British Spitfire and lacked the Falcon's maneuverability. One pilot dismissed the Arrow as "good for touring but not for war."

The Macchi MC.202 Lightning, introduced in 1941 with a 1,175-horsepower in-line engine built in Germany, was the best Italian fighter to see action in large numbers. It flew in Africa, the Balkans, the Mediterranean and Russia. But not until the Fiat G.55 Centaur and the Macchi MC.205 Greyhound were developed did Italy have fighters fast and well armed enough, with 20mm cannon, to take on the Allies' best. The Centaur and the Greyhound were just arriving in fighter wings when Italy was knocked out of the War.

Italian pilots gather for a last-minute briefing near a line of Macchi MC.200 Thunderbolt fighter-bombers. The all-metal Thunderbolts achieved their greatest success when they sank the Royal Navy destroyer Zulu during a British attack on Tobruk in 1942.

A Macchi MC.202 Lightning is silhouetted above Mount Vesuvius, near the Bay of Naples. Considered superior to the British Hurricane and the American P-40, its rivals in North Africa, the Lightning could climb to 19,000 feet in less than six minutes.

SEAPLANES TO PATROL THE MEDITERRANEAN

The Italians used a variety of patrol planes in trying to keep the Mediterranean "our sea." One of the most useful, the Imam Ro.43 floatplane, was an all-metal two-seater biplane that could be launched by catapult from a ship's deck, then retrieved later by crane.

The big, ungainly-looking Cant Z.501 Seagull flying boat was called "Mama, help!" reportedly because of the fear it inspired in children who saw it flying low over Italy's beaches. The Seagull was slow and built of wood, but its range of 1,500 miles made it valuable for convoy-escort and antisubmarine runs as well as for reconnaissance missions.

The Cant Z.506B Heron, a trimotored seaplane, was faster and better-armed than the Seagull—and was renowned as a rescue plane. From 1940 to 1942, Herons plucked 231 downed airmen from the sea.

In 1943 the Italians planned to send a new and more powerful seaplane on a one-way transatlantic mission. Two Cant Z.511s were to fly under U.S. radar and launch human torpedoes against ships in New York harbor. But Allied planes destroyed the craft before they could leave.

An Imam Ro.43 is catapulted from an Italian warship. The floatplane's folding wings enabled cruisers to carry two—and battleships up to four—of the aircraft, which had a range of 680 miles.

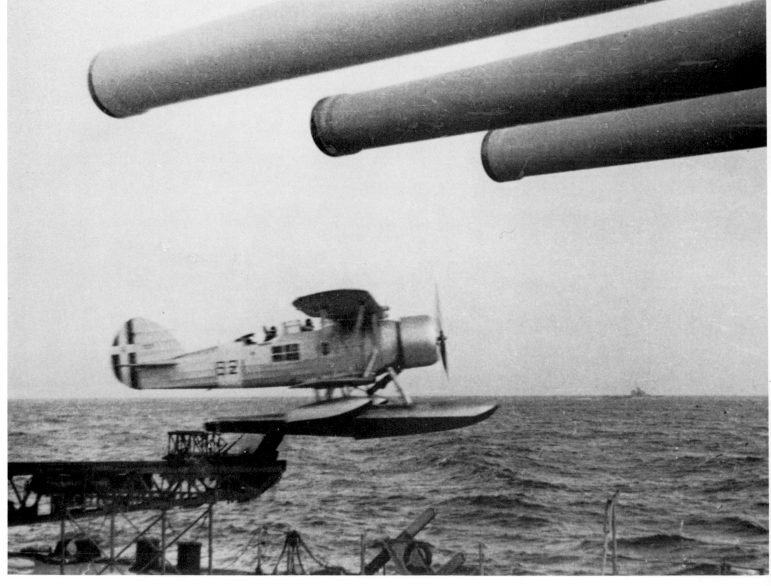

As though lifted by a giant fan, a Seagull flying boat rises over the Italian shoreline. The Seagull carried three machine guns—two mounted on its hull and one, reachable only by a ladder, on the wing behind the engine.

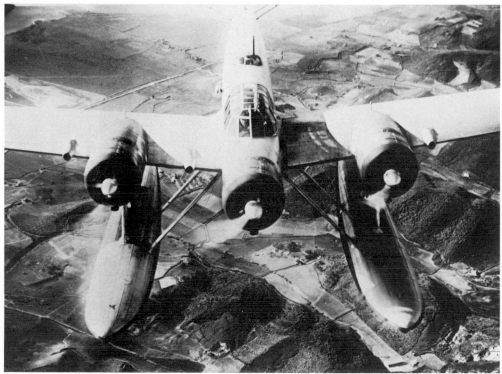

Heading inland, a Heron seaplane flies over Italy's coastal farmland. A gondola mounted under the Heron's fuselage housed the bombardier and either 2,745 pounds of bombs or a single 1,764-pound torpedo.

Paratroopers stream earthward from the rear cargo doors of an SM.82 Kangaroo bomber-transport during a training exercise over the Italian countryside.

A KANGAROO WITH REACH AND PUNCH

One of Italy's best planes was the appropriately named SM.82 Kangaroo. A tri-motored bomber-transport, it had a commodious hold for carrying equipment or troops. The craft also boasted two world records for distance and speed, demonstrating that it could make a long hop in a short time.

The Kangaroo originally was intended to be used only as a transport. The plane's fabric-covered metal fuselage—the wings and the tail were made of wood—could carry six tons of cargo, loaded through a pair of large rear doors. A metal floor divided the fuselage into upper and lower compartments, but the floor could be removed to accommodate especially bulky loads. The Kangaroo had space for 40 fully equipped paratroopers, 600 gallons of fuel or—with the floor taken out—a single Fiat CR.42 Falcon with its wings and spare parts stored alongside. In all, the SM.82 transported some 50 Falcons from Italy to air bases in Italian East Africa, a trip the single-engined fighters could not have made under their own power.

As a heavy bomber, the Kangaroo could carry an equally impressive load—eight 1,100-pound bombs or twenty-seven 220-pounders. With a range of 1,865 miles, the bomber could execute surprise night attacks on British-held cities and ports as far away as Palestine.

Even the Germans, who were generally contemptuous of the Italians' planes, were favorably impressed by the Kangaroo. Almost half of the 875 Kangaroos that the Italians manufactured wound up flying in the Luftwaffe.

Italian soldiers wait to board a Kangaroo painted in the camouflage scheme the British called "sand and spinach."

Nestled in the hold of a Kangaroo, a Fiat Falcon is ready to be ferried to the front. The Falcon's wings and stabilizers are fixed to the bulkhead at right.

An Italian bomb specialist decorates bombs for delivery to England—including one with an umbrella (foreground) to symbolize former Prime Minister Neville Chamberlain. None of the bombs reached their intended targets.

LUCKLESS BOMBERS OVER BRITAIN

Against the wishes of Adolf Hitler and the advice of his own generals, Benito Mussolini insisted that Italy participate in the Battle of Britain. The Duce feared that the War would end before Italy had a chance to impress its powerful German ally—and win sufficient glory for itself. Thus in September of 1940, seventy-three Fiat BR.20 Stork medium bombers were based in German-occupied Belgium to join the attack on southeastern England.

The Italians soon wished they had remained at home. The bomber crews, miserable in the drizzly Belgian climate, had a hard time learning to fly in the equally soupy weather over the English Channel. The Storks themselves were no match for British attack planes and ground defenses; they were slow, under-gunned and cursed with fabric-covered wings that were easily shredded by enemy fire. And their fighter protection was inadequate.

The results were predictable, and embarrassing. In four months, the Storks flew only two daylight raids and a few night missions. They frequently carried bomb-loads of just 1,500 pounds per plane—and those few bombs fell more often in the sea or in coastal marshes than on their targets. In less than 300 hours of flying time, some 20 Storks—more than one fourth of the Italian force—were destroyed.

A Royal Air Force corporal measures his hand against a shell hole in the rudder of a Stork bomber that was shot down near Woodbridge, England, in November of 1940. One member of the Stork's six-man crew was killed and the other five were taken prisoner.

In tight formation, Italian BR.20 Stork bombers head for the English coast. Although they proved ineffective in the Battle of Britain, the Storks were later used as bombers in Greece, North Africa and the Soviet Union before being relegated to transport and reconnaissance duty.

Cruising at 13,000 feet, a Kingfisher bomber is camouflaged on the sides and top and painted light gray on the bottom to decrease its visibility from below.

A NIMBLE KINGFISHER MADE OF WOOD

A much better medium bomber than the Stork was the Cant Z.1007 Kingfisher. Its three 1,000-horsepower engines gave it a top speed of 275 miles per hour, and it could climb to 13,000 feet in nine and a half minutes—only two thirds the time the Stork required. The Kingfisher could also carry more than twice the payload of the Stork—up to 4,400 pounds of bombs, or two 1,000-pound aerial torpedoes for anti-shipping missions.

But the Kingfisher had drawbacks, too. It carried two 7.7mm and two 12.7mm machine guns but was vulnerable to head-on attack, and neither its fuselage nor its fuel tanks were protected by armor plate. The plane's pilots had to depend upon its speed and its ability to perform well at high altitudes to elude enemy fighters.

The scarcity of strategic metals in Italy dictated that the Kingfisher be made entirely of wood—a fact that left the plane at a disadvantage in air-to-air combat and lessened its efficiency in extreme climates, where the wood might turn brittle or rot. Nevertheless, some 560 Kingfishers were manufactured, and they saw duty everywhere the Italians fought, from East Africa to the Russian front.

A gunner aims the 7.7mm machine gun in the Kingfisher's underbelly.

Framed by two 12.7mm machine guns, a radio operator, one of the Kingfisher's crew of five, mans his post in the crowded waist section.

On a grassy Italian airfield, seven ground crewmen wheel an aerial torpedo armed with a 440-pound warhead toward an SM.79 Sparrowhawk bomber.

A VERSATILE HUNCHBACK TO PLAGUE ALLIED SHIPS

Italians affectionately named their most successful bomber, the fast and durable SM.79 Sparrowhawk, *Gobbo Maledetto*, or "Damn Hunchback," because of the hump on its fuselage behind the cockpit. The hump housed two 12.7mm machine guns; a gondola under the fuselage held another machine gun and the bombardier.

The Italians built more Sparrowhawks than any other combat plane. The 594 Sparrowhawks already flying in 1940 constituted almost two thirds of Italy's bomber force, and during the War an additional 600 came off the line.

These versatile trimotors also made fine assault and reconnaissance planes. One was even turned into a radio-guided flying bomb. In August 1942 it was launched—unsuccessfully—against British warships off the Algerian coast.

Italy had no aircraft carriers from which to attack enemy shipping. The Sparrowhawk filled that gap as a land-based torpedo bomber. Carrying one or a pair of torpedoes under the fuselage, Sparrowhawks plagued Allied convoys all over the Mediterranean—so effectively that by the end of the War every Sparrowhawk still flying had been assigned to torpedo duty.

Crewmen align a torpedo beneath a clamp set in the underside of the Sparrowhawk's wing before hoisting the weapon into place.

A torpedo secured to its belly, a Sparrowhawk is ready to raid Allied shipping. Thus loaded, the plane had an 1,180-mile range.

The British cargo ship Empire Guillemot sinks off Cape Bon, Tunisia, on October 24, 1941, after being torpedoed by an Italian Sparrowhawk bomber. By 1943, Italian planes had claimed 72 Allied warships and 196 merchantmen and had damaged 500 more.

3

An emperor's secret journey
The Duce's orders: "Hold out for three months"
A cavalry charge into British guns
Machine guns thrown out for officers' luggage
The seven-week battle at Keren Plateau
The hit-and-run tactics of Wingate's irregulars
"Never have so many lost so much to so few"
The Duke of Aosta's last stand
Haile Selassie's carefully timed entrance
Mussolini's bid to be "at Hitler's side in Russia"
Early successes for an ill-equipped expedition
On the home front, Christmas without cheer
Malta: the invasion that never was

On June 23, 1940, a small, middle-aged man traveling under the alias Mr. Strong boarded an RAF Sunderland flying boat at Poole Harbour on England's south coast. Nine days later, after a journey that included a harrowing flight over German-occupied France and a furtive stopover in Alexandria, Egypt, Mr. Strong arrived in Khartoum, the capital of the Sudan, which was ruled jointly by Egypt and Great Britain. Only a few people in the Nile port city of 42,000 were aware that the mysterious Mr. Strong was Haile Selassie, Emperor of Ethiopia, who had fled into exile when Italy conquered his kingdom in 1936. The British hoped that the diminutive Lion of Judah would be able to rally his 10 million people to rise up against their Italian masters, in concert with an Allied invasion. Until the British were ready to move, however, Haile Selassie would be forced to bide his time in Khartoum.

Despite bombastic Italian propaganda that described Fascist suzerainty in Ethiopia as the proud beginning of a new Roman Empire, few countries were more ripe for invasion. Viewed from within, Mussolini's "empire" was not what it seemed to be from a distance, reported Robert E. Cheesman, a British diplomat who had served in Ethiopia. "Minerals that could have justified the lavish expenditure on sea bases, public works, roads and bridges had not been found in quantities that would repay the cost of the necessary machinery," he wrote; "the expected discovery of oil had not been made; trade was negligible; public security was nonexistent, and in consequence revenue from agriculture could not be collected; nor did these conditions tend to attract foreign capital, in spite of strenuous efforts by the Italian government."

Italian armed forces in East Africa were equally deficient. On paper, the troops in Ethiopia and in Italy's contiguous possessions—Italian Somaliland and Eritrea—appeared to be a formidable force: 370,000 soldiers, sailors and aviators, and nearly 400 aircraft. Against them, the British had only 19,000 men under arms in neighboring British Somaliland, the Sudan and Kenya. The British forces—like the Italians, made up largely of colonials—were generally well trained, however. By contrast, 70 per cent of the men under Italian command were African troops, called askaris, who were poorly drilled and whose families often traveled with them, even into battle. "They were fierce hand-to-hand

CALAMITY ON FOREIGN FIELDS

fighters with bayonets, swords and daggers," said one Italian officer, "but they did not know what to do when they came under heavy shelling and strafing."

Most of the African and many of the Italian troops were equipped with obsolete rifles that the Allies had awarded to Italy as reparations after World War I. The mainstay of the Air Force, the CR.42 Falcon biplane, had a top speed of only 270 miles per hour. "When the English bomb us," an Italian pilot was later to complain, "our fighters cannot follow them, as their bombers are faster than our fighters."

Even Mussolini, who liked to think that the Italian Army was made up of latter-day Roman legions, had few illusions that his East African forces would be able to hold out for long if the Allies invaded. "It will be sufficient if the Empire holds out for three months," he had told the Duke of Aosta, Viceroy of Ethiopia and commander of Italian forces in East Africa, shortly before declaring war in June 1940. In effect, Mussolini was relying on a swift German victory in Europe to save his East African holdings. Then, when Hitler divided up the British Empire, Italy might well add Kenya and Tanganyika to its possessions. "It was," said Foreign Minister Ciano with relish, "the chance of 5,000 years."

Italy moved quickly in East Africa to seize that chance. On July 4, taking advantage of his overwhelming edge in manpower, Lieut. General Guglielmo Nasi struck westward from Ethiopia into the eastern Sudan—300 miles from Khartoum—and easily captured several border towns. Over the next six weeks, Nasi also overran British Somaliland, on Ethiopia's northeastern border, forcing the British to evacuate by sea from Berbera, the capital.

The victories were fuel for the Duce's propaganda machine, but they did little to gladden the Duke of Aosta, who had attended British schools, including Eton, and had a healthy respect for his enemy. He warned his military commanders that he expected the British to waste little time in building up their forces in East Africa in order to move against them. Aosta believed they would try to squeeze the Italians in giant pincers, from Eritrea in the north and Italian Somaliland in the southeast; he also felt uneasy about western Ethiopia, where his troops were thinly scattered in mountainous terrain. Like Mussolini, Aosta sensed that Italy's colonial forces would eventually be reduced to fighting a holding action while waiting for victory in Europe.

The Italians would hold on for much longer than three months, however. During most of the following year, in a campaign conducted over a desolate landscape of mountain and desert that was all but unknown to the outside world, Italian forces would fight desperately to save themselves—and Mussolini's African empire.

The British began their offensive on November 6. Some 7,000 troops under Brigadier Sir William Slim attacked at Gallabat, one of the Sudanese towns the Italians had captured in July. Slim planned to storm Gallabat with a combined infantry and tank assault, then sweep across a dry riverbed into Ethiopia and take the neighboring village of Metamma. But the Italian Air Force thwarted his plan by shooting down five Gladiator fighters from Slim's small force on the first day of battle. Deprived of air cover, Slim's infantrymen were an easy target for strafing and bombing; 42 of them were killed and 125 wounded. Chagrined, Slim ordered a withdrawal; the first substantial British attack against Italian East Africa had been beaten back.

Prudently, the British selected a new target: Kassala, a Sudanese town 180 miles to the north that also had been in Italian hands since July. Taking Kassala would open the way from the north into the heart of Eritrea, including the capital, Asmara, and Massawa, the colony's largest Red Sea port. But before the British could act, the Duke of Aosta in early January of 1941 ordered both Gallabat and Kassala abandoned. He had not been deceived by the relative ease of the victory at Gallabat; he realized that next time the British with their modern armor might make short work of his poorly equipped forces on the plains of the Sudan and western Eritrea. The Duke ordered General Luigi Frusci to withdraw his 50,000 men to more rugged terrain at Agordat and Barentu, respectively 150 and 100 miles east of Kassala.

Frusci could not maintain even those positions for long against increasing British numbers. By January 27, 1941, two Indian divisions under the command of Major General William Platt had reached Agordat, which the Italian 4th Colonial Division defended from two hills that ran east to west; at the same time, two brigades of Indian infantry were detached to move south toward Barentu. The British first tried to outflank the Italian positions at Agordat from the north, but finding an impassable river in their path, they decided instead to take the eastern hill in a direct attack.

Three days of hard fighting ensued. At one point, reported a correspondent for a Milan newspaper, an Italian officer led a cavalry charge straight into the British guns. "Lieutenant Renato Togni charged down the hill on a white horse," he wrote. "His men galloped to within 100 feet of the guns, firing from their horses and throwing hand grenades while our artillery, turning 180 guns on the British, fired at ground level." Only by laying down a concentrated field of heavy machine-gun fire did the British repulse Togni's charge.

The failure of that gallant attack broke the spirit of the Italian resistance; the eastern hill fell on January 31 after British tanks flushed out and destroyed several Italian tanks that had been poised for a counterattack on the plain between the two hills. By late afternoon, the British had also taken the western hill and had cut a road leading to the Keren Plateau, a forbidding barrier of hills to the east. Meanwhile, the two Indian infantry brigades had attacked at Barentu through a heavy minefield. Quickly they routed the Italian 2nd Colonial Division, which abandoned its vehicles and fled toward the Keren Plateau, the next likely British target.

The plateau protected the vital road that connected Asmara and Massawa. The Duke of Aosta, from his distant headquarters at Addis Ababa, was confident that the Italian forces would be able to hold it; for the moment, the Duke was worried more about logistics and politics. In all of East

Africa he had only 67 serviceable aircraft—not the 400 he was supposed to have. With the Suez Canal closed to them, the Italians had to bring in new planes one at a time as air cargo—a slow process. Fuel and truck tires also were in short supply; to conserve tires, which wore out quickly on the primitive roads, infantrymen often had to travel long distances on foot—making quick movements of troops all but impossible.

Politically, the Italians also had deep concerns. The Duke was aware that the British were recruiting an army of Ethiopian refugees in the Sudan. He felt compelled to tie down a large part of his armed forces to keep the local Ethiopian population in check. Clearly an internal revolt was simmering, one that lacked only a leader.

On the afternoon of January 20, 1941, a creaky British Valentia troop transport rumbled to a landing on a strip hacked out of the bush at Um Iddla, a dry riverbed on the frontier between the Sudan and Ethiopia. A tiny figure dressed in khaki and wearing a large pith helmet stepped out of the plane and marched resolutely toward a flagpole that had been erected in the middle of the riverbed. No longer incognito, Haile Selassie was returning to his occupied land.

"I am now entering Ethiopia to crush our common enemy," the Emperor announced to an entourage that included two of his sons, members of his court, a few British offi-

cers and a reporter from the London *Times*. Haile Selassie raised the red, green and gold flag of Ethiopia to the top of the flagpole. A timely breeze caught the banner, and as it did, a bugle sounded. Several of those present toasted the moment with warm beer, the only beverage available.

The following day, Lieut. Colonel Orde Wingate of the British Army, who had accompanied the Emperor from Khartoum, set out with a small scouting party toward Belaia, a 7,000-foot plateau that the Italians had never been able to conquer. Wingate's party reached the plateau after a 10-day journey through snarled underbrush and stupefying heat. There to greet them was Brigadier Daniel Sandford, who had made the same trek the previous summer to prepare Belaia as a military base and to persuade local Ethiopian leaders to rise against the Italians.

Sandford had been followed by a cadre of Sudanese and Ethiopian troops whose mission was to train local tribesmen. By the time Wingate arrived, however, they had trained no more than a handful of men. Most of the Ethiopian chieftains were waiting for Haile Selassie to appear before they risked an open fight. "When he comes, no one will be afraid," insisted one leader. "But until he comes, who will not be afraid?"

Haile Selassie reached Belaia on February 6 after a journey every bit as difficult as Wingate's; at times, he had lent a royal shoulder to extricate his truck from the thick brush. Shortly after his arrival, a chieftain named Jambare Mangasha proclaimed his support and that of his 4,000 warriors. Over the next few months, several other leaders pledged their fealty to the Emperor; they would fight for him, both with the British and on their own. Wingate, for his part, would forge Sandford's Sudanese and Ethiopians into a deadly army of irregulars. (Later in the War he would command a similar force in Burma.) Wingate christened his African army Gideon Force, after the Biblical hero who defeated 15,000 men with an army of 300. It was an apt name, given the numerical superiority of the Italians around them.

To the south, in Kenya, British numbers were increasing rapidly. By the end of 1940, Lieut. General Sir Alan Cunningham had raised an army of 75,000 men recruited from Great Britain's African colonies—including troops from South Africa, Kenya, Rhodesia, the Gold Coast and Nigeria.

One of his first priorities was to capture El Wak, a fortified town near the border of Kenya and Italian Somaliland. In itself, El Wak was a negligible speck on the map that might easily be bypassed. But Cunningham chose to attack it with a small force in what one British correspondent called "a most useful tryout for the invasion of Somaliland."

On December 16, 1940, Gold Coast and South African troops approached El Wak. They had reached the outskirts of the town when suddenly the Italians defending it opened fire. "Shells came down the road, hitting and bouncing with a nasty thump and going by," noted one South African officer, "making such a noise that you thought you could stretch out your hands and touch them. Everyone looked absolutely flabbergasted that the Italians had fired first. It had all been so peaceful, and anyway, it was we who were raiding the Italians; it seemed definitely unfair."

Despite intermittent firing by the defenders of El Wak, the British force managed to advance through thick brush. "Suddenly we found ourselves right on top of the Italian wire—where we had no business to be," recalled a South African soldier. He dived for cover as engineers set off charges, known as Bangalore torpedoes, to blow gaps in the wire. "Tanks came through the gap behind us and went straight into action," the soldier wrote. "The Italians' morale was so shaken by the unexpected appearance of the tanks and our troops advancing steadily through their fire that they seemed to collapse completely."

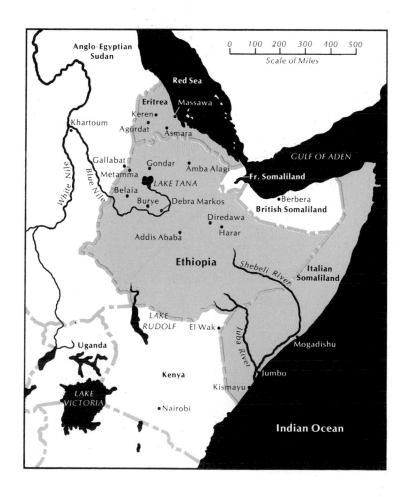

Towering over his troops, Italy's Duke of Aosta, six feet four inches tall, talks with an officer after inspecting a company of colonial levies in May 1940. The Italians had 200,000 such troops in East Africa.

At the height of its hegemony in East Africa, Italy controlled Ethiopia, Eritrea and Italian Somaliland (shown in red), as well as British Somaliland, captured in August of 1940. To retake their territory and end Italian rule in the area, the British planned a two-pronged campaign, attacking from the Sudan in the northwest and Kenya in the south, while a guerrilla force conducted a series of raids on western Ethiopia.

As a tryout, El Wak had been an easy victory, and British propagandists made much of it. When Mussolini heard how Italian troops had fled, he fired his commander in the sector, Lieut. General Gustavo Pesenti, who was also Governor of Italian Somaliland. The Duce replaced him with Major General Carlo De Simone, who had been on the Duke of Aosta's staff in Addis Ababa. But more than a change in command was needed to stop the British. Cunningham sent part of his army north of El Wak to clear out several Italian strongholds in southern Ethiopia. Early in 1941 he set out with the bulk of his command toward the Somalian port of Kismayu on the Indian Ocean.

Cunningham met little opposition on the road to Kismayu; he reached the city on the evening of February 14— to find that the Italians had already abandoned it. Three days earlier the Duke of Aosta, fearing that De Simone's men could not hold out for long, had ordered the Kismayu garrison to well-fortified positions on the banks of the Juba River, a dozen miles to the northeast.

British forces had only to cross an antitank ditch and cut through some barbed wire to occupy Kismayu. The retreating Italians had left the port city a shambles; many of the soldiers had been more concerned with saving their personal possessions than with making an orderly retreat. One soldier returned to his barracks after disabling an antiaircraft gun to find that his room had been ransacked by others. "It took only a few minutes," he noted, "to produce the effect that Attila himself had passed this way."

The Italians moved some of their artillery, but in the rush to evacuate they left behind large stores of other weapons and supplies. In one telling incident a gunner was ordered to throw machine guns out of a truck and reload it with the suitcases of officers. The unit commander who discovered the blunder when he regrouped his men at Jumbo, a village on the far bank of the Juba River, could only lament to his diary: "Here we are, 500 men without a machine gun. The soldiers are asking, 'How are we going to stop tanks?' "

In fact, General De Simone was relying on the Juba River to stop the enemy. He had neither the men nor the arms to halt the British all along the river, which flows for some 800 miles from Ethiopia across Italian Somaliland to the Indian Ocean. But at Jumbo the river was 200 yards wide and crossable only by a single pontoon bridge, which De Simone's engineers were quick to blow up. Moreover, the British would have to approach Jumbo through thick thorn brush and slog over miles of high sand dunes. De Simone decided to make a stand here, realizing that if the British broke through his lines, there would be only a few Italian positions between them and Mogadishu, the capital of Italian Somaliland.

A brigade of South African troops that had split off from Cunningham's main column as it approached Kismayu tried to cross the river at Jumbo on February 14 but was pinned down by fierce artillery fire; Italian gunners hurled nearly 3,000 shells at the South Africans in less than three hours. The South Africans began looking for another place to ford the river. They found it 10 miles upstream at Yonte, an old ferry crossing where the water was only waist-deep. The South Africans crossed at dusk on February 17 and beat off a heavy Italian counterattack the following morning. Once over the river, the South Africans could approach Jumbo from the rear; they captured it on February 19, and three days later another South African force took the town of Jelib, 50 miles north.

With the fall of Jumbo and Jelib, Italian resistance along the Juba River collapsed and thousands of troops fled into the countryside. "Armored cars are everywhere," wrote an Italian officer in his diary. "From Jelib one can hear the rattle of machine-gun fire without reply from our own troops, who have surrendered as they see the futility of continuing to fight."

British columns swept across Italian Somaliland, meeting almost no resistance as they advanced. The motorized Nigerian 23rd Brigade covered 235 miles in three days to reach the outskirts of Mogadishu on February 25. Pilots flying advance reconnaissance noted few signs of life in the usually busy port city. They spotted several airplanes sitting on the tarmac at the local airfield, but close inspection revealed them to be derelicts. In the clear green waters north of the harbor they saw a large ship lying half-submerged; in their haste to evacuate, the Italians had scuttled it.

When probing British troops reached Mogadishu, they found that the Italians had fled northward, once more leaving great quantities of supplies—including 430,000 gallons of fuel. "Sudden attacks by the enemy and by local inhabitants encouraged by the prospect of loot prevented our moving this fuel," one Italian officer later explained. At the Mogadishu airfield, the British uncovered a prize almost as valuable as the fuel: a handbook listing the size and location of every airfield and landing strip in Italian East Africa.

The occupying troops also discovered that several members of the Italian garrison had not retreated but had instead changed into mufti, hoping to blend in with the Italian civilians who remained in Mogadishu. The British had little trouble identifying the deserters in their new clothes. "White stripes from ear to ear revealed where their chin straps had been," recalled one Commonwealth soldier. "We left them alone; they were quite harmless and as prisoners they would only have complicated things."

After Mogadishu's capture, Cunningham turned northwest into Ethiopia. Before the spring rains transformed the roads to muck, he intended to capture the city of Jijiga, 660 miles distant—where he suspected De Simone was headed—and then attack the Italian garrison at Harar, Ethiopia's capital in ancient times. Moving with dispatch, the British took Jijiga on March 17. Harar fell shortly after that, and De Simone retreated once again, this time to Gondar, a mountain citadel built in the 17th Century. Once there, he dug in for a long siege.

While Cunningham slashed northward, the British organized an amphibious assault force for an attempt to recapture British Somaliland. On March 16, four ships of the Royal Navy began shelling the port of Berbera, which they had evacuated the previous summer. Later in the day, British troops landed without opposition—the Italian 70th Colonial Brigade had pulled out of the city. The campaign against Berbera also dealt a massive blow to Italian air power in East Africa. In anticipation of the landing, South African warplanes had attacked the airfield at Diredawa, 300 miles away, destroying scores of planes on the ground.

The loss of the Diredawa air fleet had a telling effect on Italian morale. "Our forces and the national and native population are aware of our complete incompetence in the air," the Duke of Aosta complained in a letter to Mussolini. Some askari troops, he said, now simply deserted rather than fight, explaining that "they had been employed to fight men and not airplanes." The Duke also expressed his fear that the situation at Keren, the plateau city where for several weeks his forces had been holding off the British, was about to come to a head.

On January 12, 1941, the Duke had sent a detachment of the elite Savoia Grenadiers to help defend Keren, which both British and Italian strategists considered the key to Eritrea. The Viceroy had warned his commander on the scene, General Frusci, that should he fail, "everything will crumble." General Platt, in overall command of the British Commonwealth forces at Keren, was forecasting "a bloody battle" against both the enemy and the terrain. "It will be won," he said, "by the side which lasts longest."

On February 2, an advance party of British and Indian troops reached the hills surrounding Keren. Between them and the city, however, lay the 3,500-foot-deep Dongolaas

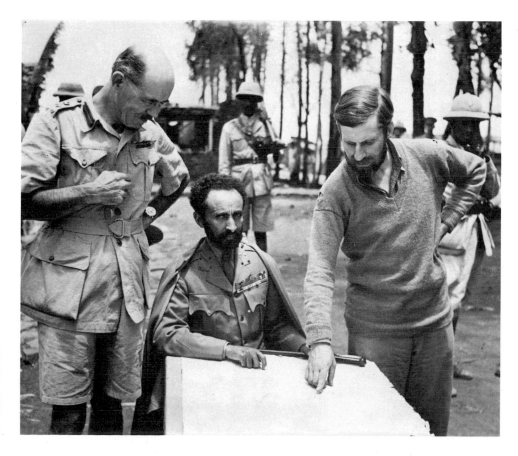

Emperor Haile Selassie plots strategy with his British advisers, Brigadier Daniel Sandford (left) and Lieut. Colonel Orde Wingate, whose unorthodox tactics in western Ethiopia led one Italian to call him grudgingly "the Napoleon of guerrilla warfare."

Gorge, a barren, time-eroded valley passable only by a narrow zigzag road. Guarding the road were sheer peaks that rose more than 2,000 feet above the floor of the valley. The Italians had placed 100 artillery pieces on the peaks; they had blown up portions of the road and salted the rest with land mines. If the British were to take Keren, they would have to do it hill by hill.

Soon the Italians in Keren could see the enemy arriving in force on the far side of Dongolaas Gorge. "The English forces were spreading out in the valley," noted Renato Loffredo, an Italian correspondent. "Armored cars, trucks and jeeps maneuvered freely, brashly even, showing their strength and numbers. The slopes of Keren must have impressed those who were about to attack them. You could clearly see the British commanders standing up in the jeeps looking through their binoculars at the mountains."

Arrayed against 30,000 British Commonwealth forces the Italians had three brigades of colonial levies, three battalions of the Savoia Grenadiers and the remnants of units that had escaped from Agordat and Barentu—an estimated 23,000 men all told. Many of them did not seem fit for battle, in Loffredo's view. They had been "tried by severe combat and worn down by continuous marches through the most difficult passages."

On February 3, the British launched their first attack. The Indian 11th Infantry Brigade, backed by heavy artillery fire, stormed Sanchil and Brig's Peak, two rugged hills on the west side of the gorge. The Indians captured both peaks, then lost them to Italian counterattacks. After stiff fighting, they took and held a nearby hill known as Cameron Ridge, which gave them a staging area for operations all along the west side of Dongolaas Gorge. The Italians knew they had to retake the ridge.

At 10 o'clock the following night, in freezing cold, a company of Savoia Grenadiers and askaris began a counterattack on Cameron Ridge. After creeping silently almost to the enemy positions, the Italians began lobbing grenades. The Indians responded with heavy machine-gun fire. In the dark, the situation became confused and desperate. "The Indians were unable to close their ranks," said one Italian, "and the fighting became man to man. Rifles were used like clubs. The Indians advanced, swinging them about their heads." The grenadiers drove off the Indians with a volley of hand grenades and braced for the next attack. It came from a company of Scottish troops who hit the Italians and askaris from an unprotected flank.

Suddenly, wrote Loffredo, "a group of askaris found themselves in the middle of a group of Scots, tall, robust and strong." The African soldiers, who "were slight, if resolute," seemed doomed until a group of grenadiers rushed to their aid, throwing grenades as they charged. "One Scot, stunned by a hand grenade, found two grenadiers on top of him who finished him off," said Loffredo. But another, "a terrible Scottish sergeant, advanced, firing his gun in two powerful hands with the butt in his stomach. A hand grenade stopped him. A second arrived. The first exploded between his feet, the second on his chest."

Then it was the British who rallied. "They held light machine guns like rifles and fired rapidly and powerfully, cutting down everything in front of them," reported Loffredo. At length the Italians retreated under the withering fire.

The fight for Cameron Ridge was only a preview. Grisly hand-to-hand fighting continued over the next seven weeks. The British advanced inch by inch—scrambling over huge rocks and boulders and tearing through razor-sharp scrub grass to gain the smallest bit of ground. Food, water and ammunition had to be hand-carried up the steep terrain. And when the British managed to take a hill, they often were so exhausted that they fell easily to counterattacks.

On March 15, the British captured a heavily fortified emplacement called Fort Dologorodoc, on the east side of the gorge. That night and again the following night, the British tried to take Brig's Peak and Sanchil—without success. The Italians also repulsed attacks on two other hills within a mile of their stronghold, forcing the British to withdraw. During the attacks, however, British engineers had examined the roadblocks in Dongolaas Gorge and reported they could clear the road if they were given heavy covering fire. General Platt agreed and set March 25 as the date for the assault, which would allow him 10 days to bring in additional ammunition and supplies.

Meanwhile, the Italians repeatedly counterattacked Fort Dologorodoc in an intensive effort to retake the hill. Between March 18 and 22, they stormed the fort seven times, suffering heavy casualties in each charge. General Frusci complained daily in his reports to the Duke of Aosta that the strength of his force was shrinking under enemy air attacks and artillery fire.

The Duke relayed Frusci's complaints to Rome and added a few of his own. The situation all over East Africa was becoming increasingly perilous, he wrote. He had few serviceable aircraft or antitank weapons left; he had even sent two of his personal heavy-caliber elephant guns to Keren in the slim hope that they might help slow the British armor. Furthermore, Aosta noted in anger, the 300,000 Italian civilians under his rule were unwilling to make sacrifices. He demanded to know how long he would have to endure.

The response from Rome was both hopeful and blunt: The Axis forces in North Africa expected to overrun Egypt by the autumn of 1941; it was imperative that he keep fighting at least until then to tie down Allied units that might be used to slow the Egyptian campaign.

At Keren, however, Italian resistance was nearly at an end. On the morning of March 25, as Platt had planned, the British began laying down concentrated mortar, artillery and machine-gun fire. Indian infantrymen stormed Italian positions near the roadblock, knocking them out and taking 500 prisoners.

By the following day, the British engineers had blasted a clear path through the roadblock. That night General Frusci withdrew most of his troops and artillery, leaving only a small force to cover his retreat. At 8 o'clock the next morning, March 27, British tanks entered Keren. During nearly two months of fighting, more than 3,000 Italian nationals had been killed and 4,500 wounded; the British counted 500 killed and some 3,000 wounded.

Almost without pause, the British turned their attention to Frusci's retreating columns, subjecting them to almost continuous strafing as they tried to reach Asmara. The Italians "were so exhausted and dispirited," noted one South African pilot, "that sometimes they did not even move off the roads when strafed." Ground troops, following in the wake of the air attacks, met little resistance from the dazed Italians. On April 1, civil authorities in Asmara surrendered to entering British troops. Platt wired the British command in Khartoum that he was in the capital of Eritrea, pointing out that his message was "not, repeat NOT, an April fool."

The easy British occupation of Asmara only strengthened the resolve of Admiral Mario Bonetti, the Italian commander at the port of Massawa, some 60 miles distant. On March 31, he had ordered the six Italian destroyers anchored at Massawa to attack Allied targets in the Gulf of Suez, then scuttle themselves to avoid capture. None of the ships managed to do any damage. Over the next few days, one ran aground and capsized, British planes sank two others and the Italians scuttled the other three. In the meantime, when Platt discovered that the phone line between Asmara and Massawa had been left intact, he tried to talk Admiral Bonetti into surrendering. Bonetti replied that his orders from the Duke of Aosta forbade surrender, and hung up.

Platt then ordered the advance on Massawa to commence. By April 5, Indian infantrymen had broken through the outer defenses of the city and encircled its landward sides while RAF bombers attacked Italian gun positions. On April 8, Bonetti decided to surrender his garrison of 9,500 men. In the three-month drive through Eritrea, the British had destroyed six Italian divisions and had taken 40,000 prisoners and 300 guns.

The pincers were closing on what remained of Italy's African empire. On March 30, Cunningham had taken Diredawa, which left him a clear path westward toward Addis Ababa. And in the Gojjam Province of western Ethiopia, Wingate's Gideon Force was making inroads. Wingate's aim was to clear a string of Italian fortifications along the 300-mile-long road from Lake Tana to Addis Ababa. When news that Wingate's irregulars were in the area reached the commander at the northernmost of those forts, he decided to abandon his position—for he believed local rumors that put the strength of Gideon Force at several thousand men. (In fact, it numbered only 300.) But before he retreated, the Italian officer did his best to slow down the enemy; he commandeered virtually every mule in the area. Gideon Force therefore had to use camels, which were less sure-footed on the treacherous mountain trails. Thousands of camels were worked to death during the campaign in western Ethiopia.

On March 4, an hour after dawn, one of Wingate's patrols reached the fort at Burye—just in time, said a British officer, to see "the entire Italian strength come milling out in full force with truckloads of infantry and a few armored cars, cavalry and artillery." Accompanying the Italians, he said, were "swarms" of colonial troops.

As it turned out, that pell-mell retreat from Burye to Dambacha, a fort 40 miles distant, would lead to one of the few Italian victories of the East African campaign. On March 6, the column fleeing Burye came upon a battalion of Ethiopian irregulars. The Italians smashed through them without even breaking formation, inflicting severe casualties as they went. The easy victory, however, did little to boost the Italians' morale. No sooner had they reached Dambacha than they abandoned both it and neighboring Fort Emmanuel and retreated to the safety of Debra Markos, which boasted a large fort and several outlying strong points. General Guglielmo Nasi, the hero of Italy's sweep through British Somaliland in 1940, had 12,000 men under arms at Debra Markos. He also had the support of a local prince, Ras Hailu, who commanded several thousand warriors.

Colonel Wingate realized that if Nasi's force broke out and took the offensive, his own tiny outfit would be annihilated. Wingate decided to try to pin down the garrison at Debra Markos. He gambled that if he made enough hit-and-run raids from the woods surrounding the fort, Nasi would be convinced that he was facing at least a division. Gideon Force made its first raid at 3 a.m. on March 20. Three platoons crept up on Italian picket lines on the slopes leading to the fort. They threw grenades at the sentries, then lobbed mortar shells into the fort's interior. After causing substantial consternation, they retreated.

Subsequent raids followed a similar pattern: Forty to 50 of Wingate's men would steal up to Italian campfires and open fire with machine guns. When the Italians learned to cope with that technique, Gideon Force shifted its tactics to employ grenades and bayonet charges—the men always vanishing into the woods before dawn.

Wingate's bluff succeeded. The askaris deserted in droves and Nasi, certain that he was outnumbered, never did attack. After suffering Wingate's harassment for two weeks, he abandoned Debra Markos on April 4 and made for the citadel at Gondar, where General De Simone's army had been holding out since early March. Along the way, Nasi's force was hounded by Ethiopian tribesmen loyal to Haile Selassie. They took a toll of more than 1,200 casualties before Nasi reached Gondar several days later. One observer called the march "a Moscow in miniature," a reference to Napoleon's 19th Century retreat from Russia.

Wingate entered Debra Markos on the day the Italians left, and received the surrender from a doctor who had stayed behind with his wounded. As Wingate was inspecting the fort, a telephone began ringing. He turned to Edmund Stevens, a correspondent for *The Christian Science Monitor*. "You speak Italian," he said. "Take the call."

"But what shall I say?" asked Stevens.

"Say that you're the doctor," replied Wingate, "and tell them the British have captured Debra Markos and a division 10 thousand strong is heading for the Blue Nile crossing."

Stevens picked up the telephone and repeated the message to a startled Italian switchboard operator; then he added a touch of his own: "If you want my advice and you value your skin, you'll pack up and get moving." The 8,000 Italians stationed along the Nile River in the vicinity of Debra Markos did just that, abandoning their positions and heading north into the interior. The ploy was typical of Win-

Italian colonists in Asmara, the capital of Eritrea, look on in silence as a British column enters the city on April 1, 1941, after the local commander surrendered without a fight.

Italian merchant ships lie half-submerged at Massawa, Eritrea (right). Before giving up the Red Sea port on April 8, 1941, the Italians scuttled more than a score of ships and dumped tons of supplies into the harbor.

gate's campaign of bluff and bravado, of which British Foreign Secretary Anthony Eden later quipped: "Seldom have so many lost so much to so few."

Two days after Wingate took Debra Markos, Haile Selassie entered the city and received the surrender of the renegade Ras Hailu and his warriors. At the same time General Cunningham, driving from the east, entered Addis Ababa and radioed Wingate to detain the Emperor at Debra Markos. "There are 25,000 Italians in Addis Ababa," Cunningham warned. "If the Emperor arrives, the natives will go wild and start looting and raping, and the Italians will all be killed. So keep the little man out." If the Emperor insisted, said Cunningham, Wingate was to use "everything short of force" to stop him.

A few days earlier, the Duke of Aosta had left Addis Ababa with the bulk of his home force for the northern highland strong point of Amba Alagi. There and at Gondar the Italians would make their last stand. "It only remains for us to resist wherever we can and for as long as we can," the Duke wired Mussolini. The Duce replied: "Resist to the last limits of human endurance."

The Duke of Aosta's stronghold at Amba Alagi, like that at Keren, was situated high on a rugged mountain. Amba Alagi was more than 11,000 feet above sea level; it commanded several slightly lower hills and a narrow hairpin road known as the Toselli Pass. At Amba Alagi and atop the other hills, the Duke commanded 5,000 troops—many of whom were airmen, sailors and policemen with little combat experience—and 30 heavy guns. Most of his African soldiers had

fled. "The Eritreans are tired," he noted sympathetically in his battle diary. "They have been waging war for six years nonstop and have had enough. They have gone home."

The British commander, General Ashton G. Mayne, believed that the Italians were spread too thin to retain control of their stronghold for long; by stretching them even thinner, he hoped to create a weak spot and exploit it. On May 4 and 5, British troops supported by concentrated artillery fire captured three Italian positions west of Amba Alagi. Three days later they took two more hills to the south. And on May 10, they captured a hill east of the Duke's command post. Now the Duke was nearly surrounded; all the British had to do was play a waiting game—bombing and shelling the Italians in their fixed positions.

"Constant firing all day long," wrote the besieged Duke. "We spend the day jumping from one rock to another, belly to the ground, with grenade splinters coming from all sides and volleys from machine guns that hit the rocks behind us, splattering us with pieces of stone. We are covered with dust and dirt from the explosions."

Later Aosta reported: "Every three minutes, a plane dives on us, shooting with its front machine gun, then drops stick bombs on us and finally gives us another firing from the rear gun." The noise was unbearable, said the Duke, adding ruefully, "I wish this diary could have a sound track."

On May 14, Mussolini wired the beleaguered Viceroy that he could give up if he could not care adequately for his wounded. Three days later, the Duke capitulated. Italian troops at Gondar, under Generals Nasi and De Simone, were spared for a time by the rainy season, and would hold

out for another six months before surrendering. Nevertheless, the Duke wrote accurately that after almost a year of unrewarded resistance, "the great adventure of the empire is about to end."

Haile Selassie had in fact written finis to the Italian adventure in East Africa nearly two weeks earlier. On May 5, 1941—five years to the day after Marshal Pietro Badoglio's entry into Addis Ababa as a conqueror—Haile Selassie returned to his capital in triumph. Colonel Wingate had procured a magnificent white stallion for the Emperor to ride. But Haile Selassie rejected Wingate's romantic vision for a sardonic one: He rode into the city in an Alfa Romeo limousine, made in Italy.

On June 22, 1941, at 3 a.m. on a Rome night, a German diplomat brought Foreign Minister Ciano a letter from Hitler to Mussolini. Ciano immediately telephoned the Duce and informed him of the letter. "I have just made one of the most serious decisions of my life," Hitler had written. "I have resolved to put an end to the hypocritical game of the Kremlin." With that, Mussolini learned that Operation *Barbarossa*, the German invasion of the Soviet Union, was under way. The Italian leader was infuriated at the manner in which Hitler had notified him of such a momentous undertaking. "I would not wake my own servants in the middle of the night," he groused. Nevertheless, he was determined that Italy gain a share in the expected German victory. He told an aide, "I must be at the side of Hitler in Russia."

Mussolini's desire to send troops to Russia was both symbolic and self-serving. He wanted to show the world that Italy—in spite of the painful loss of its East African holdings—was still a power to be reckoned with. He also wanted to partake in the plunder from a campaign that many military experts predicted would take Germany no more than three months to win.

Four days later, on June 26, Mussolini mounted a reviewing stand in Verona to watch 60,000 Italian soldiers parade past on their way to Russia. "These divisions are superior to the Germans in men and equipment," the Duce boasted. "I should not hesitate to say that in all Europe, there are no soldiers so perfect."

The soldiers were hearty enough; their equipment was not. Most of them were equipped with World War I rifles.

The Pasubio Division strides with confidence past Mussolini in Verona before departing for Russia in 1941. Reinforcement troops sent the following year were less optimistic, and they often marched off to the front singing a dirge entitled "The Black Flag."

They were outfitted in lightweight uniforms with cloth leggings that also dated back to the last war—for no one thought they would have to face the rigors of the Russian winter. They also were appallingly short of such basic items as radios, binoculars, compasses and maps.

Italian officers told their men not to worry. "The Russian population is primitive, the same as the African," they said—ignoring the lessons of the recent African campaign. "Just as in Ethiopia, a few trinkets will be enough to win the people over."

During the next few months, Mussolini got the victories he yearned for. His troops joined the German command in early August in the Ukraine and helped to drive the Red Army back several hundred miles across the Dnieper and Bug Rivers. "If the weather is good, this war will end soon," wrote one soldier to his family. "It will last until September at most." Others were equally optimistic in their letters home. "Mussolini and Hitler have assured us that Russia will be done for by winter," wrote an infantryman. "Such men don't speak nonsense to the world. They are quite sure of what they say."

Anxious to see his men in action before the fighting ended, Mussolini accepted an invitation from Hitler to visit the Russian front. But when he arrived on August 25 at the Wolf's Lair, Hitler's retreat at Rastenburg in East Prussia, Mussolini appeared pale and drawn. He clearly was not at his best—in part because he was still mourning the death of his son Bruno, who had been killed in a military airplane crash a few weeks earlier. Still, the Duce managed a warm greeting for his host, for he wanted to persuade Hitler to accept more Italian troops in the fight against the Russians.

For most of the day, Mussolini was treated to a Hitler monologue, a device the Führer often used when he wished to avoid saying "no." Each time Mussolini tried to bring up the subject of greater Italian participation in Russia, Hitler would ignore him and speak, instead, of the stupidity of Roosevelt and Churchill in supporting the decadent Soviets, and of the glorious victory that Italy and Germany would soon be sharing.

When Mussolini tired of Hitler's fulminations, he would interrupt with a torrent of words of his own, centering on the glories of ancient Rome; the Emperor Trajan had campaigned 18 centuries earlier at Uman, he bragged, in the very place that Italian troops now occupied. (Actually, Trajan's legions had fought in modern-day Rumania, more than 400 miles away.)

The next day, Hitler and Mussolini flew to the Ukraine. There was no fighting going on at Uman when the two dictators arrived, so a parade was arranged for Mussolini; a crack team of *Bersaglieri*—Italy's light infantry—wheeled past him on motorcycles, shouting "Duce!" He beamed with pleasure at the display. Later, however, the commander of the expeditionary force, General Giovanni Messe, took Mussolini aside to complain: His men lacked proper arms, had little fuel and few motor vehicles—and supply trains from Italy were few and far between.

Mussolini could only shrug and tell Messe to try to get along with what he had. Still, the general's frank account disturbed Mussolini. His mood worsened when Hitler went off to chat with German soldiers, leaving the Duce to his own devices. "Hitler might have taken me with him when he went to speak to his own troops," Mussolini snapped peevishly to an aide. "Did you notice how unsoldierly the Führer looked when he was among his men?"

Still irritated by the snub, Mussolini managed to have the last laugh on the return flight to the Wolf's Lair. He persuaded the pilot to let him fly the plane. Hitler assented, and then had to endure a stomach-wrenching series of swoops and steep banks as the Duce played childishly with the controls. Later, Mussolini would insist that an account of his joy ride be included in the official communiqué of the meeting.

On the train back to Rome, Mussolini was visibly depressed. Hitler had refused his offer of additional Italian troops and had made it clear—in attitude if not in words—that he regarded the Italians as poor relations to be humored and kept out of trouble. Hitler had good cause to feel that way; in the past year he had pulled Mussolini out of two potentially disastrous situations. When the Italian invasion of Greece failed, the Wehrmacht had come to the rescue. In Libya, Marshal Rodolfo Graziani had fled before a British force that was outnumbered more than four to one. Graziani had beseeched Saint Barbara, the patron of artillery, to save him; but it was Hitler who did the saving. In February 1941 he sent Lieut. General Erwin Rommel to North Africa with a panzer division and a motorized infantry division,

DEATH OF A FAVORITE SON

Behind a flower-laden hearse carrying his son Bruno, Mussolini walks with his family and other mourners through the streets of Pisa as onlookers pay their respects with the Fascist salute.

Like parents in wartime everywhere, Mussolini lived under the threat of personal tragedy. On August 7, 1941, an aide rushed up to him as he entered the Palazzo Venezia. "There has been a crash at Pisa, Duce," the man said. "Your son Bruno has been injured and his condition is critical."

Mussolini was stunned by the news that Bruno, 23, a captain in the Air Force, had been hurt. "Is he dead?" the Duce asked. Yes, the official admitted, recalling later that at that moment, "Something switched off inside Mussolini forever."

The Duce was proud of his eldest son Vittorio, 24, who was also a test pilot at Pisa, and of his daughter Edda, 30, a socialite turned Red Cross work-

er who was serving in Albania. But the dashing Bruno had been his favorite; the two had delighted in roughhousing together and in singing impromptu duets from Italian operas.

A few hours later, Mussolini heard the details of Bruno's death from Vittorio. Bruno had been testing a new bomber, the P.108B, when one of its four engines failed at an altitude of only 300 feet. His last recognizable word, reported Vittorio, was "Papa."

Thousands lined the roads as Bruno's funeral cortege passed. Mussolini endured the proceedings stoically, but later he remarked to an aide, "I appear calm in front of you because that is how I have to show myself. But inside I am torn with grief."

and by mid-April the British, except for a 35,000-man garrison in besieged Tobruk, had been swept out of Libya. Rommel technically was under Italian command, but the North African victory had been won by German arms.

Chafing at his role in Hitler's shadow, Mussolini characteristically jumped at the chance in December of 1941 to honor the Tripartite Pact with Japan and declare war on the United States after the raid on Pearl Harbor. "What does this new event mean?" Mussolini asked rhetorically. "Every possibility of peace is receding further and further into the distance; to speak of a long war is a very easy prophecy to make." Somewhere in that long war, he believed, Italy might yet find its destiny.

On December 11, Mussolini announced his declaration of war against the United States from the balcony of the Palazzo Venezia. The audience seemed sullen; many Italians, after all, had blood ties in America. Mussolini, who had been known to orate for hours from the balcony, sensed the crowd's mood and cut his speech to less than five minutes.

War with the United States was just one more burden for Italians to bear in that cheerless season. On the home front, Mussolini had forbidden newspapers to mention Christmas, which, he told Ciano, "only reminds one of the birth of a Jew." Food, coal and other necessities remained in short supply. "The Christmas holidays are coming," wrote one civilian to a relative in the Army, "but what kind of Christmas will we have? I cannot remember one like it for anxiety and sadness. We will probably be making bread from ashes because the flour ration per person, 150 grams, is not sufficient. Meat, too, is very scarce. We are bearing everything with resignation."

Militarily, the situation was no better. In November, British planes and submarines operating from the island of Malta had manhandled Italian convoys to North Africa, sinking 13 cargo ships and three destroyers. Less than half of the 79,000 tons of food and equipment the Italians shipped had reached its destinations. At one point, the government resorted to shipping fuel across the Mediterranean on hospital ships. Meanwhile Rommel, who was starved for supplies, had been forced back steadily by a British counterattack that eventually cost his command 33,000 men captured. By the middle of December, the British had relieved Tobruk and had driven Rommel out of the easternmost Libyan province of Cyrenaica.

In Russia, the Red Army had halted the Axis advance just outside Moscow. Italian soldiers were now shivering alongside equally ill-prepared Germans on the frozen steppes.

In early January of 1942 came a glimmer of hope: The Italians managed to get a convoy through to Tripoli, enabling Rommel to begin a new drive. Caught off balance, the British Eighth Army fell back almost 300 miles before it regrouped along a line in eastern Cyrenaica. Egypt lay tantalizingly close, and Rommel was determined to take it. He made repeated requests to Hitler for more men and matériel. Hitler always refused, telling his frustrated general that the forthcoming summer campaign in Russia was his first priority. He did promise, however, to remove a serious threat from the Germans' unprotected rear—the British base at Malta. He was sending the battle-tough Fliegerkorps II—the 2nd Flying Corps—which had seen heavy action on the Russian front, to bomb the island into submission.

Japanese Foreign Minister Yosuke Matsuoka, accompanied by his Italian counterpart, Galeazzo Ciano, receives a lance salute from cavalrymen during a visit to Rome in March 1941. Matsuoka's trip paid dividends in December when Mussolini—though not required to by treaty—joined Japan in declaring war on the United States.

Until now, the Germans and Italians had been able to send no more than a few planes a day against Malta. But with the arrival of Fliegerkorps II in Sicily, Axis planes began to bombard the island around the clock. On a single day, the 8th of March, 152,000 pounds of bombs fell on Malta. But bombs alone could not subdue the base, and Hitler's Naval chief, Admiral Erich Raeder, convinced him that the only solution was to invade the island.

This invasion would be a joint operation. In April, Italian and German commanders developed a plan, code-named Operation *Hercules,* that they intended to carry out during the July full moon at the latest. The Germans would provide air cover and drop a parachute division commanded by General Kurt Student, whose men had successfully overrun Crete in a similar operation in 1941. The Italians would also send in a parachute division and would bombard the island from the sea.

In early May, Marshal Ugo Cavallero, Mussolini's current Armed Forces Chief of Staff, outlined the details of Operation *Hercules* to Ciano. Before it could begin, Cavallero reported, the Germans and Italians under Rommel's command were to open a major drive toward the Egyptian border; then they would halt until Operation *Hercules* was launched. When Malta at last was neutralized—and the Axis lifeline in the Mediterranean had been made secure—Rommel would proceed into Egypt.

"I know that it is a difficult undertaking," Cavallero confided to Ciano, "and that it will cost us many casualties. But I consider it absolutely essential for the future development of the War. If we take Malta, Libya will be safe."

In late May, Rommel launched his attack in eastern Libya. When the British withstood his initial thrust, he concentrated his armor in an area that would later become known as "The Cauldron" for the seething battles that took place there. Rommel broke through the British lines against surprisingly light opposition. The British commander, General Neil Ritchie, had refused to commit his tanks to The Cauldron en masse lest Rommel, who was earning his reputation

as the Desert Fox, outflank him. Rommel now had a clear path to Tobruk and he took it, capturing the key port city on the 21st of June.

At Tobruk, the Germans took 33,000 prisoners, thousands of gallons of fuel, 2,000 serviceable vehicles and enough food to sustain 30,000 men for three months. His immediate supply problems solved, Rommel urged Hitler to let him drive into Egypt immediately instead of waiting for Malta to fall. Field Marshal Albert Kesselring, Rommel's superior in the German hierarchy, argued that Operation *Hercules* should go ahead as scheduled. But, as Kesselring peevishly put it, Rommel exercised "an almost hypnotic influence on Hitler, which made him incapable of an objective judgment on the military situation."

On June 23, Hitler wrote to Mussolini, urging that Rommel be given a free hand to proceed immediately into Egypt. "Destiny has offered us a chance that will never be repeated in the same theater of war," Hitler argued. "If the remnants of this British army are not followed by every soldier to his last breath, the same thing will happen that deprived the British of success when, within a very short distance of Tripoli, they suddenly stopped so that they could send troops to Greece."

Hitler concluded with an emotional pep talk: "Therefore, Duce, if in this historic hour I can give you a piece of advice straight from my eager heart, it would be: 'Order operations to be continued until the British forces are completely annihilated, as far as your command, and Rommel, think they can do it militarily with their forces. The goddess of fortune passes only once close to warriors in battle. Anyone who does not grasp her at that moment can very often never touch her again.'"

Mussolini, who had come to trust Rommel more than his Italian generals, found Hitler's appeal irresistible. He set aside the plan for invading Malta and instead ordered Rommel—still technically under his command—to drive into Egypt. Here, at last, was the campaign that the Duce was sure he could win.

MOBILIZING THE HOME FRONT

oman school children display coin banks outside the King's palace on National Savings Day, part of a government campaign urging Italians to be thrifty.

SCRIMPING THROUGH YEARS OF WANT

Benito Mussolini recognized Italy's dependence on foreign imports as a major threat to his military ambitions. In 1934 he began a campaign called *autarchia,* or self-sufficiency, to make the country as economically autonomous as possible. It was a difficult goal for a nation whose industry's survival depended on steady transfusions of oil, coal and metals from abroad.

Mussolini planned to make *autarchia* work by reducing imports and by colonizing nearby, weaker countries to exploit their natural resources. The plan backfired after Mussolini invaded the African kingdom of Ethiopia in 1935. The members of the League of Nations censured Italy for the unprovoked attack by cutting off its financial credits and refusing to sell it armaments. Mussolini responded by refusing to trade with the member nations. At home, the Fascists arranged exhibitions featuring a wide range of indigenous minerals and textiles, hoping to convince the public that Italy was indeed self-sufficient. But the most persuasive propaganda failed to hide the fact that the country could not afford to sacrifice its foreign trade and at the same time support Mussolini's military adventures.

Severe shortages became evident as soon as World War II began, but the Italians pitched in to make do with what they had. Collection drives were organized in which young people went from house to house gathering coins, scrap metal and wool for recycling. Buses and automobiles were converted to run on wood, charcoal or compressed gas. Businessmen used teams of oxen to plow urban gardens for food to supplement their families' government rations. When the military draft created Italy's first labor shortage, women took over jobs formerly done by men—driving tractors, operating streetcars and manufacturing war goods.

Nevertheless, the nation's economic condition deteriorated. Italians told the story of a man who asked a merchant for a fig and was told that it cost a lira, the basic unit of currency. "What? A fig is not worth a lira," the man indignantly exclaimed. "You mean," the merchant corrected him, "the lira is not worth a fig."

An exhibition of Italian minerals in 1938 trumpets two prominent Fascist themes: "Self-sufficiency," and the view that "Mussolini is always right."

Curious citizens inspect a bus that ran on the fumes of burning wood, a fuel Italians turned to when oil imports shrank to one fifth their previous level.

Two new cars with wood-burning engines, a Fiat (left) and a Bianchi, are exhibited at the Mayoralty Building on Capitoline Hill in 1939. Their engines were inefficient, stalled regularly and emitted a terrible stench.

Passengers climb through a window to board a packed trolley car in Rome. Italy's public-transportation system, already inadequate because of the shortage of fuel, became even more overcrowded when worn-out buses could not be replaced and taxis were restricted to emergencies only.

Newlyweds in Rome embark on married life aboard a bicycle built for two. Strict gas rationing, in addition to laws that discouraged driving personal automobiles, made the bicycle a primary mode of transit.

A Fascist Youth member wheels a cart marked "A tuft of wool for the soldiers" to a collection center in April 1942. Much of the wool collected was mattress stuffing removed from beds at home by school children.

CAMPAIGNING TO COLLECT PRECIOUS SCRAP

Before the Ethiopian War, Italy was importing almost all the textile fibers and more than half the metals its industries used. By 1940, the years of trade restrictions and military campaigning had nearly exhausted the nation's reserves of iron, copper, tin, nickel, wool and cotton.

The Fascist Bureau for the Distribution of Scrap as early as the mid-1930s pressed citizens to donate domestic articles that contained metal to a state-run collection drive. The media extolled examples of personal sacrifice, such as playwright Luigi Pirandello's contribution of his 1934 Nobel Prize medal, and Mussolini's offering of several heroic busts of himself.

Similar drives gathered cotton and wool goods for recycling to replace tattered Italian military blankets and uniforms. The scarcity of cotton and wool had one beneficial side effect: It encouraged the development of substitute textiles derived from flax, hemp and broomstraw.

*Members of Fascist Youth groups in prewar Rome gather up an
assortment of scrap metal—everything from pots and pans and bedsteads
to a display of military medals (lower right).*

Citizens in Rome crowd the stairway outside the Bureau of Welfare as they wait for ration cards.

"EAT TO LIVE, DON'T LIVE TO EAT"

The greatest problem the Fascists faced by 1941 was feeding 45 million Italians. Their solution was to stretch out their scant food supplies. Rationing cut the prewar consumption of staples such as rice and pasta by half. The poor and the middle class added to their rations by cultivating "war gardens" and raising rabbits and chickens; the rich coped by buying food on the black market at exorbitant prices.

Social unrest grew apace with the shortage of food. Shoppers often waited all day in ration lines guarded by police, only to be told that supplies had run out. Their surly mood was not improved by government posters that urged: "Eat to live—don't live to eat." When the diet of some Italian troops was reduced to mule meat and boiled grass, the government seized livestock to feed the Army. The farmers' resultant plight inspired a cartoon showing one farmer disguising his pig as a cat.

Shirt-sleeved citizens of Milan harvest grain in a city park. Gardens were planted in every open space, including the grounds of cathedrals and monuments.

A waiter accepts ration cards from Roman diners. Portions became so meager that one joke had customers asking: "Waiter, did I or did I not have a meal?"

A MANPOWER GAP FILLED BY WOMEN

During the 1930s, when about one million Italian men were consistently without employment, most women had little chance of landing a job. Those who tried had to overcome the traditional disapproval of women in the workplace. Mussolini encouraged women to stay at home and produce prospective soldiers for his armies.

By 1942, however, a severe manpower shortage caused by military conscription forced the Duce to reverse himself. "Your duty," he told female workers, "is resistance on the home front." Women responded to the call, taking jobs in public service or in war industry; in some factories they eventually constituted a majority of the labor force. Many Italians welcomed the change in women's status: The extra income helped thousands of families cope with the war-inflated economy.

A woman industrial worker—a rare sight before the War—fastens a fabric covering to the frame of a CR.42 fighter in the Fiat aeronautics plant in Turin.

A ''tram lady,'' awkward in the thick cork-soled shoes that became common when leather was banned, switches her streetcar onto another set of tracks.

EASTWARD TO THE DON

Italian cavalrymen ride past a farm near the Don River in October 1942. The old-fashioned horse soldiers were effective on the broad Russian steppes.

A GALLANT EXPEDITION'S NIGHTMARISH END

On the day Hitler launched Operation *Barbarossa*, June 22 1941, an envious Benito Mussolini resolved to send an Italian expedition to fight alongside the Germans in Russia. He insisted that glorious victory rather than embarrassment and defeat would be Italy's portion this time. A few weeks later 60,000 Italian troops entrained for Vienna and points east to join a campaign that many felt would be a romp.

At first it seemed like one. Italian units linked up with the advancing Wehrmacht east of the Dniester River in early August. They fought well, helping to push the Russians across the Bug and Dnieper Rivers, then struck into the mineral-rich Donets basin. But the Italians' logistics were a nightmare. They were short of trucks, weapons and even warm clothes—which were considered unnecessary since Russia was to be conquered by wintertime. What artillery they had was outdated, and their antitank weapons were not strong enough to penetrate Soviet armor. The better-supplied Germans were understandably reluctant to share equipment—yet they were quick to criticize when shortages hurt the Italians' performance.

Far from giving up, however, Mussolini upgraded the expedition to a full army in July 1942. The Italian commander General Giovanni Messe, protested acidly: "If we can barely equip 60,000 men how are we to supply more than 200,000?" Again the soldiers fought vigorously and bravely joining in the drive to the Caucasus and even undertaking a daring cavalry charge that kept open the way to the Don River and Stalingrad.

Then winter and shortages took their toll. A determined Red Army stopped the Axis advance at Stalingrad and broke through the thinly stretched Italians along the Don. The Italians retreated, fighting desperately to avoid encirclement then trudged more than 300 miles westward through deep snow, implacable winds and 30°-below-zero temperatures to the new Axis lines. Many survived only with the aid of peasants who fed and clothed them as they fled. By spring when the terrible retreat was over, fully half of the Italian force had been lost to the Red Army and the Russian winter

A child offers a Fascist salute to Italian troops in the Ukraine, where many peasants, chafing under Soviet rule, welcomed the invaders as liberators.

ound for the Russian front, Italian troops take lighthearted leave of Italy in July 1941. Some 225 trains took the expedition to its staging base in Rumania

RUNNING BATTLES ON THE RUSSIAN PLAINS

The Italians entered the fighting in Russia on August 12, 1941. The next weeks and months were a heady period of progress, interrupted by intense seesaw battles in the towns, along the rivers, amid the endless fields of sunflowers and wheat.

The Soviet troops assigned to deal with the invaders struck irregularly, often at night, and then retreated. They left blown bridges, mined roads, poisoned wells and burned villages in their wake to slow the Axis onslaught.

Worse than any of these Soviet tactics was the simple physical difficulty of moving supplies and troops across the sodden land—which turned into a white swamp with the first blizzards in early October. Nevertheless, some Italian units covered as much as 250 miles in a single week, advancing so rapidly that at one time Italians were strung out along a 500-mile line.

Bayonets fixed, Italian soldiers move through a thatched-hut village near Poltava in September 1941.

Italian combat engineers strike at a Russian strong point near a small factory. The Italians regularly asked their German allies for the toughest assignments.

Caught in the open on a frozen river in the Ukraine, Italian infantrymen hug the ice to fend off a Soviet counterattack in December 1941.

Covered by their comrades, Italian infantrymen rise from their foxhole to throw grenades during fighting on the Dnieper River in 1942.

THE ITALIAN CAVALRY'S GLORIOUS LAST CHARGE

The year-long Axis advance continued to eat up territory and collect prisoners and abandoned supplies right to the banks of the Don River. But there, in August 1942, the Soviets stiffened. From a bridgehead near the river town of Serafimovich they launched a fierce counterattack designed not only to turn back the Italian units hold-ing the Don but also to stem the flood of men and matériel headed for Stalingrad, some 80 miles southeast.

The outmanned and outgunned Italians were ordered to stand and fight to the death—and they did, beating back Soviet heavy tanks with the homemade incendiary bombs that the Russians (who also used them) called Molotov cocktails. In the fighting at Serafimovich the Italians lost 1,700 men, but they captured 1,600 prisoners and a huge cache of Soviet arms.

Then the Italians regained the offensive. Elements of the Savoia Cavalry, a regiment with a long tradition of service to the Savoy monarchy, came upon a Soviet force on the Isbuschenski steppe. Reconnaissance showed the Soviets to number about 2,000—with artillery and mortar support. Still the 600-man Italian regiment struck, counting on surprise to even the odds.

Early on August 24 one squadron hit the Soviet front on foot, while a second rode around the enemy lines on horseback and

By 9:30 a.m., the War's last great cavalry charge had ended in a clear Italian victory. Two Soviet battalions were wiped out, and another was sent packing across the Don, leaving behind 500 prisoners of war, four big guns, 10 mortars, 50 machine guns—and a collapsed offensive.

In a swirl of dust, the Savoia Cavalry charges furiously into battle on the Isbuschenski steppe on August 24, 1942. The heroic charge completely surprised a superior Soviet force, which had hoped to encircle and annihilate the Italians along the Don River.

Plume-helmeted Bersaglieri—Italy's elite light-infantry troops—inspect an American-made Grant tank captured from the Soviets in the summer of 1942. The Italians supplemented their scant supplies with booty they collected—including 14 tanks, two armored cars, 10 field pieces and thousands of rifles taken during the battle of Serafimovich.

Thousands of Soviet prisoners of war dot a temporary holding camp near the Don River in September of 1942. At upper left, recently arrived prisoners stand in line as they wait to be processed

RETREAT THROUGH A FROZEN HELL

Through the autumn of 1942 the Italian Eighth Army braced itself along the Don. The men built bunkers and gun sites linked by trenches, sometimes unearthing vegetables that supplemented their slim rations. They laced the riverbanks with barbed wire and piled up scrub as a noise alarm against infiltrators. As winter came on they slung buckets of hot coals under their machine guns to keep them from freezing and reduced guard shifts to 30 minutes—all a man could stand in the numbing cold.

Meanwhile the Soviets were massing their armies. In mid-December, when they outnumbered the Italians 4 to 1, they attacked. Wave after Russian wave swept across the frozen Don. The Italians committed what reserves they had, including railroad workers and service personnel, but they could not hold. The Hungarians and Rumanians fighting beside them fled. Crack Italian alpine divisions hung on until late January, 1943. Then, nearly encircled, they too retreated.

The Italians had little left to fight with. Their few trucks, out of fuel, were abandoned along with tons of supplies. Their weapons frequently were worthless: ancient carbines, and grenades that refused to explode. The soldiers slogged on for weeks. One of them wrote that before he collapsed, delirious, in the snow, he saw visions of "a table laid with wine, spaghetti, grapes and figs" back in sunny Italy. He was among the lucky ones; his comrades made him get up and keep walking.

White-clad Italian alpine troops move forward to counter a Soviet attack in December 1942.

An alpine patrol skirts the top of a ridge. Such ski troops protected the flanks of the Italian columns as they retreated during the winter of 1942-1943.

An Italian driver stands by his all-weather transport—a captured Soviet camel.

Holding a grenade in each hand, an Italian infantryman keeps watch in his shallow trench. The soldier's rifle had been designed half a century earlier.

Italian soldiers whose truck has run out of fuel hurry on foot (above) to avoid the fate of the snow-covered dead at left. The retreat from the Don in January 1943, in freezing cold and under constant attack, was agonizing. "We walked along with our heads low, one behind the other, mute as shadows," wrote a survivor. "Every step seemed a mile and every second an hour; it was endless."

4

A vision of glory on a white stallion
Bad news from El Alamein
Himmler plays detective
A challenge from "the first of the traitors"
The national diet: gray bread and rubbery cheese
Trouble from a "Rasputin in skirts"
Winter death march in the Caucasus
Mussolini sweeps his government clean
Barren dialogues between dictators
Sicily: Invasion haunts the homeland

Toward the end of June 1942, Benito Mussolini received a coded telegram that bore joyous news: The German and Italian forces driving deep into Egypt were on the verge of capturing Alexandria and Cairo, beyond which lay easy access to the strategic Suez Canal. After a string of humiliating defeats, the Italian Army would share a great conquest. Characteristically, the Duce decided to be on the scene in person at the moment of victory; it would be a time at last for glory. On the morning of June 29, with an entourage large enough to fill five transport planes, Mussolini flew to Tripoli to await the final breakthrough of the Axis in the desert.

The plan for what to do with Egypt had already been made: Hitler had agreed to Italian domination, and Mussolini had named an Italian civil administrator to govern the country. For himself, the Duce envisioned a triumphant entrance into Cairo. He would lead his troops into the vanquished capital riding a magnificent white Arabian stallion, while wearing at his waist the gilded sword of Islam, a symbol of conquest given him by Italo Balbo when Balbo was Governor of Libya. A hymn of victory had been composed for the occasion.

But the good news from the desert proved illusory. Even as Mussolini crossed the Mediterranean, Field Marshal Erwin Rommel's panzer army, its supplies stretched to the limit, bogged down in the face of fierce British resistance at El Alamein, just 60 miles from Alexandria and 210 miles from Cairo. The days wore on, but the situation at the front remained stagnant.

The Duce established himself at Beda Littoria, 500 miles behind the front lines, to await the promised triumph. It was as close as he ever got to the fighting. Trailed by journalists assigned to report glowingly on his activities, he passed the time in meaningless inspections of troops, hospitals and prisoner-of-war camps. He hunted partridge in the desert with a submachine gun and amused himself at times by training the weapon on British captives being marched to the camps. One day the newsmen found him strutting about a truck full of haggard British soldiers, the submachine gun slung over his shoulder. Scowling, the Duce addressed their Italian guard: "If you see any hostility, you must fire without warning. You must hate the enemy. Be on the lookout and shoot at the first sign of revolt."

A NATION ON THE BRINK

Such posturing failed to endear Mussolini to his combat troops. The rumor circulated in the ranks that he was bad luck, since his arrival had coincided with the British counterattack that stopped the Axis advance. The Germans, for their part, sneered at Mussolini behind his back for his ill-timed bid to steal the limelight from Rommel, to whom the victory would rightly belong.

After Mussolini had chafed for three weeks in the desert, his patience wore thin; on July 21 he flew back to Italy, dejected and humiliated. Though he left some personal luggage in Tripoli so that he could return on short notice, the opportunity would never arise. The Axis offensive in North Africa was finished; Mussolini and Italy now faced a long procession of defeats, each of which buried deeper the Duce's dream of a Mediterranean empire. He came to realize during his trip to the desert that the War had reached a turning point: "The wheel of fortune turned," he wrote. Winston Churchill, his more eloquent rival, would call that summer of 1942 "the hinge of fate."

Mussolini returned from North Africa a physical wreck. His imposing body, so long a national symbol of health and vigor, had taken on an aged and beaten look. The Duce was racked by stomach pains that no one seemed able to diagnose. One of his many physicians believed he had contracted amoebic dysentery during his stay in the desert. Another asserted that his problem was the reappearance of the ulcer that had plagued him for years. Injections were prescribed by two doctors, and countermanded by a third.

Rumors circulated that Mussolini had cancer and was dying. Another story—sparked by his sexual excesses—maintained that he was suffering the terminal stages of syphilis. In any case, the medication given him by his doctors did no lasting good; for the rest of his life he had to endure bouts of severe pain.

In an effort to regain his health, Mussolini left Rome with his mistress, Clara Petacci, to rest at Riccione, his favored resort on the Adriatic coast. There he remained in virtual isolation until the early autumn, while his prolonged absence left the leaderless Italian government in a state of paralyzed indecision. This was only the first of many escapes from responsibility that the dictator would indulge in.

Mussolini, in fact, was suffering from more than stomach pains. His disappointment over the cumulative failures of Italian forces in the War had pushed him into a deep depression. His characteristic zeal, his buoyant energy and optimism, had given way to a fatalistic apathy from which he would rarely emerge.

Giuseppe Bottai, his old comrade in the Fascist movement, was appalled by the extent of Mussolini's decline. After a visit, Bottai described him as "gray, ashy, with sunken cheeks, troubled and tired eyes, his mouth revealing a sense of bitterness. The man seems not so much ill as humiliated, sad, and unable to struggle against his advancing years. One would like to take his hand and speak to him, but he is no longer the man he was. The road to an exchange of confidences has been barred. Even to ask after his health arouses his suspicion."

The news of Mussolini's poor health set off alarms in both Italy and Germany. As the Fascist hierarchy well knew, the regime depended for its existence on this one man, whose collapse or death might bring a new order and their own ruin. King Victor Emmanuel, for his part, began casting about cautiously for a possible successor to the Duce, talking with such old-time Fascists as Bottai and Dino Grandi, who might be able to steer the nation through the chaos that would follow Mussolini's permanent absence. The Germans were equally concerned. They realized that the death of Mussolini might take Italy out of the War and thereby expose Germany's southern flank to an Allied attack.

The anxiety of the Germans spurred a visit to Rome by Heinrich Himmler, the head of the SS, on October 11, 1942. The Duce made a special effort to impress his important visitor. Dressed in his finest civilian clothes, he did his best to convince Himmler that nothing had changed, that he was firmly in charge of the Fascist Party and the people of Italy, and that the nation was resolute in its effort to win the War. Himmler, however, carried his investigation further. He spent the next three days sleuthing about Rome, conferring quietly with pro-German Italians such as the guileful Chief of Police, Carmine Senise, and the Minister of the Interior, Guido Buffarini. From these sources and others he got a more pessimistic report of the state of Italian morale. He learned that the Italians were grumbling more than ever about food rationing, inflation and shortages, and that they were weary of the War. Senise also warned Himmler that if the situation continued to deteriorate, the Royal Family could not be trusted to keep faith with the Axis.

On his return to Berlin, the SS chief relayed that warning to Hitler, and added his own appraisal: Italy would remain an Axis partner—so long as Mussolini remained alive. Himmler's report was all the warning Hitler needed; from now on, Germany would maintain constant scrutiny over Italy and be ready at any time to take over its wavering ally. Nor were Germany's intentions lost on Mussolini, who remarked ruefully to his son-in-law, Foreign Minister Ciano: "The people are now wondering which of two masters is to be preferred, the English or the Germans."

Into this atmosphere of gloom and suspicion came bad news of historic significance from Africa: On October 23, the British Eighth Army attacked at El Alamein, and soon the outgunned and outsupplied Axis forces had begun to retreat. The Italian infantry, especially the troops on Rommel's southern flank, were left to struggle on foot through the desert or surrender in place. As a result, 16,000 Italians were captured in 14 days.

Mussolini responded to the military disaster with resignation. "We must regard Libya as probably lost," he told Ciano laconically. "From certain points of view this is an advantage, because North Africa has cost us our merchant fleet and now we can better concentrate on the defense of our mainland territories."

On the heels of the British breakthrough at El Alamein came more ominous news for the Axis. At 5:30 a.m. on November 8, Ciano was roused from sleep by a telephone call from German Foreign Minister von Ribbentrop. The Allies—including large numbers of Americans—had landed in force at Casablanca, Oran and Algiers. This was not just a move to outflank Rommel; it was an intensive effort to clear the Germans and Italians from North Africa. As the Americans advanced from the west and the British from the east, the Axis forces would find themselves caught in an ever-tightening vise.

Hitler reacted immediately by dispatching strong air and ground units to Tunisia to smash the American and British forces before they could become well established. Mussolini responded similarly, and Axis strength in Tunisia eventually amounted to more than a quarter of a million men. Both

leaders were certain they knew what was at stake—and it was more than a victory in the desert. They were convinced that if the Allies succeeded in wresting North Africa from the Axis, they would use it as the launching point for an invasion of Italy. And Italy offered an avenue into the heart of Germany itself.

Hitler suspected that merely the threat of an attack on Italy might encourage the Italians to rid themselves of both Mussolini and Fascism, and then make the best surrender terms they could with the Allies.

Mussolini was bitterly discouraged by the latest events. "In Italy," he wrote later, "the repercussions of the American landing in Algiers were immediate and profound. Every enemy of Fascism promptly reared his head; the first of the traitors, minor figures, even though some were national councilors, emerged from the shadows. The country began to feel the strain. As long as only the English were in the Mediterranean, Italy, with Germany's help, could hold firm and resist, though at the cost of ever-greater sacrifices; but the appearance of America disturbed the weaker spirits."

The Duce had ample reason to be concerned about the strain on his people, for Italians were tired of living with defeat abroad and deprivation at home. Throughout 1942, intermittent Allied bombing of Italian cities, the severe shortages of food and consumer goods, and skyrocketing prices combined to make the nation miserable—and to kindle a hatred of Mussolini's regime.

Food supplies had dwindled inexorably since the beginning of the War for several reasons: Italy, having few natural resources of its own, was forced to trade food to Germany for the oil and gasoline needed to run its war machine. Italy's armed forces necessarily claimed first priority on what food was available. The Allied blockade, moreover, cut off shipments by sea, and thousands of Italian farmers were either in military service or had taken jobs in the cities.

All this meant that by the middle of 1942 staple foods were extremely scarce and severely rationed on the home front. Because of a wheat shortage, bread and pasta—the mainstays of the Italian diet—were made with fillers that turned them a dirty, dark gray color, barely recognizable in appearance or taste. The strict rationing of fats, including butter, had caused the famous Italian cheeses, such as provolone, Gorgonzola and Parmesan, to disappear from the marketplace. They were replaced by low-fat cheeses that had the taste and consistency of rubber. Olive oil, once abundant, became a precious substance; eggs were doled out, one per person per week; fruits and vegetables became equally scarce.

To make matters worse, the cost of living had doubled since Italy entered the War, which meant that a family's meager ration of food now cost twice as much. This was particularly hard on Italian workers, whose wages were frozen when the War began.

For those who could afford to pay outrageous prices, a vigorous black market provided food enough to lay a decent table. The peasants who worked the gardens and farms of Italy became the suppliers for a bootleg food industry. Great numbers of city dwellers streamed to the farms carrying empty suitcases, which they were determined to fill at any expense. Many of the more enterprising peasants came regularly to the cities with their contraband, delivering it to steady customers much like a milkman making his rounds.

The journalists Eleanor and Reynolds Packard, who continued to live in Rome until their repatriation to the United States in 1942, recalled the daily visits of the profiteers: ''Almost every morning, two or three bootleggers would come to our home before we left for the office and offer us legs of lamb, goats, chickens, ducks, eggs by the dozen, and butter. It was just a question of paying more. At first, it was double, but as rationing became more and more strict, it mounted to five times the legal price. None of these bootleggers felt like he was doing anything wrong or unpatriotic. The War was unpopular, the people were indifferent anyway, and here was a good opportunity to make big profits.''

OVRA, or the secret police, tried to combat the trafficking in black-market food by mounting special teams to search farm carts headed for the cities and inspect the packages and suitcases of travelers at railroad terminals. The bootleggers adjusted quickly to the latter threat; for a small fee, they handed their contraband to uniformed soldiers on the trains before reaching the station, knowing full well that OVRA did not stop military men and scrutinize their goods. Then the bootleggers would retrieve their packages in the street outside the station.

To further discourage profiteering, the regime meted out stiff penalties—frequently, 5,000-lira fines and three years or more in jail. In one extreme instance, a baker received a sentence of 24 years for black marketeering in flour. Mussolini added another deterrent by declaring that those convicted could expect no amnesty at the end of the War. At the urging of former Fascist Party Secretary Roberto Farinacci, he even imposed the death penalty for profiteering; but, fearful of the public's reaction, he never carried it out. The black market continued to flourish.

Through the winter of 1942 the average Italian was not only hungry, but cold. Italy had no coal mines of its own, receiving nearly all its coal from the Germans. But barely enough arrived to keep the Italian war industries going. Houses and apartments in Rome and other cities were limited to five hours of heat per day; hot water was available only three times a week for apartment dwellers, and cooking gas was cut off except at mealtimes.

The Italians were also running out of clothing. Many of their textile factories had shut down for lack of raw materials, and those still operating could barely meet the demands

Wearing a white leather jacket and helmet, Mussolini bounds from the transport plane he had copiloted to Tobruk in late June, 1942, anticipating a triumphal entrance into Egypt.

of the military, let alone the civilian population. As a result, a man was allowed to purchase either one suit or one pair of shoes per year, but not both. And if a woman bought the single heavy winter coat to which she was entitled, she was unable to buy any more clothing that year except handkerchiefs and underwear.

The clothing shortage had been escalated by German tourists in Italy. Early in the War, when apparel was plentiful, thousands of German tourists swarmed across the border to buy the goods that they could not get at home. "It was not unusual," wrote Eleanor and Reynolds Packard, "to see a German woman buy five or six dozen pairs of silk stockings at a time. They and the German men bought shoes, suits, dresses, underwear, ties and hats in wholesale quantities." By the time the regime responded by decreeing the rationing of clothes, many shops were half-empty and production had slowed to a crawl.

As the shortage grew more acute, prices climbed. A pair of shoes that cost $30 before the War now fetched a whopping $60. A black market flourished in clothing as it did in food. From under the counter merchants offered their best customers more articles than their ration coupons entitled them to—at a price. For the working class, however, there was little escape from going threadbare. Many poorer Italians traded their ration coupons to the wealthy for castoff coats, shiny-bottomed trousers and worn-out shoes.

The Italians did not suffer such privations in silence. As their grumbling grew loud enough to reach even Himmler's ears, the regime, which could do little to change the realities of the situation, sought to placate the people with propaganda. The Ministry of Popular Culture initiated a campaign lampooning the shortages and high prices, and jokes and cartoons began to appear in the popular magazines and newspapers. *La Stampa,* a Turin daily, ran a cartoon of a man begging on the street; he is nearly naked except for a pair of glistening new shoes. A passerby asks him why he has to beg, since he can afford to buy new shoes. The beggar replies: "That's why I'm so poor."

Another cartoon showed two tramps in conversation. One says, "A taste for alcohol brought about my downfall. What was your weakness?" The second tramp replies: "A taste for eggs fried in butter."

The campaign provoked more resentment than laughter. Italians saw through their government's transparent attempt to lure them away from the facts. To them, being cold, hungry and shabby was not at all funny. The government's propaganda machine also failed to achieve another of its major goals: to convince the people that the Italian armed

forces were firmly in control of the War. On Mussolini's orders, the press and radio distorted the truth about the progress of the War—but to such a degree that the lies were evident to the man in the street.

"Our official communiqués, from the very start of the War, emphasized and exaggerated the virtues of our own forces and belittled those of our enemies," wrote Rear Admiral Franco Maugeri, who had become Chief of Naval Intelligence. "Every successful skirmish or patrol was magnified, rhapsodized and blown up until it took on the proportions of Gettysburg or Trafalgar. And the news of Allied victories was played down or entirely omitted. We began to doubt, then to distrust and finally to disbelieve the official statements put out by our government."

As time wore on, more and more Italians tuned their home radios to the BBC and the Voice of America to get another picture of the War, even though listening to foreign broadcasts was a prison offense. When it became apparent to the regime that its broadcasts were being ignored by the public, Mussolini tried to force people to listen. He ordered that radios in all public places—the cafés, bars and theaters—be tuned to the official news bulletins at 1 p.m. and 6 p.m. each day, and that all patrons stop eating, drinking or talking and stand at attention for the duration of the newscast. But no one in Italy, except perhaps the most ardent Fascists, felt like standing at attention for Mussolini, particularly in those places where they were trying to find relaxation.

Having failed to win back the public's ear through discipline, the government tried a ruse to revive interest in the official broadcasts. It created a heckler known as the "Ghost Voice," who would break in on Fascist radio commentators while they were on the air. In a typical exchange, the Ghost Voice would interrupt the official announcer with a comment such as: "I dare you to tell us what is happening in Italy." And the announcer would reply with a confident chuckle: "It's raining, which is good for our crops."

Initially, the Ghost Voice caught the attention of the people, who tuned in by the millions. But once it became apparent that the heckler never asked pertinent questions, and that he always lost out in the exchange of quips with the announcer, the people realized that the act was faked and that the two opponents were actually broadcasting from the same studio. Italians stopped listening, and the regime abandoned the scheme.

The deepening anger Italians felt toward their government was sharpened by the personal excesses of the Fascist hierarchy—the leaders who might have won sympathy by setting a spartan example for the nation. Several high-ranking Fascists had taken advantage of their positions to attain enormous wealth through questionable business deals. Ciano, whose possessions included vast real-estate holdings, had emerged as perhaps the richest man in Italy.

While most Italians shared the deprivations brought by war, the Fascists flaunted their wealth and privilege. Mussolini himself followed a lean regimen, subsisting mainly on fruits and vegetables, but his eating habits were imposed by a delicate stomach, not by a sense of duty. His underlings, on the other hand, openly ignored the rationing laws. Ciano had a table reserved every night on the terrace of the fashionable Albergo Ambasciatori on the Via Veneto. He and a beautiful companion—usually not his wife—could be seen dining there on succulent cuts of meat, forbidden to ordinary restaurant-goers all but one night a week.

Another favorite haunt of the high Fascist officials was Ascenzio's, the finely appointed restaurant where money or power could buy any forbidden delicacy. On one occasion, an overzealous police officer arrested the owner, Ascenzio, for flagrant violation of the rationing laws, and Ciano had to bail him out of jail. The matter was hushed up, and not a word of it appeared in the heavily censored newspapers. But the story got around, and ordinary people who had to pay outrageous prices for food on the black market or go hungry had one more reason to be disgusted with the Fascist regime.

Then there was the continuing Petacci affair, which had become an open scandal. Not many Italians blamed Mussolini on moral grounds for keeping a mistress; the practice was all too common. But they resented the way Clara Petacci meddled in political affairs for the benefit of her family members and friends. Admiral Maugeri described her as a "Rasputin in skirts." She used her influence with the Duce to have government officials promoted or demoted, as they struck her fancy. And Clara made certain that her brothers and sisters, uncles, aunts and friends all fed heartily at the public trough.

Teen-age boys in Rome publicize a wartime fashion decreed by Fascist authorities: short pants for youths under 16. Italy's Federation for Male Clothing declared that shorts were "hygienic"; more important, they required less fabric than long trousers or knickers.

Mussolini, who earlier had tried to launch Clara's sister, Myriam, as an opera singer, now intervened in the Italian movie industry to ensure that Myriam would achieve her latest ambition, to become a movie star. The Duce browbeat producers and edited film critics' reviews to pave Myriam's way to acceptance.

During the summer of 1942, when hungry Italians were punching new holes in belts already tightened, Myriam Petacci decided to marry. Her wedding, an extravaganza by any standard, was offensive to the deprived Italians. Wedding gifts piled high; the elite of the government attended the ceremony, and Mussolini presented an ornate silver banquet service to the bride and groom. After the wedding he rewrote and censored press accounts of the event.

Not long afterward, the Venice Film Festival, which featured Myriam Petacci's movie, *Ways of the Heart,* provided the Petacci clan and several high-ranking members of the Fascist Party with another opportunity to disgrace themselves in the eyes of the Italian public. Gustavo Piva, the Fascist Party's local secretary in Venice, was aghast at the antics of his own party's elite. ''The hierarchs and their women lived together for weeks in luxury apartments,'' Piva complained later in a speech before a party convention. ''They poured through the city like a tide of mud, an insult to the population in its war effort. If I had to say where the rot begins and ends, I would be utterly lost.''

During that same summer, Mussolini was repeating a catch phrase to Fascist Party members at every opportunity: ''At all costs,'' he admonished, ''we should become a serious nation.'' The irony of his words was not lost on his beleaguered country.

By the autumn of 1942, with the campaign in North Africa turning sour, Mussolini had reached the conclusion that the key to Axis survival lay in a diplomatic move on the Eastern Front. Aided by Italy, the Germans had tried to capture the oil fields of the Caucasus while seizing the strategic city of Stalingrad. The advance had come to a halt, prompting the Führer to divert more and more men, arms and planes from the Mediterranean to regain the momentum in Russia. However, it was no longer the Axis troops who were advancing, but the Russians. Viewing the precarious situation in the East, Mussolini decided that the War hinged on making a political settlement that would end the conflict with the Soviet Union. Then the Axis could concentrate its forces in the Mediterranean to smash the Allies in North Africa—and in Europe as well, should they risk an invasion.

To promote this notion, Mussolini sent Ciano on December 16 to confer with Hitler at Rastenburg, the Führer's headquarters in East Prussia. After listening to a tedious lecture by Hitler, who exhorted the Italian Navy to greater effort in the Mediterranean, Ciano presented the Duce's proposal for making peace with the Russians. Hitler simply ignored the proposition. He would not consider even retreating, much less talking peace with the Russians. Doggedly the Führer clung to the notion that the Axis could win the War on both fronts.

Hitler in this instance would have been better advised to listen to Mussolini, for even as the Rastenburg talks proceeded, Soviet armies launched a counteroffensive, surrounding the German Sixth Army at Stalingrad and routing the Italian Eighth Army north of Voroshilovgrad.

In the Piazza Navona in Rome, off-duty Italian soldiers watch a dramatic performance staged in a portable ''little theater of the people'' in 1942. The traveling show was sponsored by the Opera Nazionale Dopolavoro, the state agency responsible for public entertainment.

For the hapless Italian soldiers, the Soviet offensive was the culmination of a season of horrors. Stretched in a thin screen along the Don River, with only one rifleman for every 20 feet and one machine gun for every mile of front, the Italians had been coping under impossible conditions. Food was short, and ammunition was so scarce that soldiers had been ordered not to fire without receiving permission from higher authority. Temperatures fell to 30° and 40° below zero; the cheap shoes issued to the Italian troops had long since worn out and the icy winds knifed through their thin overcoats. When the Russians struck in overwhelming force, the Italians fell back and their retreat became a death march. They abandoned their wounded and fought their way through Russian partisans, spurred by reports that the Soviets were shooting captives.

The Germans, as they had done in North Africa, treated the Italians as subhumans. They stole the Italian trucks and threw wounded Italians into the snow to make room for themselves in vehicles or in peasant huts. During a 300-mile flight across the frozen Russian steppes, the Italians lost 115,000 men dead and 60,000 captured. Those who managed to survive as forced laborers for the Germans were in time to receive a few boxes from Italy, marked with the message: "Apples from the Duce, sunshine from Italy." The token sustenance only hardened their hatred of the regime that had sent them east to die.

As the debacle in Russia was taking shape, Ciano took note in his diary of the rancor that existed between the Germans and Italians conferring at Rastenburg: "The atmosphere is heavy. To the bad news was added the sadness of that damp forest and the boredom of collective living in the command barracks. There isn't one spot of color, one vivid note." The Germans, Ciano added, immediately placed the blame for the disaster in Stalingrad on the Italians, accusing them of cowardice under fire. As an example, he related an acrimonious exchange between a German and an Italian diplomat: The Italian asked if his countrymen in the field had suffered many losses. "No losses at all," the German replied. "They are running."

As the defeats piled up, Mussolini became a man detested in his own country. In the movie theaters, when his image appeared on the screen, no longer did the audience respond with the customary cheer: "Long live the Duce!" Instead there was total silence. Bitter jokes circulated about him. According to one fanciful story, a delegation of anti-Fascists traveled from Milan to Rome intending to assassinate the Duce, only to return home in disgust when they saw that they would have to stand in a line of people waiting to do the same thing.

The cynical humor was symbolic of an antigovernment resistance that was becoming more brazen as it spread. The Communist underground newspaper, L'Unità, announced the formation of a National Action Front to fight Fascism; the Front, a coalition of Communists, Christian Democrats, Socialists and members of other political parties, formed the nucleus of a movement that would later take arms against both the Fascists and the Nazis in Italy. In the meantime, L'Unità's clandestine readership was increasing ominously.

Resistance appeared in another quarter as well: the highest circles of Mussolini's government and the armed forces. Members of the Fascist hierarchy met openly to discuss how to get rid of Mussolini and extract Italy from the War. On January 8, 1943, as Italian troops in Russia were struggling to save themselves, Ciano lunched with Bottai and Farinacci, two dissidents whose names were being circulated about Rome as the leading candidates to succeed the Duce. Ciano found them bitter and exasperated, as he noted in his diary. Bottai told him sarcastically: "In 1911 Mussolini said that we should give up Libya. It has taken him 32 years to keep his word."

Roman gossip produced other candidates for succession: Marshals Ugo Cavallero and Pietro Badoglio, who could provide military backing for a new government, and Dino Grandi, whose experience as a diplomat might serve Italy well when the time came to get out of the War.

Though plots and cabals abounded, no one yet was ready to act—except Mussolini himself. The Duce, having suffered a recurrence of his gastric problem, isolated himself in January at his country home, La Rocca della Caminate. Even while away from Rome, he kept abreast of the scheming through a network of informers who visited him daily. As the reports of opposition grew more frequent and alarming, Mussolini realized that he would have to act to save himself. His plan was simple and Draconian: a sweeping purge of the government.

On January 31, Mussolini returned to Rome—and struck. His first move was to sack Marshal Cavallero as Armed Forces Chief of Staff, making him a scapegoat for Italy's military setbacks and removing him from access to power. Mussolini replaced him with General Vittorio Ambrosio, a quiet, skilled and highly respected military man. This shift delighted Ciano, for he had long despised Cavallero and for months had been working for his downfall. Ciano's satisfaction did not last long, however, for he was the next to be purged: On February 5, Mussolini personally fired his son-in-law as Foreign Minister.

"The moment I enter the room," Ciano wrote of the encounter, "I perceive that he is very much embarrassed. 'What are you going to do now?' he begins, and then adds in a low voice that he is changing his entire Cabinet. Among the various personal solutions that he offers me, I choose to be Ambassador to the Holy See. It is a place of rest that may, moreover, hold many possibilities for the future. And the future, never so much as today, is in the hands of God."

Mussolini's purge continued. Most of his Cabinet members learned of their "resignations" through a public radio announcement. One of them, Giuseppe Gorla, the Minister of Public Works, was on a railroad inspection trip. At Naples, he was astonished to see railway workers uncouple his official private car; when he asked why, he was told that he had just resigned. And there was evidence that Mussolini's new appointees had not been carefully screened: Carlo Tiengo, the new Minister of Corporations, was named to the post while he was in a mental institution. After a few days on the job, he was delivered back to the asylum.

By sweeping the government clean, Mussolini intended not only to depose his possible successors, but also to distract public attention from the War and demonstrate to the world that he was still the man in charge. This last notion was shattered in dramatic fashion only a month after his new government was installed.

On March 5 at 10 a.m., the workers at the Fiat aeronautics plant, a vital factory in Turin, laid down their tools and walked off the job; it was the first industrial strike in Italy since the Fascists came to power in 1922. The walkout soon spread to other important factories in Turin and encompassed more than 100,000 workers. Later that month, at the urging of *L'Unità*, the employees of the Pirelli tire factory in Milan joined the general strike.

On the first day of the strikes in Turin, Mussolini called out troops of the Fascist militia and sent them to the plants. He maintained daily contact with the city's authorities, but the government seemed helpless to stop the walkouts. Despite having sworn personal loyalty to the Duce, the militiamen were in sympathy with the workers and refused to bully them back to their jobs. As Italian Police Chief Carmine Senise put it: "Everyone took part in the strike, Fascists and

non-Fascists, even those who were members of the militia."

Before the last of the strikes were settled in April, 300,000 workers had mobilized and several war industries had ground to a halt. It was a clear message to the government that an anti-Fascist movement existed and was ready to march. As a concerned Farinacci wrote to Mussolini: "The party is absent and impotent, and now the unbelievable is happening. Everywhere, in the trams, the theaters, the air-raid shelters, people are denouncing the regime, and not only this or that party figure, but the Duce himself. And the most serious thing is that no one reacts. Even the police do not function, as if their work was now useless. We are facing a period when events may become agonizing. Let us defend our revolution with all our strength."

Nothing that Mussolini might do to defend Fascism at home could help the worsening military situation abroad. In the East, the Soviets were preparing massive spring offensives. In Africa, Italian and German troops were being pushed inexorably into a cul de sac in northern Tunisia, their backs to the sea. The strenuous effort to supply the Axis forces in Tunisia was failing miserably: During the month of March and again in April, Italian convoys in the Mediterranean suffered losses of nearly 50 per cent.

In response to the burgeoning crisis, Mussolini indulged once more in foolish optimism. On March 26 he wrote Hitler: "It should be realized that the Anglo-American landing in North Africa has been fortunate for us in that it has created a new strategic situation. Now we have the possibility of converting what was a lucky, not to say easy, enterprise into a catastrophe that could have incalculable consequences for the development of the War, especially in the United States." To inflict this catastrophe on the Allies, Mussolini had devised a scheme that was ludicrous, given the sorry state of his armed forces. He proposed that the Axis send troops through Spain and capture Gibraltar, seizing the Balearic Islands in the process, to gain control of the western Mediterranean and the Allied supply routes.

The Germans viewed Mussolini's plan for what it was: the quixotic illusion of a beaten man. Their opinion of Mussolini had sunk to its lowest possible depth. As Hitler and his aides prepared to meet with the Duce in a summit conference in Salzburg, they received a report on what to expect from Mussolini. The assessment, prepared by Prince Otto von Bismarck II, grandson of the Iron Chancellor and German Ambassador in Rome, painted a pathetic picture of the once-dynamic Italian leader. "I do not foresee, on the part of Mussolini, any particularly embarrassing request," Prince Otto wrote. "His fleet does not exist, his army is problematical, his future is even more so. He feels himself to be weak. Hitler thinks and talks only of military matters, and this is not a favorable platform for Mussolini. He has remained a dilettante."

The Germans were not the only ones aware of Mussolini's weaknesses. The astute General Ambrosio had long since realized that Mussolini's lack of resolve in his dealings with the Germans had placed Italy in enormous peril. Preparing for the conference at Salzburg, Ambrosio and others who had the ear of the Duce tried to convince him that he must face down Hitler and extract some vital concessions: Mussolini must persuade Hitler to withdraw his armies from the Soviet Union and throw them into the breach in the Mediterranean to stave off an Axis collapse there. Only a victory in North Africa, they insisted, could save Italy from the inevitable—an Allied invasion of the homeland.

On the afternoon of April 6, Mussolini and an entourage of military and diplomatic advisers entrained for Austria. On the journey northward, the Duce's stomach ailment recurred and he writhed in pain. By the time he reached Salzburg he was doubled over with cramps. Referring to recent Italian losses at-sea, he muttered to one of his party, "There is a name for my disease. It is convoys."

When Hitler and Mussolini presented themselves on the staircase of Salzburg's Klessheim Castle, an ornate edifice richly decorated with furniture and tapestries looted from France, the onlookers were startled at their appearance. Both were pale and drawn, with tired eyes and halting steps. "Like two sick men," one of the Italian delegation whispered to a colleague. "You mean two corpses," the other replied. Mussolini, in fact, was so sick that the conference was suspended for a day to allow him to regain his strength.

The meeting at Klessheim Castle might as well have been suspended indefinitely, for all the good it did the Italians. Though the talks between Hitler and Mussolini took place in strict privacy, and no record was made, Mussolini later said he insisted that Hitler find a way to end the war in Russia and reinforce the Mediterranean. Hitler, according to the Duce, "played the same old record," citing Soviet losses up to then of 11.3 million men, and Soviet vulnerability to a decisive blow in the near future. "I could not raise with him peace feelers of any kind," Mussolini told an official of the Foreign Ministry.

Whatever transpired between the two leaders, it was clear to everyone that the Duce again had fallen under the spell of Hitler's eloquence and persuasive charm. Buoyed by the Führer's self-confidence, Mussolini finished the four days of talks in a state of euphoria. Hitler smugly took credit for the transformation. He later remarked to Goebbels: "When the Duce came out of the train at Klessheim, he looked like a beaten old man. When he left, he was full of energy, ready for anything."

Mussolini's temporary uplift was shared by no one else in the circle of power in Italy. General Ambrosio and other military leaders, the new Secretary of State for Foreign Affairs, Giuseppe Bastianini, the Fascist Party hierarchy and

A British soldier in Sicily scans the town of Villa Rosa, in which almost every building has been painted by Mussolini loyalists with slogans that read "Duce, come back to us!" and "Duce, return!" Other Sicilians, however, welcomed the British and American troops as liberators.

members of the royal court all were angered and dismayed by Mussolini's failure at the Klessheim meeting. It seemed clear to them all that only the removal of the Duce could save Italy. Mussolini's opponents in Rome, who had quietly awaited the outcome of the conference, now buzzed with new fury. When General Ambrosio returned home, he assigned one of his top aides to develop a plan for the Duce's eventual arrest.

Mussolini made a few hasty and superficial moves to swing the party and the home front behind him once again. He sacked the Italian Chief of Police, Carmine Senise, for failing to stop the March strikes. He fired Fascist Party Secretary Aldo Vidussoni and replaced him with an old ally, Carlo Scorza, who reorganized the *squadristi* bludgeon squads of the 1920s with fresh recruits and sent them out with orders to club anyone who was not wearing the Fascist emblem. And as a last resort, the Duce fell back on oratory, his once-shining skill.

On May 5, 1943, for the first time since December of 1941, Mussolini addressed the public from the familiar balcony of the Palazzo Venezia. The occasion was the seventh anniversary of the capture of Addis Ababa—which had long since been lost by the Italians. His audience was a special one, a group of diehard Fascists who had just come from a rally of their own.

"I know that millions and millions of Italians are stricken with an indefinable sickness," Mussolini declared, "and the name of it is the African sickness. There is only one way to cure it, and that is to go back there. And we will go back there!"

The crowd responded with a cheer, and when the noise subsided, Mussolini's voice rose higher: "I hear, vibrating in your voices, the proclamation of your old and incorruptible faith: faith in Fascism, certainty of victory."

"Vinceremo!" the crowd replied. "We shall conquer!"

But oratory was no longer enough; Mussolini had been outpaced by events. The end had come for the Axis forces in Africa. On May 8, Tunis fell, and five days later the remnants of the Italian and German armies—nearly 275,000 men—surrendered to Allied troops on Cape Bon peninsula. Mussolini's press announced the catastrophe in bold and ludicrous headlines: "All Resistance Ends in Tunisia by Order of the Duce."

The surrender in North Africa triggered the Germans to unilateral action. As early as March, during the wave of labor strikes in northern Italy, members of Himmler's SS had begun to infiltrate Italian territory and to send back to Berlin reports on civilian unrest and the plots against Mussolini that were being discussed. Hitler became convinced that the Germans could no longer rely on Italian forces to resist an Allied invasion. Now that such an invasion was likely, Hitler determined to defend Germany, if necessary, by making Italian soil his front line. He ordered that the Wehrmacht be alerted for Operation *Alaric:* the German occupation of Italy.

On June 12, the Italians suffered another ominous blow. The island of Pantelleria, an obvious Mediterranean steppingstone to the Italian mainland, was attacked by an Allied invasion force. Pantelleria was a natural fortress garrisoned by 12,000 Italian fighting men. But when the island commander radioed Mussolini that his forces had no drinking water, the Duce tamely acquiesced in the commander's request for permission to surrender without a fight. As it turned out, no water shortage existed—the Italians there were just sick of the War.

"They are knocking at the gate," said Mussolini of the Allies. And the only uncertainty that confronted Axis strategists was where the next blow would fall. The Germans guessed that the Allies might invade through Sardinia or Greece. Mussolini thought otherwise; at a gathering of Fascist Party chiefs in late June, he hinted darkly that the British and Americans would likely land in Sicily, just off the toe of the Italian boot. "The minute the enemy starts to debark," he growled, "he must be stopped stone cold on the beach."

The Duce was right. On the night of July 9, Allied parachutists descended on Sicily; within hours, waves of landing craft inundated the eastern and southern coasts of the island. The invaders were not stopped on the beaches. Instead, they drove inexorably across the island.

There was no doubt now in Italian minds that the mainland would be next; and it was also clear that Italy no longer possessed the means to defend itself. As Mussolini had once remarked, there was only one question remaining for speculation: Who would become Italy's master, the Allies or the Germans? In either case, the bell was tolling for the Fascist regime.

CAMPAIGN OF FEAR

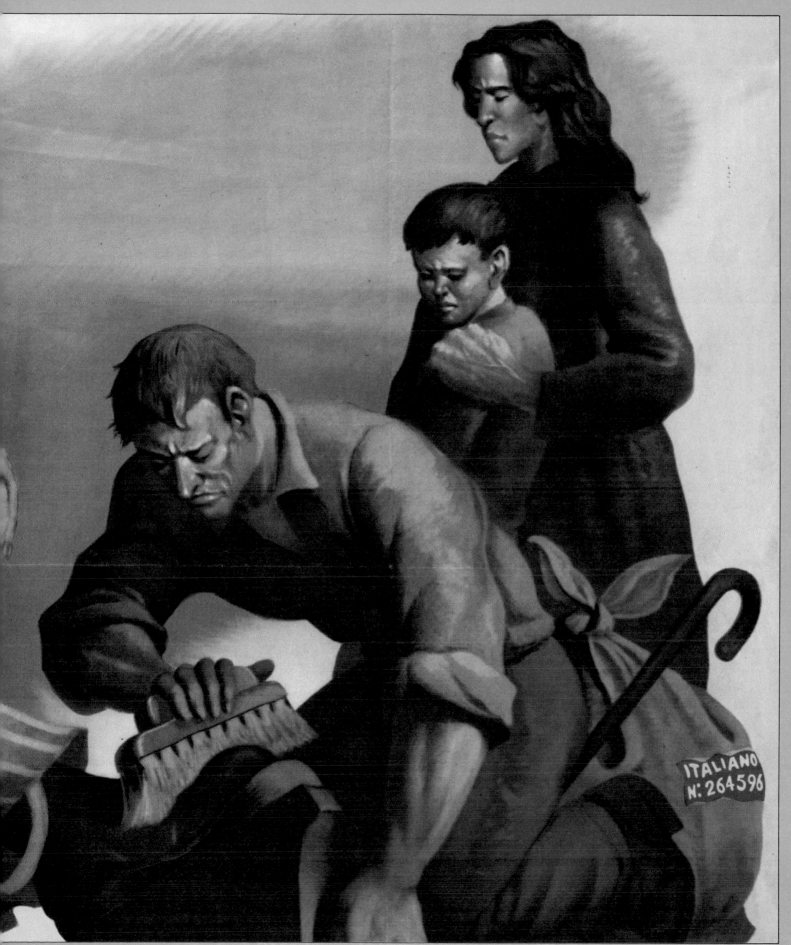

An Italian father shines the shoes of an imperious Uncle Sam in this 1944 poster, which warned that slavery awaited any who welcomed the Allied invaders.

ITALIANO
N.° 264596

VISIONS OF HORROR TO RALLY THE PEOPLE

A bloodied Italian child stands in shock over a dead playmate in a poster that accuses American bombers of dropping booby-trapped pens.

When Italy entered the War, its propaganda artists were among the first to go on the offensive. To inspire the people, illustrators produced posters calling for a new Roman Empire in which Italian warplanes would set London ablaze and Italian soldiers would destroy the fearsome Russian bear. Later, as Axis fortunes began to wane, Fascist propagandists were forced to strike a different note in an effort to keep the people united behind the war effort: They pictured Italy as a beleaguered country threatened by unspeakable horrors. Posters featured heroic men, victimized children and stoic mothers, and each Allied nation was shown to embody a particular danger.

The British Empire became a rapacious spider eager to ensnare Italy in its web. Propagandists assured the public, however, that the British could never succeed; their vitality had been sapped by such Anglo-Saxon vices as psychoanalysis, golf (an "anti-Mediterranean sport") and the afternoon tea break.

The United States was presented as a cruel foe whose aircraft indiscriminately bombed schools, churches and hospitals, and whose insensitive troops would plunder Italy's treasures. In one poster, a GI was shown carrying off the statue of the *Venus de Milo,* on which he had slapped a two-dollar price tag.

Russians were portrayed as godless mongrels who would snatch screaming children from their mothers' arms and destroy the Italian family. Parroting one of the Germans' favorite themes, the Italians lumped Communism with Jewry and the Freemasons in what they branded the "international plutocracy."

In 1943, Italy was invaded and Mussolini was exiled from Rome. The remaining Fascist propagandists turned their talents to promoting the Duce's new government in the north. They denounced King Victor Emmanuel as a traitor to the nation for capitulating to the Allies. And they urged Italians to work and fight alongside the Germans— who had, in reality, become their occupiers. It was a final call to arms.

In an emotional appeal against surrender to the Allies, a mother wearing her dead boy's war medal pleads, "Don't betray my son."

"Defend him!" exhorts a poster that depicts a squalling Italian baby threatened by Jews, Communists and Freemasons.

Squatting on the bones of the war dead, a brutish Red Army soldier wielding the symbolic Soviet hammer prepares to deliver the death blow to a world dripping blood.

A mother defends her youngster from a malevolent spider, its legs forming the spokes of the British Union Jack. Italian artists also portrayed Britain's John Bull as an octopus and as a glutton who had swallowed the world.

The menacing figure of a stereotyped Jewish Bolshevik looms against the New York skyline in a 1942 poster censuring the recent alliance of the Soviet Union and the United States.

PATRIOTIC APPEALS FOR A FLAGGING CAUSE

In 1944, Mussolini tried to raise an army to support the puppet regime, backed by German arms, that he had set up in northern Italy. His propagandists appealed to patriotism and manliness, themes that had been successful in the heady first days of the War. Recruiting posters maintained that a ravaged Italy could still redeem itself in the eyes of the world, and featured tiger-fierce soldiers rushing into battle. Other posters stressed cooperation with Italy's German comrades-in-arms.

But the posters and their rhetoric failed to stir a populace weary of the War and wary of the Germans, who treated them as a conquered people. Italian men by the thousands fled into the countryside rather than fight for Mussolini's flagging cause.

After dropping from the sky as boldly as the eagles behind him, a paratrooper brandishing a grenade charges into combat in this recruiting poster for an Air Force commando unit.

"To arms for honor," proclaims a poster seeking volunteers for the 10th Light Flotilla, a Navy commando unit that managed to recruit 4,000 men after the armistice. They were diverted to fight anti-Fascist Italian partisans.

A pair of baleful eyes emphasizes the message of this poster for Mussolini's Republican National Guard: "The world watches us—let us arise again, we are still in time."

"And you . . . what are you doing?" demands
a poster that sought to shame Italian men
into enlisting in the army of Mussolini's newly
established republic in northern Italy.

LA GERMANIA È VERAMENTE VOSTRA AMICA

''Germany is truly your friend,'' reads a Fascist poster. Few Italians believed its message as they watched the Germans plunder Italy.

5

Allied bombers over the Eternal City
A fateful meeting of the Grand Council
A new leader declares, "The War is continuing"
Clandestine maneuvers to switch sides
An American general's secret survey of Rome
Plucking the Duce from a mountaintop prison
The birth of a short-lived republic
Four days of uprising to liberate Naples
A hard winter for "summer partisans"
"Justice for the Italian people"

Once Allied troops landed successfully on the beaches of Sicily in the early hours of July 10, 1943, it was clear to most Italians that the end was near for Italy as an Axis belligerent. With its Navy nearly immobilized, its Air Force reduced to a shadow, and its battered Army suffering from a loss of will, Italy was virtually without military potential. The dominant wish of the Italian people was to walk away from the War—to be able to disengage from both their German partner and their Allied enemy without having their country either fought over or occupied.

It was Italy's tragedy that this wish had little chance of being fulfilled, and no one knew so better than Benito Mussolini. On July 19, in a moment of political lucidity, he stated the case succinctly to his ministers and aides: "Perhaps you think that this problem has not been consciously on my mind for a long time. Under a seemingly impassive mask there is deep torment, which tears my heart. I admit the hypothesis: to detach ourselves from Germany. It sounds so simple. One day, at a given hour, one sends a radio message to the enemy. . . . But with what consequences?" Having posed the question, Mussolini answered it himself: "The enemy rightly will insist on a capitulation. And what attitude will Hitler take? Perhaps you think he will give us liberty of action."

Hitler of course would not give up Italy without a fight. But if Mussolini saw his country's dilemma clearly, he was less astute about his own. He seemed not to realize that the Allied invasion of Sicily had made many of the men around him determined to disengage not only from the War but from the man who got them into it.

For King Victor Emmanuel, the dangerous course of trying to depose the dictator was complicated by his overriding concern to preserve the House of Savoy, which had ruled part or all of Italy for nearly 1,000 years. The King was on a tightrope; on one side of him were the remnants of Fascist power, still strong enough to crush a coup d'état and blot out its perpetrators. On the other side was a burgeoning array of anti-Fascists who would certainly judge the monarchy by how it acted in this momentous hour. The King was convinced that Mussolini had to go, and he possessed the Constitutional authority to remove him; but he was not yet sure that it was safe to do so.

Less worried about the monarchy, but equally deter-

SURRENDER WITHOUT PEACE

mined to shake up the government, was a group of old-line Fascists led by one of the original members of the party, former Foreign Minister Dino Grandi. Another prominent member of this cabal was the Duce's own son-in-law, Count Galeazzo Ciano. The group was not of one mind. Some of its members saw a need to rid the country of Fascism and renounce its ties with Germany. Others, among them Roberto Farinacci, were strong pro-Nazis who wanted only those changes that would improve Italy's prosecution of the War.

At a tense meeting with the Duce on the afternoon of the 16th of July, 15 of the discontented Fascist leaders—not including either Grandi or Ciano, who were prudently absent—made the first overt move against Mussolini's absolute rule. In effect, they asked the dictator to cede some of his powers in the interest of making the regime more efficient. Every man present had his heart in his mouth, for their proposals might well be considered treason by the Duce—and although he had lost much of his aura of power, he still controlled OVRA, the secret police. After listening to their complaints, Mussolini curtly agreed to convene the Fascist Grand Council to take up the matter.

To the Duce, such a meeting seemed safe enough, for in his view the council had no power of action; it was only advisory, and he had not even bothered to convoke it for years. Even if the council did vote to redistribute some of his powers, he was confident he could ignore its initiatives and go on doing as he pleased. Not until five days later did Mussolini learn that Dino Grandi was circulating a resolution to end the Duce's one-man rule by restoring the authority of the Grand Council and other government agencies, and returning supreme military command to the King.

Mussolini drew some encouragement during these eventful days from a hoped-for meeting with Hitler, one he was sure would lead to improvements in Italy's fighting capacity. But again he was out of touch with reality. Far from being prepared to send the Italians more aid, Hitler was outraged by reports that entire divisions of Italian soldiers were surrendering in Sicily without firing a shot; he had come to believe that German forces would have to take full command of the situation in Italy.

Hitler summoned Mussolini to meet him at the northern Italian town of Feltre on July 19. Following the opening formalities, the Italian delegation sat restlessly through a two-hour monologue by Hitler, interrupted only briefly by the news that Rome had been bombed by the Allies with terrible loss of life. At lunch, the Duce's top aides privately urged him to explain firmly to Hitler that Italy must leave the War. But later in the day, when the two dictators met in private, Mussolini let himself be carried away by Hitler's talk of new weapons that would reverse the course of the War and ensure an Axis victory. Finally venturing to speak, Mussolini, rather than declaring Italy's urgent need for peace, asked for more military aid. Later, quite pleased with himself, he reported to his aides: "I had no need to make that speech to Hitler, because this time he has firmly promised to send all the reinforcements we need."

While Mussolini was getting his pep talk from Hitler, General Vittorio Ambrosio, Armed Forces Chief of Staff, was handed a list of demands by Field Marshal Wilhelm Keitel, his German counterpart. The list amounted to an ultimatum giving Germany effective control over the defense of the Italian mainland. Hereafter, Italian commanders would be little more than figureheads, and the Germans would be free to deploy any German or Italian troops necessary for a savage defense of Italian territory. Thus, unknown to many of those plotting to remove the Duce, the hope of keeping Italy from becoming a battleground went glimmering.

The Rome to which Mussolini returned from Feltre was shocked and demoralized. Italians had believed that their Eternal City, with its thousands of churches and its millennia of irreplaceable art and architecture, would never be bombed. The presence of the Vatican alone, they thought, would be enough to spare the city the fate of London, Rotterdam, Berlin and their own industrial centers in the north.

They still thought so on the morning of July 19, despite an overnight shower of leaflets warning that Rome would be bombed that day. At 11 a.m., air-raid sirens began to wail. The first of 500 American planes were dropping bombs on the railroad station, the marshaling yards and the Littorio and Ciampino airfields.

Before the all clear sounded three hours later, a black Mercedes limousine carried Pope Pius XII to the neighborhood of the 13th Century Basilica of San Lorenzo Outside-the-Walls. Stray bombs landing there had taken much of the

155

raid's overall toll of 1,400 dead and 6,000 injured. The Pope moved among the victims, joining other priests in administering last rites to the dying. Many in the crowd kissed his white robe, which had become stained with grime and blood. Then another limousine arrived, carrying King Victor Emmanuel, dressed in the gray-green uniform of a marshal. As the King started to get out of his car a woman spotted him and screamed for the attention of the crowd. "He's come to see the massacre," she shouted, and others took up the cry. Badly shaken at being jeered by his people, the monarch retreated into his limousine and rode off to chants of "We want peace!"

This distressing experience pushed the King off his political tightrope—Mussolini must go. When in a few days the Grand Council voted against the Duce, as the King fully expected it to do, he decided to use their action as the justification for removing the dictator. And he settled on Mussolini's successor: the respected Marshal Pietro Badoglio, who had been inactive since being relieved by the Duce as Chief of the Armed Forces General Staff in December 1940, after the failure of the Greek campaign.

When Mussolini, clad in the black shirt of the Fascist militia, appeared for the meeting of the Grand Council on the afternoon of Saturday, July 24, Fascist Party Secretary Carlo Scorza sprang to his feet and cried, "Saluto al Duce!" All 26 members of the council stood and raised their right arms in the Fascist salute.

The expression of loyalty notwithstanding, Mussolini was no longer among friends. Grandi had spent the previous hour cementing support for his motion to separate the dictator from his powers. Yet Grandi was gravely worried. Before coming to the meeting he had taken the precaution of going to confession, making a new will, and strapping a hand grenade to his thigh—he did not intend to be taken alive by Fascist torturers if the coup failed.

Mussolini opened the meeting with a two-hour lecture tracing the history of the War; he then launched into an attack on Grandi's motion, which would strip the Duce of his authority over the ministries that ran the country and would remove him as Commander in Chief of the Armed Forces. A round of debate followed. Impassive through most of the criticisms of his rule, Mussolini could not suppress an expression of rage when his son-in-law, Ciano, announced his support for the motion.

After nine hours of disputation, Mussolini demanded a roll-call vote, thus forcing each member of the Grand Council to make his position clear. Needing a simple majority of the 26 members, Grandi's resolution got 19 votes. At 2:40 a.m. Sunday, Mussolini adjourned the meeting. Grandi felt like a man who had been reprieved from the firing squad. As soon as he was alone, he carefully removed the hand grenade from inside his trousers.

Mussolini, who was in the habit of seeing the King regularly on Mondays, requested an audience for that Sunday afternoon, July 25. He wanted to lose no time in having the action of the Grand Council set aside. Victor Emmanuel was waiting for the Duce in the doorway of his drawing room in the Villa Savoia, and the two men entered together. For this visit, the King had instructed his military aide, General Paolo Puntoni, to stand listening just outside the door, ready to intervene if he was needed.

As Puntoni later reconstructed the fateful encounter, Mussolini attempted to take the initiative, but the King cut him off, saying: "My dear Duce, it's no longer any good. Italy has gone to bits. Army morale is at rock bottom. The soldiers don't want to fight any more. You can certainly be under no illusions as to Italy's feeling with regard to yourself. At this moment you are the most hated man in Italy."

Then the diminutive King made his crucial point: "All Rome already knows about the Grand Council resolution, and they are all expecting a change."

Caught unaware, the Duce said, "But if Your Majesty is right, I should present my resignation." Quickly the King replied, "And I have to tell you that I unconditionally accept it." Mussolini's 21-year rule was over.

The King had orchestrated the moment well. As Mussolini left the palace, he was firmly offered armed "protection." His own driver having been taken away, he was driven to a carabinieri barracks, not yet comprehending that he was under arrest.

Within the next few hours the King formally appointed Badoglio as Prime Minister. Troops of the regular Army secured government offices and communications facilities to head off any threat of a countercoup. A few Fascist leaders were arrested, but most of those still loyal to Mussolini had

At his home in Rapallo, Ezra Pound composes pro-Fascist commentaries on stationery emblazoned with Mussolini's motto, "Liberty is a duty, not a right."

FASCISM'S RABID AMERICAN VOICE

One of Mussolini's most fervent promoters was Ezra Pound, the American poet and expatriate who had lived in Italy since 1925. Pound lionized the Duce as "an opportunist who is right" and declared that Thomas Jefferson "was one genius and Mussolini is another."

Pound met Mussolini only once, but he bombarded the Duce with advice on economics and politics. When the War came, Pound volunteered to make radio broadcasts to Allied countries to counter "London lies." He directed his first broadcast to the United States on January 23, 1941, urging Americans to avoid Europe's war. His messages were rabidly anti-Semitic:

"Had you the sense to eliminate Roosevelt and his Jews," he told Americans after Pearl Harbor, "you would not now be at war." He took potshots at President Roosevelt, calling him "stinkie," and characterized Prime Minister Churchill as senile.

For each broadcast, Pound was paid 350 lire, about $17, barely adequate to cover expenses, let alone justify the political risks. In 1943 a U.S. grand jury indicted Pound *in absentia* for treason. Undeterred, he continued writing in support of Fascism until the War ended.

On April 30, 1945, Pound was arrested by Italian partisans. He insisted that they deliver him to U.S. custody, and he spent the next six months in a detention camp near Pisa with 3,600 hardened soldier-criminals. For part of that time, the 60-year-old poet lived on execution row in a

wire cage six feet square. Eventually he was flown to Washington, D.C., for trial.

Julien Cornell, Pound's attorney, found the "poor devil very wobbly in his mind." A jury decided he was incompetent to stand trial, and the court confined him to a Washington mental hospital.

For the next 12 years, Pound's admirers—among them T. S. Eliot, Dag Hammarskjöld, Ernest Hemingway, Archibald MacLeish, Robert Frost and Clare Boothe Luce—fought for his release. In 1956 *Life* argued that Pound's acts had "aged to the point of requital, parole or forgiveness."

On April 18, 1958, Pound had his last day in court. Ruling that the poet would never recover sufficiently to face trial, the judge dismissed the treason indictment. Pound returned to Italy, where he spent the remaining 15 years of his life.

fled Rome following the Grand Council vote. At 10:45 that night, Italian radio interrupted its programing to announce the change of government. This news was followed by the first announcement from the new Badoglio government, one that went largely unnoticed by the Italians and was largely disbelieved by German officials trying to absorb the shock of the Duce's sudden downfall: "The War is continuing. Italy, the jealous guardian of her age-old traditions, remains loyal to her pledged word."

Italy's towns and villages rejoiced at the fall of Mussolini. Men and women still in their nightclothes poured out of their homes into the hot summer night to embrace and fill the air with cheering. Men stood on each other's shoulders to pull down the emblems of Fascism, and before long the sidewalks and streets were littered with framed photographs, busts and statuettes of the former Duce.

The new government, all of whose members were tarred with the Fascist brush to one degree or another, moved quickly to stop the demonstrations. Anxious lest the country enrage Germany by declaring peace through public acclamation, Badoglio invoked force to restore order. In several cities hundreds of people were shot.

Within days of taking office, Badoglio began the intricate process of trying to extract Italy from the War without further bloodshed. The nearest point of contact with Allied officials was the Vatican, but the British and American representatives there did not have secure communications with their governments. Contact would have to be made beyond Axis borders. The man chosen for the job was General Giuseppe Castellano, an aide to Armed Forces Chief of Staff Ambrosio. The King, fearing for his own safety, refused to give the envoy written credentials, which left Castellano to gain the attention of Allied diplomats with nothing stronger than a letter of introduction from Sir D'Arcy Osborne, Britain's representative to the Vatican. Castellano decided he would approach the British Ambassador to Spain to deliver his message.

Castellano's task was monumental. Italy hoped to do an about-face, substituting ally for enemy and—somehow—gaining the status of an Allied belligerent. Allied policy, however, held Italy to be an enemy, one that, like Germany and Japan, had to be beaten into submission. The British

government, though publicly committed to demanding Italy's unconditional surrender, yearned to strike at Germany through what Churchill had called the "soft underbelly" of Europe and would have preferred to negotiate for Italian assistance. But the Americans, sensitive to the Soviet Union's demands for a second front, were opposed to diverting men and matériel to Italy from the planned invasion across the English Channel; they were therefore not inclined to go easy on the collapsing enemy. The Germans, for their part, were determined regardless of political developments to make Italy an impregnable defensive barrier against invasion from the south.

Traveling incognito by train, General Castellano reached Madrid on August 15. There he managed to make an appointment with British Ambassador Sir Samuel Hoare, probably the only diplomat who had not fled to the seashore to find relief from Madrid's 114° F. heat. Castellano delivered his message: Italy wished to renounce its ties with Germany and join the War on the side of the Allies. But Italy could do so, said Castellano, only if Allied troops landed on the mainland, and in sufficient strength to protect Rome from German occupation. Then Italy would willingly sign an unconditional surrender, announce it publicly, and enter the lists against Germany.

To demonstrate his good faith, Castellano offered to brief Allied military personnel on the disposition of German forces in Italy. At the same time, he warned that Hitler was rapidly pouring fresh troops into Italy, which would lose its ability to change sides if the Allies did not act quickly.

Ambassador Hoare had no authority to negotiate with the Italians, but he promptly informed London of his interview with Castellano and made arrangements for the next contact to take place in Lisbon, a neutral capital friendlier than Franco's Madrid. Castellano, still traveling under an assumed name, reached Lisbon on August 16 and got in touch with Sir Ronald Hugh Campbell, the British Ambassador there. Campbell prudently kept the Italian envoy at arm's length for two days—long enough to confirm Castellano's credentials and for the Allies to agree on a response.

Italy's proposition, as delivered by Castellano, collided head-on with the Allies' avowed stance, which was not to negotiate with any enemy who had not surrendered unconditionally. Specifically, the Allies wanted Italy to earn their good will by signing an armistice and then doing whatever it could to resist the Germans and obstruct their preparations for the coming Allied invasion.

Moreover, the Allies intended to impose a surrender that had two parts, only one of which the Italians were to know about before signing the armistice. Known as the Short Terms and the Long Terms, both parts had been prepared well in advance by a joint British-American commission. The Short Terms were a list of 121 standard military items, including cessation of hostilities, return of Allied prisoners, surrender of the fleet and air force, and the establishment of an Allied military government. Only the last item hinted at the Long Terms to come. It read: "Other conditions of a political, economic and financial nature with which Italy will be bound to comply will be transmitted at a later date." Those conditions, which included such items as prohibiting the manufacture of armaments and control by occupation authorities of all means of communication, clearly did not define the relationship of cobelligerents. Rather they were the rules of a conqueror for the conquered.

On August 19, American Major General Walter Bedell Smith and British Brigadier Kenneth D. Strong, representing the Allied Supreme Command, arrived in Lisbon by way of Gibraltar and handed the Short Terms to Castellano. Authorized to negotiate only a change of sides, Castellano took the Short Terms back to Rome, along with a promise from Smith to ask General Dwight D. Eisenhower, the Allied commander in chief, to give Italy at least two weeks' notice of the date of the invasion. Actually, the invasion was only 15 days off, and the Allies had no intention of telling anyone, much less an Italian general, the date, location or strength of the assault.

Castellano was received in Rome as the bearer of bad tidings. Far from winning cobelligerent status, he had returned with proof of Italy's total political prostration. Badoglio's Foreign Minister, Baron Raffaele Guariglia, was incensed because Castellano had promised the Allies active military assistance against the Germans, a decision he was not authorized to make. Indeed, his offer far exceeded what the Italians were willing to commit themselves to. Although the Italians desired cobelligerent status, with all its postwar benefits, they knew very well that the Italian Army would be powerless against the Germans.

As much as anything, the Italian leaders in Rome wanted a commitment from the Allies to protect them—and the capital—from the Germans. Faced with the Allied demand for acceptance of the Short Terms, the Italians responded that they could not risk announcing an armistice until the Allies had landed north of Rome, preferably with at least 15 divisions. They were unaware that the entire invasion would be carried out by only eight divisions—the remaining Allied strength in the European theater was being saved for an eventual invasion of France.

Meeting with Castellano on August 31 at Cassibile, Sicily, General Smith made a counteroffer—but one tied to a 48-hour ultimatum. Italy must surrender immediately; then the Allies would drop a U.S. airborne division near Rome to help secure the city, provided the Italians were able and willing to keep the Germans at bay for a time. When Castellano returned to Rome the same day with this offer, the Italians' response was to agree to the surrender if they could have more time to prepare to face the German reaction. Back went Castellano to Cassibile on September 2 with the Italian counteroffer. At this point General Smith, running out of patience, demanded that Italy sign the surrender at once or get ready to withstand an all-out Allied attack.

Events were moving too fast for the Italians. On September 3, while they pondered Smith's ultimatum, General Sir Bernard L. Montgomery landed two divisions near Reggio di Calabria—on the toe of the Italian boot, just across the Strait of Messina from Sicily. Later that day the Badoglio government radioed explicit authorization for Castellano to sign the surrender. No sooner was the document completed than Smith handed Castellano the Long Terms; once more the Italian emissary would be the bearer of bad news.

Having swallowed the bitter pill of surrender, the Italians became concerned with protecting as much of their country as possible from the Germans—and they began to have second thoughts about facilitating the American airborne landing near Rome. They had information that the main Allied landings would come well south of the capital.

Planning for the airdrop had been going forward at the Allies' headquarters in Algiers. But Major General Matthew B. Ridgway—commander of the 82nd Airborne Division, which was to make the drop—was skeptical about the promised Italian assistance. The 82nd's artillery commander, Brigadier General Maxwell D. Taylor, and Colonel William T. Gardiner of the Troop Carrier Command were dispatched on a secret mission to Rome. They were to make final arrangements with the Italians and, more important, evaluate the situation and decide whether or not the operation should take place.

The two officers arrived at the port of Gaeta in a British PT boat escorted by the Italian corvette *Ibis*. They were met by Rear Admiral Maugeri, Italy's Chief of Naval Intelligence, and made the 85-mile trip to Rome with him in an ambulance. The Americans were carrying a large amount of Italian currency, and a radio hidden in a suitcase. Both men also carried sidearms and were in full uniform, covered by plain raincoats. By plan, they were pushed around and given harsh orders by their Italian escort, as though they were enemy pilots pulled from a plane that had gone down offshore. They devoutly hoped that prisoner-of-war status would be granted them if they had the bad luck to fall into German hands.

In Rome, Taylor and Gardiner soon learned that the Italians were wavering again. Taylor informed Marshal Badoglio in the early hours of September 8 that the airdrop and the main invasion were to take place the next day and that the Italians were expected to announce the armistice beforehand. Badoglio reacted by sending a message to General Eisenhower repudiating the surrender. Taylor, in turn, used his radio to flash the code word "innocuous," signaling cancellation of the airdrop.

Eisenhower's response was angry and unequivocal: If the Italians reneged on the agreement, the consequences would be grave. "No future action of yours," he radioed, "could then restore any confidence whatever in your good faith, and consequently the dissolution of your government and your nation would ensue."

Without waiting for Badoglio's reply, Eisenhower proceeded to broadcast the official Allied announcement of the Italian surrender. The announcement came at 6:30 p.m. on September 8 while the Italian Cabinet was in conference with the King on how to respond to Eisenhower's ultimatum. Faced now with the choice of confirming the surrender or being warred upon by both the Germans and the Allies, the Italians bowed to the inevitable. At 7:45 p.m. Badoglio announced the surrender to his nation, officially ensuring that Italian forces would not resist the Allied landings the following day.

The surrender did not come as a surprise to the angry Germans. From the moment he was told of Mussolini's downfall in July, Hitler had expected the worst. Even before he found out about Badoglio's pledge to continue the War against the Allies, he had told his chief of operations, General Alfred Jodl, "Undoubtedly in this treachery, they will proclaim that they are loyal to us; but of course they will not remain loyal."

Accordingly, the Germans had begun preparations to withdraw their four divisions in Sicily—where Axis resistance ended on August 17—to the mainland and to send other forces through the Alpine passes to occupy the north.

Fleeing Rome after the armistice, King Victor Emmanuel III (second from right) talks with aides on board the Italian corvette Baionetta en route to the Adriatic port of Brindisi—and safety—on the 10th of September, 1943. A German warplane flew over the ship in mid-voyage, but passed on without attacking.

Field Marshal Rommel, commanding the troops assembled in the Alps, seized control of the passes, but Field Marshal Kesselring, commander of all German forces in the south, temporarily dissuaded Hitler from more drastic steps—such as occupying Rome, arresting the King and Badoglio, and restoring Mussolini. Kesselring argued that such moves would push Italy into the Allied camp before German strength could be spread effectively throughout the country. If the Germans went along with Badoglio's charade, while rapidly deploying troops under the pretext of preparing for a joint defense, they would be in a better position to hold the country when the other shoe fell.

Now, with the armistice an accomplished fact, the Germans moved swiftly to take over Italian positions. They disarmed Italian soldiers by the tens of thousands; Italian officers who objected were shot. Thus, when the Allies landed, they confronted not neutralized Italian troops but determined Germans. So began a campaign that was to drag on for 20 bitter months, until just before the ultimate collapse of Germany itself.

The Germans failed to get their hands on Italy's Navy. Complying with the Short Terms of surrender, columns of battleships, cruisers, destroyers and smaller craft steamed from their bases on Italy's west and east coasts toward Allied ports at Malta and in North Africa, in some cases just a step ahead of the frustrated Germans. Their escape was not complete. The Luftwaffe found and sank the battleship *Roma* at sea with a loss of about 1,400 of its crew. Most of the fleet, however, reached haven with the Allies.

The Allies began to come ashore at Salerno and Taranto on September 9. German officials in Rome expected the British and Americans to strike there as well, so they moved troops to secure routes of withdrawal northward, should it become necessary to evacuate the city. The King, Prime Minister Badoglio and their retinues had already fled Rome, leaving before dawn on the 9th. Their departure left Italy's armed forces leaderless at the moment when they most desperately needed guidance on how to react to German—as well as Allied—moves.

The government entourage turned out to be right in fearing for its safety. Kesselring had no intention of pulling out of Rome unless driven out. Instead he deployed his forces to make the capital secure.

German troop dispositions blocked the escape routes that had been prepared for the King and Badoglio. So just before first light, they began a roundabout trip that took them to Pescara on the Adriatic coast, then by ship to Brindisi, which the Germans had just evacuated and Montgomery's troops had not yet reached.

Wherever the Germans took control, life became harsher and more dangerous for all Italians, and particularly for Jews. Mussolini had never subscribed to Hitler's extreme racial theories, and Jews had been among the original Fascists. Even when the Duce instituted anti-Jewish laws in 1938 to curry favor with Hitler, the impact was social and economic, but not life-threatening.

With the German occupation of Rome, however, the situation changed almost overnight. SS chief Heinrich Himmler informed Lieut. Colonel Herbert Kappler, the senior Gestapo officer in Rome, that the city's 8,000 Jews were to be rounded up and deported to concentration camps in Eastern Europe. Kappler thought such a move politically unwise, and he joined several German diplomats and generals in a halfhearted attempt to block it. At the same time, however, he extorted a ransom of 50 kilograms—about 110 pounds—of gold from the Jewish community in exchange for a promise of safety. It was a promise he had no intention of keeping; once the gold was in German hands, nothing stood between the Jews and doom but the willingness of other Italians to help them.

On the 16th of October, a Gestapo sweep through Rome netted more than 1,000 Jewish men, women and children. They were sent to Auschwitz, where only 16 of them would survive the War. The Gestapo's subsequent report to headquarters in Berlin complained that Italian police could not be used in the sweep because of their "unreliability," and that Roman citizens in general displayed "outright passive resistance, which in many cases amounted to active assistance" to the Jews.

On the orders of Pope Pius XII, the Vatican—whose extraterritorial status was respected by the Germans—gave shelter to some 4,700 Jews in its monasteries and convents all over Rome. Many others were hidden by private citizens. Throughout German-occupied Italy, Jews were subjected to deportation to death camps or to random attacks by Gesta-

Italians lay down their arms at dawn on September 9, 1943.

CAPTIVES OF A ONETIME ALLY

When Italy made peace with the Allies in September of 1943, many of its soldiers found life worse rather than better. The German divisions that controlled much of Italy took the armistice as a betrayal. They moved quickly to seize and disarm the Italians to avoid having to fight them.

Thousands of Italian soldiers escaped to fight again—with the Allies or as partisans. Others shed their uniforms and dissolved into civilian anonymity. But most —615,000 in all—were shipped to internment camps in Germany. There they faced either slave labor or enlistment in combat units of the new Fascist republic. Barely 1 per cent of the embittered Italians chose to rejoin their former allies; of those who remained in the camps, 30,000 died of hunger, exposure and overwork.

Under a German guard's watchful gaze, Italian prisoners fill a stadium in Bolzano

northern Italy before being shipped to Germany. Several divisions in the Balkans chose—at heavy cost—to fight the Germans rather than surrender.

po and SS men and by Fascists still loyal to Mussolini. Before the War was over, some 9,000 of Italy's 45,000 Jews had been killed.

While the German Army tightened its hold on the country, Hitler was doggedly attempting to locate, and liberate, his ally Mussolini.

One of the Badoglio government's first priorities had been to sequester the Duce where no one could find him. The Italians knew that Hitler would not take Mussolini's removal lightly, and that he would surely try to snatch him back and use him to set up a new Fascist government. Even before the Duce's fall, Hitler had foreseen, following the Feltre meeting, the likelihood that he would have to prop up Mussolini—perhaps as "governor of northern Italy."

From the time of the Duce's arrest, a high-stakes game of cat and mouse was waged between the Italian Military Intelligence Service (SIM) and German intelligence agents, who had been assigned by Hitler to find Mussolini and pluck him from the Italians' grasp. SIM's technique was to keep moving Mussolini from place to place and to confuse the Germans by disseminating false information throughout the country regarding his whereabouts.

Mussolini's keepers first moved him on the night of July 27 from the *carabinieri* barracks in Rome to the tiny island of Ventotene in the Gulf of Gaeta, some 40 miles west of Naples. But because the island had no suitable lodgings, they proceeded to the isle of Ponza, 25 miles farther west. A Luftwaffe fighter detachment on the island informed German intelligence of Mussolini's presence, but the Italians learned of the danger and moved the ex-dictator again. Foiled, the Germans next followed a false lead to the port of La Spezia, southeast of Genoa.

On August 17, Hitler's agents almost caught up with their prize. From a letter sent by one of the men guarding Mussolini, the Germans learned that the Duce was now on still another tiny island, La Maddalena, just off the northeastern tip of Sardinia. SS Lieut. Colonel Otto Skorzeny, assigned to carry out the rescue, made plans to launch an amphibious landing on the island from a U-boat. But at the last minute he and his commandos were ordered instead to execute a parachute drop on a different island—the result of another false lead planted by SIM.

After this delay, Skorzeny flew over La Maddalena himself to confirm Mussolini's presence, surviving a crash into the sea in the process. A seaborne raid on the island's harbor three days later, August 29, was too late by a day. Warned by Skorzeny's overflight, the Italians had moved Mussolini again, this time to Gran Sasso d'Italia, a ski resort high in the Apennines, northeast of Rome; normally the resort was reachable only by a cable-drawn railroad.

Mussolini's captivity at Gran Sasso lasted for 15 days. While there he tried to commit suicide by slashing his wrists rather than risk being handed over to the Allies. Then the Germans found him, with the help of a tip from their command post at Lake Bracciano 18 miles northwest of Rome: A seaplane had landed on the lake in secretive circumstances. Shortly thereafter, the SS intercepted an Italian radio message about the completion of "security arrangements" at Gran Sasso. Hot on the trail now, the Germans pieced together evidence that someone of importance had been driven two thirds of the way across the country from the seaplane dock at Lake Bracciano to Gran Sasso. They concluded that they had discovered Mussolini's latest place of confinement.

On the afternoon of September 12, eight gliders carrying Skorzeny and his men crash-landed near the resort and extracted the ex-dictator from his captors without firing a shot. Caught by surprise, the *carabinieri* guarding Mussolini refrained from fighting, evidently because the Germans had come accompanied by a *carabinieri* general and because their own officers had misinterpreted their orders from Rome. With Mussolini in hand, Skorzeny's commandos faced the problem of getting him off the mountaintop. For this they brought in a tiny Fiesler-Storch plane that they hoped could take off from the only available airstrip, a short downhill stretch of grass that ended at a precipice. Mussolini, a pilot himself, was leery of the enterprise, especially when Skorzeny insisted on jamming his six-foot-seven-inch frame into the plane along with the pilot and the Duce. Greatly overloaded, the plane bounced across the grass, hit a rock, dropped over the edge, then gradually gained altitude and flew off safely toward Pratica del Mare, a village about 16 miles south of Rome. There, Mussolini was transferred to a larger plane and eventually was flown to Hitler's headquarters at Rastenburg.

After the multiple shocks of being deposed, seeing Fascism overthrown, being held prisoner and hearing of Italy's surrender, Mussolini was rapidly giving way to age and ill health. He was only 60 years old, but the personal energy that had always given his public appearances so much impact was gone; he struck those who saw him as having literally shrunk in size. When ushered into Hitler's presence at the Wolf's Lair on September 15, he had only one request: He wanted to go home.

Hitler would not hear of it. In a harsh two-hour lecture, the Führer told Mussolini exactly what he thought his responsibilities were—in effect, to reestablish the Fascist state. A necessary first step, he said, was to exact official vengeance on the "traitors" in the Grand Council who had voted against him. Mussolini now understood that he was in Hitler's power.

On September 23, Mussolini left Germany with a German escort, not even sure where he was being taken. He was delivered first to his home at La Rocca delle Caminate, where he proclaimed himself head of the Italian Social Republic, then on to Lake Garda near the little town of Salò, which was to be the capital of the new state.

There, in luxurious villas on the western shore of the lake between Salò and the town of Gargano, the various ministries of the Italian Social Republic established their offices. The restored Duce, along with his wife, Rachele, their surviving sons and their grandchildren, lived in the Villa Feltrinelli, a large building that Mussolini considered "gloomy and unfriendly." Soon Donna Rachele was driven to a fury of jealousy by the news that her husband's mistress, Clara Petacci, had settled in nearby. Clara, like Mussolini, had been rescued by the SS from imprisonment by the Badoglio government; she was sent to be near her lover on the direct orders of Hitler, who believed the Duce should not abandon his faithful paramour. One day Rachele went to Clara's villa to confront her, and their two-hour argument ended with both women in tears. Informed of the incident, Mussolini prudently spent that night in his office.

In this comic-opera setting, Mussolini kept up the pretense of governing his phantom nation. Each morning, promptly at 8:45, he was at his desk to begin a day of reading documents, receiving visitors and talking incessantly about how he had been let down or betrayed—by his countrymen and by the Germans. He wrote articles in defense of his dictatorship and sent them to Italy's leading newspaper, the *Corriere della Sera* of Milan.

Yet he almost never concerned himself with serious administration of the government, and indeed there was little to administer. The territory of the Italian Social Republic consisted nominally of all land under Axis control—in late September, 1943, all of Italy except Sicily, Sardinia and the lower third of the mainland. Yet outside a pitifully few square miles around Salò, the Germans were treating Italy as a conquered country. Hitler had appointed gauleiters for the South Tyrol and the Venezia Giulia districts, both of which had once been part of Austria. The rest of Italy was divided into an operational sector in the north and a sector in the south formally designated "occupied territory."

The Salò Republic, as it was generally called, had virtually no effect on Italian life beyond promoting a revival of Fascist thuggery and giving a façade of legitimacy to Hitler's determination to make Italy a bloody battleground in defense of Germany's southern flank.

Restored Fascist ministers were quick to set up their own uniformed forces—the Fascist militia, the Republican National Guard, the police, the 10th Squadron of naval commandos. Peopled by old-line Fascists who had emerged from cover with Mussolini's restoration, and by teen-age hoodlums seeking license to rape and murder, these organized gangs fell with a vengeance on their enemies. In the turmoil that beset occupied Italy, their most obvious enemies were other Italians, those who had prematurely revealed their anti-Fascist sentiments after the July 25 coup d'état. These dangerously exposed people became easy marks for the Fascist gangs. But "an enemy of Fascism" could also be anyone who failed to show proper respect for a Fascist officer, or even someone on the wrong side of an old vendetta. Thus were sown the seeds of a vicious civil war that pitted Italians of every political stripe against one another in a spree of killing that threatened to disintegrate what remained of their nation.

The most prominent episode of civil bloodletting was the trial and execution of members of the Fascist Grand Council—the men who had voted to depose Mussolini. In prison in Verona were six of these men, including Count Ciano and Tullio Cianetti, who had sent a letter recanting his vote to Mussolini the day after the Grand Council meeting. The 13 other members who had voted for the resolution were in hiding, or had fled the country, or had managed to reach the Allied lines in the south.

The six men were brought to trial in an unheated courtroom in the 14th Century Castelvecchio on January 8, 1944. Nine blackshirted judges presided, but behind the scenes the affair was in the hands of the Fascist extremists who had gravitated to Salò, operating with the approval of their German masters. The verdicts and sentences were predetermined: Only Cianetti escaped the death sentence. The requisite appeals were speedily disposed of. Alessandro Pavolini, the new Fascist Party Secretary, was unwilling to take the risk that Mussolini might overturn the sentences, so he withheld the appeals, he said, to shield his chief from the "necessity of confirming the death sentence." He need not have worried. Even an emotional letter to Mussolini from his daughter Edda—Ciano's wife—did not move him to save his son-in-law.

At 9:20 on the morning of January 11, a 25-man firing squad lined up across from the five men who had voted against Mussolini—the only ones who were caught and punished for their deed. The condemned Fascists were subjected to the humiliation of being tied in chairs, with their backs to their executioners. At the last moment, Ciano managed to twist around in his chair and face the rifles. The grisly scene was made worse by the incompetence of the firing squad: The first volley wounded all five of the men but killed none of them, and the squad had to fire again. All five were finished off with a *coup de grâce* from the pistol of the commanding officer.

The Badoglio government and the monarchy, after fleeing Rome in the wake of the armistice announcement, set up operations in Brindisi, on the Adriatic coast in southern Italy. Here, in a manner that oddly mirrored the Salò Republic in the north, they existed in a state of limbo, exercising limited authority under the aegis of the Allied Control Commission, whose primary function was to create Allied military governments in newly liberated localities.

As the fighting moved northward, however, the administration of rear areas was left increasingly in the hands of the Badoglio government, which was commonly referred to as the "Kingdom of the South." This tenuous government stood to gain considerably by declaring war against Germany, but since the surrender the King had resisted Badoglio's attempts to tug him in this direction. Victor Emmanuel belatedly fixed on the "honor" of his country's obligations to the Germans. He appeared unable to comprehend that the monarchy continued to exist only because the Allies saw some value in the King as the symbolic head of Italy's

anti-Fascist movement. He even had the bad judgment—and taste—to continue referring to himself as King of Italy and Albania, Emperor of Ethiopia, a title created by a Fascist imperialism that existed no more.

Not until October 13, under intense pressure from the Allies, did Victor Emmanuel agree to declare war on Germany. The act meant virtually nothing to the Allies militarily, but it gave legitimate cobelligerent status to Italian Army units not under German or Fascist control, and gave the country a role far preferable to that of defeated enemy. Italian troops later fought the Germans in several battles, including the siege of Monte Cassino early in 1944, during which an Italian force of about 5,000 men and 500 vehicles suffered heavy casualties.

For the average Italian, living conditions rapidly worsened after the armistice. In a country already weakened by years of privation, life became a daily struggle for survival. Meat was in such short supply that almost any living thing might find itself hunted for food. The cat population in many towns and villages was all but exterminated, and even the tiniest birds—if they could be caught—were considered a great prize. Some sources of meat were so questionable that a butcher who displayed the carcass of such a delicacy as rabbit in his shop window would be careful to include the rabbit's head as evidence of the authenticity of the goods.

Italians were fortunate in having a long, sunny growing season that produced abundant fruits and vegetables. Yet the breakdown of their marketing system forced starving city dwellers to trudge miles into the countryside to forage for food growing wild. Each day the radius of land that had been picked clean grew larger, and the hike in search of something to eat grew longer.

On the Allied invasion beaches, once the beachhead was secure, priority was given to supplying the advancing troops. Thousands of tons of food, blankets, vehicles, fuel, medicines and other supplies poured into the conquered territories in quantities the Italians had never seen. One result was an epidemic of theft and black marketeering.

The black market had been active since the onset of wartime shortages, but with the collapse of government controls and the influx of Allied matériel it became a major industry. Thievery—either freelance or under the control of

organized gangs—became so prevalent that the equivalent of one shipload of supplies was being stolen for every two that reached the soldiers. But Italians were too hungry to be scrupulous about the source of their sustenance.

From its start, Italy's new Kingdom of the South had competition. The armistice and the Allied invasion had signaled the beginning of large-scale partisan activities, which hitherto had been limited mainly to political organization and propaganda work by resistance leaders in exile. In large cities from Rome northward, committees for national liberation came into being to fight both the Germans and the reemergent Fascists of the Salò Republic. In the south, less formally organized but as fiercely determined partisan bands also took matters into their own hands, attacking German units in anticipation of an early linkup with the advancing Allies.

By September 28, Allied forces were closing in rapidly on Naples. Small bands of young working-class men and women, motivated by a desire for revenge against German terror squads, rose up against their oppressors in neighborhoods all over the city. Within two days the few hundred insurgents had increased to more than 1,000. The joint pressure of the Allied presence and civil insurrection forced the Germans to abandon Naples on October 1, although not before they had looted the city of almost everything of value that could be moved and had destroyed the municipal archives,

In a Verona courtroom, six Fascist Grand Council members who voted to depose Mussolini in 1943 await sentencing for treason by the new Salò Republic. They are, from left: Marshal Emilio de Bono; labor leader Luciano Gottardi; Count Galeazzo Ciano; Agriculture Minister Carlo Pareschi; Administrative Secretary Giovanni Marinelli; and Corporations Minister Tullio Cianetti. On the 11th of January, 1944, all but Cianetti, who had changed his vote on the resolution, died before a firing squad.

In Milan, where in 1922 he launched his March on Rome, the Duce stands atop a tank to exhort members of his Republican National Guard on the 16th of December, 1944. That same day he addressed a mass rally of loyal Fascists—his last public appearance.

167

wiping out at a stroke one of the richest collections of medieval records in Europe.

The Four Days of Naples, as the uprising came to be known, was the first case of an Italian city fighting for its own liberation before the Allies arrived. It did much to restore Italian self-respect at a time when the country was under the thumb of foreigners who had little regard for it.

Though driven from Naples, the Germans had taken pains to bring grief to the city even after they were gone. They concealed long-delay time bombs in busy locations throughout the city—some set to go off weeks later. The explosion of one such bomb at the Central Post Office on October 20 inflicted 72 casualties.

Even the post-office tragedy was not the end of Naples'

ordeal. On October 23, the day the municipal electricity supply was to be restored, a German straggler turned himself in and told authorities that thousands of bombs hidden all over the city were wired into the dormant electrical system. They would go off, he said, the instant the power was turned on. The Allies, who had occupied Naples on October 1, hastily began the stupendous task of evacuating the entire city. One and a half million people—including patients near death, women about to give birth, elderly people confined to their beds, hysterical inmates of mental institutions, a hospital full of wounded Allied soldiers—all had to walk or be carried to heights above the city. There they watched with growing tension as the 2 p.m. zero hour for turning on the electricity approached. The moment came and went, in silence. At 4 p.m. the weary Neapolitans were given the all clear and permitted to return to their homes.

German vengeance assumed an even bloodier form as the partisans intensified their warfare from industrial and communications sabotage to open combat. On March 23, 1944, a group of partisans attacked a detachment of SS police in Rome, killing 32 of them. In a fury, Hitler ordered that within the next 24 hours 10 Romans be shot for every German dead. Gestapo agents began rounding up victims—captured partisans, Jews already under detention, petty criminals and ordinary citizens. In a frenzy of kidnapping they scooped up 335 men—more than even Hitler had demanded—and drove them in trucks to the Ardeatine Caves southeast of the city. There, SS troopers shot down every last man. Then they dynamited the caverns shut to hide the atrocity.

As the Allies continued their advance northward against stubborn German resistance, anti-Fascist leaders began returning from exile to the liberated areas of their homeland, and multiparty politics returned to Italian life for the first time in 18 years. Six major parties represented most of the organized partisan groups that were active against the Germans and the Fascists of the Salò Republic: Communists, Socialists, Labor Democrats, Christian Democrats, Liberals, and members of the Action Party.

The Badoglio government and King Victor Emmanuel were anathema to Italy's Communists and Socialists. Nevertheless the Soviet Union, not wishing to impede military ac-

An injured man and a boy stagger away from the blast zone moments after the explosion of a German bomb in the Naples Central Post Office on the 20th of October, 1943. The Germans had evacuated the city three weeks earlier, leaving behind scores of hidden bombs.

tion against the Germans on any front, granted recognition to the Badoglio regime on March 14, 1944. Italian Communist Party chief Palmiro Togliatti, returning from exile in Moscow, accordingly ordered a complete turnabout in his party's policy, accepting for the time being the Badoglio government and the continuation of the monarchy. Marshal Badoglio then convened a new Cabinet on April 24 that included all six parties. Since most of Italy was still under German occupation, no elections were held; each party received equal representation.

Once Rome was taken by the Allies, on June 4, 1944, the partisan parties refused to tolerate Badoglio any longer, and his government fell. He was succeeded by 70-year-old Ivanoe Bonomi, who had been Prime Minister in pre-Fascist

times. Gone too was Victor Emmanuel; hoping to save the tainted monarchy, he reluctantly gave up active rule in favor of his son, Crown Prince Humbert, whom he designated Lieutenant General of the Realm.

In the German-controlled north, partisan warfare broke out in earnest under the direction of the Committee of National Liberation for Northern Italy, composed of all the major parties except the Labor Democrats. Conditions peculiar to the north—the dangerous work of fighting the Nazis, the large numbers of urban industrial workers and the superior organization and discipline of the Communists—caused the northern partisans as a whole to be politically more radical than those of the south. The Communists—organized in "Garibaldi units"—and Socialists were the most numerous and the most effective of the northern partisans. The Communists dispatched special teams called *Gruppi d'Azione Popolare,* or *gappisti,* to carry out direct attacks on Nazis and Fascists.

Larger numbers of partisans participated in strikes and committed sabotage. In May of 1944 the partisan movement had only about 20,000 members, but with each Allied success it picked up recruits. The *gappisti* tended to look down on these latecomers as "summer partisans," and many of them indeed were former Fascists seeking the best available protective coloration.

As winter approached, the Allied drive stalled at the Germans' Gothic Line, a defensive bastion that stretched across the country south of Bologna. When it became clear that an Allied victory was not imminent, partisan strength declined. At the same time, the civil war grew more vicious as the most unregenerate Fascists and the partisan action groups intensified what both sides knew was a fight to the death.

Before the Allied offensive resumed in the spring of 1945, the forces loosely controlled by the Committee for National Liberation had begun to swell dramatically—from a low of about 30,000 in December to an estimated 200,000 by late April. Many of them were latecomers indeed. As the Allied armies swept the exhausted Germans before them, the partisans prepared for a national insurrection.

Since the fall of Rome, Mussolini had watched the course of the War with growing despair. To revive his flagging spirits he had invited himself to Germany in the summer of 1944,

Italian troops serving with the Allies file down a trench near Monte Lungo in December 1943. The following spring, the 21,000-man Italian Corps of Liberation supplied approximately 5,000 soldiers to fight alongside the American Fifth Army in the drive to liberate Rome.

169

ostensibly for the purpose of observing four new Italian divisions training there. After reviewing the troops, he proceeded to Rastenburg to meet with Hitler, arriving about 4 o'clock in the afternoon on the 20th of July. By uncanny coincidence, the Duce had chosen to visit on the day German conspirators exploded a bomb in an unsuccessful attempt to assassinate Hitler. Hitler and Mussolini, both of whom sought portents wherever they could find them, made much of the episode. Said the battered and bandaged Hitler, "What happened today is an omen of destiny. The great cause that I serve will triumph." Mussolini, as if chanting a liturgical response, answered, "After this miracle it is impossible that our cause should know defeat."

Mussolini then sat through a meeting of the Nazi leadership in which Ribbentrop and Hermann Göring traded insults, and Hitler, who had controlled himself until then, burst out in a screaming rage against his would-be assassins. Later in the meeting, Hitler agreed to permit two of the Italian divisions to return to Italy, and as Mussolini was leaving he said, "I consider you my best friend and perhaps my only friend in the world."

The Duce, who had long believed that he had been brought down by the betrayal of his generals, was able to draw a measure of comfort from the attack on his fellow dictator. When he returned to Salò he told Clara, "The Führer has his traitors too."

By March of 1945 that short-lived rise in spirits was far behind him. Even at Salò he was faced with a tightening circle of Allied armies and Italian partisans. Like Hitler, Mussolini hoped desperately that the death of President Roosevelt on the 12th of April would somehow end the War. But by that time the final Allied drive had started and the Committee for National Liberation was meeting to orchestrate its national uprising.

On the 13th, the Duce dispatched his son Vittorio to confer with Cardinal Schuster, Archbishop of Milan. He sought to strike a deal that would enable him to surrender directly to the Allies, thereby keeping him out of partisan hands, but no one was willing to bargain with Vittorio. On April 16, Mussolini decided to go himself to Milan, which was both the last remaining Fascist stronghold and the headquarters of the partisans. He still hoped to negotiate—even with these, his bitterest enemies. All this time he was unaware that SS General Karl Wolff had established contact with American representatives in Switzerland and was secretly negotiating for the surrender of German forces in Italy.

On April 21, the partisans rose in unison to take control of towns and cities the Allied armies had not yet reached. The

Committee for National Liberation had been recognized by the Allies and by the Rome government as the legal government in the north, and on April 25 it assumed open civil and military rule. One of its first acts was to decree the death penalty for all Fascist leaders. Nevertheless, Mussolini agreed to meet with representatives of the committee. This face-to-face encounter took place that same afternoon, but it came to nothing: Mussolini wanted to negotiate, the partisans wanted his unconditional surrender.

When he left the meeting, Mussolini decided to go to Como near the Swiss border, either to barricade himself for a last stand in the Alps or to escape through the mountains. He left that night in a motorcade of 10 cars. In the wake of the Duce's departure, the last of the Fascist combat units surrendered or dispersed in the dark. The Italian Social Republic had ceased to exist.

At Menaggio, on the shore of Lake Como, Mussolini composed a farewell note to his wife, Rachele. "I ask your forgiveness for all the harm that I have done you without meaning to," he wrote. Just as he finished, a car pulled up to his quarters carrying Clara Petacci, who again had refused to be separated from him.

Together, on the morning of April 27, the two set out by automobile and joined a German motorized column heading north. On the western shore of Lake Como, about 45 miles from a tunnel that would take the couple through the Alps to Austria, the convoy was stopped by partisans. Shooting broke out, followed by a parley. The partisan leader offered to let the Germans pass, but he insisted that no Italians be permitted through and that each vehicle be searched. The German captain in command of the convoy agreed to proceed to the village of Dongo, where the partisans would check for fugitives.

Mussolini concealed himself in the back of one of the trucks. He wore a Wehrmacht overcoat and helmet and pretended to be a soldier sleeping off a drunk. The inspection was careful, however, and the Duce was discovered. The partisans took him to their local headquarters, interrogated him and locked him in a peasant hut. He was soon joined by Clara, who had also been taken by the partisans.

The men holding the Duce planned to deliver him to the National Committee in Milan, but the Communist, Socialist and Action Party factions of the committee were afraid that he would then be delivered to the Allies—and that Italy would appear unable to mete out its own justice. On orders from a subcommittee of leftist partisan officials, a Garibaldi leader who operated under the *nom de guerre* Colonel Valerio—in peacetime he was an accountant named Walter Audisio—raced to stop the Dongo partisans. Early on the afternoon of April 28 he reached Dongo and demanded custody of the Duce. The local group understood what would happen if they gave their man up, for Valerio had immediately made his intentions clear.

After Valerio had browbeaten the local leader into turning over the prisoners, he burst into the bedroom where they were being kept, shouting, "I've come to liberate you!" He led them to a car and drove about a mile before stopping. Ordering them out at gunpoint, he placed them before a stone wall. As the couple stood there, Valerio declaimed: "By order of the High Command of the Corps of Volunteers for Freedom, I am instructed to do justice for the Italian people."

In the last moments of his life, Mussolini rose above his fear. Unbuttoning his coat, he ordered Valerio to shoot him in the chest. Two volleys rang out. The former Duce and his mistress were dead. They were joined in death by other Fascists rounded up and shot by the partisans, and their bodies were displayed to the world hanging by the heels from the girders of a Milan filling station.

After hanging ignominiously for a day, Mussolini's body was cut down by order of the Allied authorities and was buried in a secret location in Milan. In 1957, Mussolini was reburied next to the grave of his son Bruno in Predappio, his birthplace. He lies under a tombstone decorated with the emblem of the fasces.

A solitary Neapolitan strolls by a wall covered with official proclamations and a wishful anti-Mussolini message. Though the Duce did not die until April of 1945, he was reviled after his fall from power as a despot who had led his country to destruction.

TRAPPED BETWEEN ENEMIES

U.S. Martin B-26 Marauders bomb Nazi-occupied Florence in 1944. After Italy surrendered, the Germans exploited the area's steel and chemical industries.

HUNGER AND RUIN AS THE WAR COMES HOME

Italy's last year of war under Mussolini's dictatorship was a time of suffering and disillusionment. Allied bombers wreaked destruction on factories, homes and commercial districts in every industrial city, from Naples in the south to Turin in the north.

The relentless bombing, combined with Fascist mismanagement of scarce goods, fomented social unrest. Hungry Italians referred to the last notch on their belts as "the Mussolini hole." Venetians rioted outside the bakeries for bread and were dispersed with clubs. Sicilian peasants fired on government officials who tried to collect their wheat. Strikes involving as many as 300,000 workers crippled war industries in northern Italy.

When King Victor Emmanuel and the Grand Council forced Mussolini out of office on July 25, 1943, the streets quickly filled with exultant civilians celebrating what they believed to be the end of the War. Six weeks later, the post-Mussolini government accepted the Allies' terms of unconditional surrender.

But the War was not through with Italy. The Nazis treated the armistice as a betrayal. Determined to defend the southern approaches to the Reich, the German High Command increased its presence in Italy—eventually to 22 divisions. Rome was subjected to 24 hours of looting by German troops. The Allies, who had subdued Sicily in August, invaded mainland Italy in early September, and grimly began fighting their way north.

The misery of the Italian people increased as their country became a battleground. Life in areas that were under German military control was particularly harsh. In Naples, an early Allied target, thousands of civilians rose up to evict the Germans, who systematically booby-trapped the city before they left.

What was left of Italy's resources was commandeered by the Germans, leaving Italians to resort to beggary, ragpicking and the black market. "Whether it is we or the English who take the Italians' trousers," said a scornful Hitler of his onetime allies, "it comes to the same thing."

A German soldier eyes a Roman crowd. "With customary tact," an Italian said, "the Nazis lost no time in letting us know who was master."

A barber works amid the ruins of Cassino, the hill town south of Rome that was destroyed, along with its famous abbey, during the Allied advance in 1944.

AIR STRIKES ON FASCISM'S BIRTHPLACE

Residents of Milan watch from a distance as their city burns in the wake of an Allied air raid. Shantytowns sprang up on the fringes of the city to shelter the homeless.

Milan, the northern industrial city that had launched Mussolini on his Fascist career, became a primary target of Allied air raids. The attacks, which began in 1942, lasted into 1945. The bombers came both by night and by day, sometimes strafing workers as they bicycled between their homes and the factories where they were employed. Demoralized Milan became a hotbed of Communism and anti-Fascism.

Hitler sent antiaircraft units to Milan in 1943, but they were unable to prevent Allied raids from leveling a third of the municipal area. Eventually—as in much of Italy—the only public service still functioning was the railroads, and trains overflowed with refugees and soldiers who were fleeing the paralyzed city.

Stunned survivors console one another on a Milan street after a raid. "The people realized," a high official said, "that if the War went on, all our towns would be destroyed."

Acres of empty shells remain standing in bombed-out Milan. Of the city's 930,000 residences, 360,000 were either severely damaged or completely destroyed.

Women and children and a disabled veteran gather at the mouth of the cave where they took shelter with their belongings during the bombing of Naples.

REFUGE IN CAVES FOR STOIC NEAPOLITANS

The port of Naples was especially vulnerable to bombing because it had few anti-aircraft defenses. Hundreds of Neapolitans lived through the Allied raids of September 1943 in caves outside the city formerly used to store Navy supplies.

Once Allied troops captured Naples, in October, it became the Germans' turn to bomb the city, forcing the citizens to stay underground. A typhus epidemic caused by unsanitary conditions cost many lives.

Before they evacuated Naples, the Germans had carried out one of the most thorough demolition jobs in military history. In addition to planting hundreds of booby traps, they sealed delayed-action bombs in the walls of public buildings and littered the harbor with scuttled ships.

Neapolitans learned to steal or scavenge to survive. A black market existed, but few could pay its prices: It took a month's wages to buy a bottle of olive oil.

Surrounded by her family in a grotto near Naples, a stolid Italian mother nurses her infant.

A refugee family makes its corner of a cave more livable by fashioning a bedroom out of old blankets and suspending a bird cage from a post above it.

Italian soldiers and citizens assemble in front of a ransacked Fascist office building in Milan, where rioting left six people dead and 30 others wounded.

In Sicily, which was the first part of Italy to experience the hardships of the War at close range, civilians ransack the abandoned headquarters of an Italian infantry regiment at Agrigento in July of 1943.

EXPLOSIONS OF SUPPRESSED ANGER

The news of Mussolini's fall from power, broadcast at 10:45 p.m. on July 25, 1943, unleashed a storm of pent-up resentment. The Italian people now could openly express their disenchantment with the Fascist Party. Many who earlier the same day had worn Fascist emblems—sarcastically called "bedbugs" because of their shape—ripped them off and ground them under their heels.

By midnight, Rome was convulsed by mob demonstrations against the discredited regime. Crowds shouting "Death to Mussolini!" ransacked government offices and hunted for party leaders. So many Italian officials seeking asylum and safe passage crowded into the German Embassy that one SS colonel there described it as "a travel agency."

The uprisings spread throughout Italy. In Turin, citizens drove a truck through the front gate of a prison, liberating both political and common prisoners. Crowds in Milan confronted tanks and soldiers brandishing fixed bayonets. Sicilians looted hastily abandoned Army supply depots. And though Italians everywhere had gone hungry that summer, they found government storehouses full of huge cheeses and sacks of rice and flour.

To restore order, an interim government coalition of military officers and former Fascists ruthlessly imposed martial law. "In case of demonstrations," one Italian general told his troops, "no one is to fire into the air. Shoot to kill."

Scavenging in the wake of retreating Germans, Italian women gather flour spilled from broken crates in an overturned Army truck near the town of Finale

A black-market operator (right) in Milan sells food from a briefcase.

Neapolitans wait to fill bottles with water from an emergency supply.

AFTERMATH
IN A CONTESTED TOWN

A portrait of Mussolini lies discarded on debris cleared from the streets of Eboli, which was devastated during fighting between Allied and German troops in September of 1943. "The Germans want to use Italy as a rampart," said an Italian general, "and they don't give a damn if it ruins her."

FIRES oF INSURRECTION

Flushed from the woods after planes pinpointed their location, four former Italian soldiers surrender to the Germans near the Swiss border in September 1943.

THE VIOLENT RISING OF VENGEFUL PARTISANS

July 26, 1943, was a holiday in the Piedmont town of Cuneo, as it was all over Italy. Mussolini had been deposed by the King, and war-weary citizens turned out to hail an early end to the fighting. Only a few farsighted leaders of the half-dozen or more political factions competing to control Italy's future recognized that Italians now had a new enemy—the German Army. So it came as a shock to the revelers crowding Cuneo's Piazza Vittorio when one of these leaders, Tancredi Galimberti, a lawyer and member of the underground Action Party, shouted from a balcony: "The war goes on, but against Germany. For this war there is only one means—popular insurrection."

For the moment, no one answered Galimberti's call to arms, which was as unwelcome as it was unexpected. It took the Nazis themselves, treating northern Italy like an occupied enemy nation, to spark insurrection. Public outrage spread quickly after incidents of violence were reported such as the shooting of 16 Italian civilians in the village of Rionero Sannitico, on September 24, because an old man had wounded a German soldier he caught stealing chickens. It was fanned when the Germans, aided by Fascists loyal to the new puppet republic at Salò, began combing the cities and villages of the north for ex-soldiers and draft-age youths to fight for Mussolini.

To escape these press gangs, thousands of able-bodied men took to the hills, where Army officers and underground political leaders like Galimberti organized them into guerrilla bands. The partisan fighters ultimately numbered more than 200,000. They raided depots for weapons and used air-dropped Allied munitions to blow up trains, mine roads, and ambush German and Fascist troops.

They paid a terrible price for these small successes; more than 35,000 partisans and civilians died in savage Nazi reprisals before Italy's final liberation in the spring of 1945, when urban guerrillas rose in an orgy of anti-Fascist vengeance and—as Winston Churchill later wrote to one of their leaders—"played their part in liberating their country from the German-Fascist yoke."

Partisans in Bologna brandish weapons in April 1945. Anti-Fascist "Action Groups" of urban guerrillas specialized in bombings and sabotage.

Mourning survivors kneel before a hand-lettered memorial "to the martyrs of the Nazi-Fascist terror"—16 villagers shot for the wounding of a German.

A RAGTAG ARMY'S STRUGGLE TO SURVIVE

By early 1944, partisan bands of up to 450 men were scattered across the mountains and valleys of northern Italy, sustained by a maxim that passed from unit to unit:

"Struggle against the cold, the hunger and the terror." They received food from sympathetic villagers, paid for with promissory notes to be redeemed after the War. The Allies helped by air-dropping 6,000 tons of clothing and other supplies.

To counter their foes' massive manhunts —in one valley 3,000 partisans had to flee

12,000 German and Fascist troops—the bands split up and adopted hit-and-run tactics. A favorite was to block a mountain pass and ambush pursuers and patrols. The partisans seemed to be everywhere. In June Mussolini's officials tallied 2,200 partisan actions and reported 82,000 snipers and saboteurs at large in upper Italy.

Partisans shelter in a mountain cave near Bologna in March 1944 while a sentry stands guard. Other guerrillas risked capture by wintering in the milder plains after fragmenting into units as small as six men.

Wearing identifying red neckerchiefs, men of a Communist "Garibaldi unit," named for Italy's 19th Century liberator, dig holes and wire explosives to block a road near Cuneo. Buried under the surface, the mines were detonated when Axis trucks passed over them.

A German supply truck burns on an Alpine road after an attack by partisans in August of 1944. Hitler complained bitterly about such attacks to Mussolini, who formed special counter-guerrilla groups called Black Brigades to combat them.

Hurled from its tracks by partisan-laid explosives, a train lies dismembered on an embankment in northern Italy. A similar partisan exploit on December 20, 1943, wrecked a munitions train that was bound for Cassino, killing 500 German troops.

Guards force condemned partisan hostages to carry a placard reading, "Are these Italy's liberators or just bandits?"

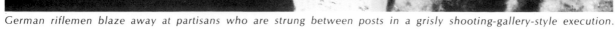

German riflemen blaze away at partisans who are strung between posts in a grisly shooting-gallery-style execution.

THE GRIM FACE OF NAZI RETALIATION

Buoyed by the Allied liberation of Rome in June of 1944, partisan ranks swelled, and incidents of sniping and sabotage multiplied. The Germans retaliated fiercely, executing at least 10 Italians for each German who was killed, and stringing the corpses from lampposts, trees and the balconies of buildings.

Air-dropped leaflets warned villagers of the consequences of helping the partisans. "Every house in which rebels are found or in which a rebel has stayed," the notices read, "will be blown up. All stores of food will be burned, the cattle taken away, and the inhabitants shot."

Emboldened by a new Allied offensive that began in late August, partisans and peasants ignored the German threats and rose to attack the enemy from the rear. But when the Allied offensive stalled, German artillery smashed exposed partisan formations, and SS units wasted the countryside. One cluster of villages, called Marzabotta, literally disappeared from the map after two SS companies herded their 1,830 inhabitants into a church and massacred them. Soon disheartened partisans, shivering in summer shirts and shorts, began creeping into the Allied lines at the rate of 50 or 60 a night, and by the end of 1944 partisan forces had dwindled to a hard core of about 30,000.

Bodies dangle from the balconies of the Rittmeyer Palace in Trieste, the Italian border city where German soldiers indiscriminately hanged 52 residents.

195

LAST-MINUTE OFFENSIVES BY URBAN GUERRILLAS

As Allied armies finally advanced on Italy's northern cities in the spring of 1945, urban partisans—most of them organized into Communist-led "Groups of Patriotic Action"—set up "antiscorch" squads to prevent the retreating Germans from sabotaging power plants, factories, bridges and dams. Street patrols flushed out snipers to clear the way for the Allies. In Bologna, Genoa, Turin, Milan and Venice, underground leaders orchestrated full-scale insurrections, expelling the Germans hours and even days before the Allies arrived.

In Turin, for instance, local Communists barricaded themselves in a factory and threw Molotov cocktails at passing German convoys. And in Genoa, 3,100 poorly armed partisans accepted the surrender of 6,000 Germans a day before the American Fifth Army reached the city.

At a street corner in Florence, partisans fire on diehard snipers lying in wait for advance units of the British Eighth Army. Street fighting in Florence lasted a week and claimed some 300 partisan lives.

In an industrial sector of Turin, where workers took over their factories to prevent sabotage by the Germans, two members of an "antiscorch" squad rush to the aid of a wounded companion in April 1945.

Armed partisans force their way into the home of a Fascist sympathizer in Venice. In the Veneto region alone, anti-Fascists rounded up 140,292 prisoners for the Allies.

SETTLING ACCOUNTS WITH MOB JUSTICE

In almost every city, violence and vengeance scarred the process of liberation, in spite of orders to the partisans from their central headquarters, the Committee for National Liberation, that local tribunals observe the strictest legality in arraigning captured Fascist officials and their sympathizers. Mob justice frequently prevailed, and hot-blooded resistance fighters and their hangers-on killed uncounted thousands of people—including Benito Mussolini and his mistress.

Some blamed revolution-minded Communist partisans for the excesses, but the multiparty committee rejected the charge. "Fascism itself," it stated, "is responsible for the explosion of popular hate." The partisan leadership justified the execution of Mussolini as "the price of a clean break with a shameful and criminal past."

As townspeople in Modena drag a Fascist sympathizer off to jail another woman threatens her with a bayonet. The prisoner was charged with shooting at partisans from a window in April 1945.

Enraged patriots confront a suspected Fascist saboteur (center) after the explosion of a bomb in a Rome tobacco shop during the Allied liberation of the capital city.

The bloodied bodies of two Italian motion picture stars lie on the floor of a house in Milan on April 30, 1945. Luisa Farida (left), Osvaldi Valenti (bottom right) and an unidentified third person were executed by partisans for recruiting Fascist spies.

Triumphant partisans drive through Bologna on April 21, 1945. American troops entering Bologna that day were surprised by the relative calm imposed on t

ity by the insurgents. Under Allied occupation, the partisans reluctantly laid aside their arms, and many of their leaders became officeholders in postwar Italy.

BIBLIOGRAPHY

Adams, Henry H., *Years of Deadly Peril*. David McKay, 1969.

Angelucci, Enzo, *The Rand McNally Encyclopedia of Military Aircraft: 1914-1980*. Transl. by S. M. Harris. Rand McNally, 1981.

Angelucci, Enzo, and Paolo Matricardi, *World War II Airplanes*, Vol. 1. Rand McNally, 1978.

Badoglio, Pietro, *Italy in the Second World War*. Transl. by Muriel Currey. London: Oxford University Press, 1948.

Barnett, Correlli, *The Desert Generals*. Berkley Publishing, 1960.

Bartoli, Domenico, *Italia Drammatica: Storia della Guerra Civile, 1943-1945*, Vols. 1, 2 and 3. Milan: Stampa Rizzoli Grafica, 1965.

Barzini, Luigi, *The Italians*. Bantam Books, 1964.

Bellomo, Bino, *Lettere Censurate: L'Ottusita' del Potere*. Milan: Longanesi, 1975.

Berreta, Alfio:
    Amedo D'Aosta: Il Prigioniero del Kenia. Milan: Eli, 1956.
    "La Battaglia di Keren," *La Seconda Guerra Mondiale*, Vol. 1. Ed. by Enzo Biagi. Florence: Sadea-Della Volpe, 1964.

Biagi, Enzo, *Storia del Fascismo*. 3 vols. Florence: Sadea-Della Volpe, 1969.

Bojano, Filippo, *In the Wake of the Goose Step*. Transl. by Gerald Griffin. Ziff-Davis, 1945.

Borgese, Guiseppe Antonio, *Goliath: The March of Fascism*. Hyperion Press, 1979.

Bourke-White, Margaret, "Naples." *Life*, January 24, 1944.

Bradagin, Marc'Antonio, *The Italian Navy in World War II*. Transl. by Gale Hoffman. United States Naval Institute, 1957.

Brown, James Ambrose, *A Gathering of Eagles*. Capetown, South Africa: Purnell and Sons, 1970.

Buono, Oreste del, and Lietta Tornatuoni, eds., *Era Cinecittà: Vita, Morte e Miracoli di una Fabbrica di Film*. Milan: Bompiani, 1979.

Caporilli, Pietro, ed., "La Battaglia del Don." *7 Anni di Guerra*. Rome: Edizioni Ardita, May 17, 1964.

Carter, Barbara Barclay, *Italy Speaks*. London: Victor Gollancz, 1947.

Cederna, Antonio, *Mussolini Urbanista*. Rome: Editori Laterza, 1981.

Chabod, Federico, *A History of Italian Fascism*. Transl. by Muriel Grindrod. London: Weidenfeld and Nicolson, 1963.

Churchill, Winston S., *The Second World War*:
    Vol. 3, *The Grand Alliance*. Bantam Books, 1950.
    Vol. 4, *The Hinge of Fate*. Houghton Mifflin, 1950.

Ciano, Edda Mussolini, with Albert Zarca, *My Truth*. Transl. by Eileen Finletter. William Morrow, 1977.

Ciano, Galeazzo, *The Ciano Diaries: 1939-1943*. Ed. by Hugh Gibson. Doubleday, 1946.

Collier, Richard, *Duce! A Biography of Benito Mussolini*. Viking, 1971.

Collier, Richard, and the Editors of Time-Life Books, *The War in the Desert* (World War II series). Time-Life Books, 1977.

D'Aquino, Maria Luisa, *Quel Giorno Trent'Anni Fa*. Naples: Guida Editori, 1975.

Davis, Melton S., *Who Defends Rome?* The Dial Press, 1972.

Deakin, F. W., *The Brutal Friendship: Mussolini, Hitler, and the Fall of Italian Fascism*. Harper & Row, 1962.

De Felice, Renzo, and Luigi Goglia, *Storia Fotografica del Fascismo*. Rome: Editori Laterza, 1981.

Del Boca, Angelo, *The Ethiopian War: 1935-1941*. Transl. by P. D. Cummins. The University of Chicago Press, 1969.

Delzell, Charles F., *Mussolini's Enemies: The Anti-Fascist Resistance*. Howard Fertig, 1974.

Delzell, Charles F., ed., *Mediterranean Fascism: 1919-1945*. Walker, 1970.

Diggins, John P., *Mussolini and Fascism*. Princeton University Press, 1972.

Eggenberger, David, *Dictionary of Battles*. Thomas Y. Crowell, 1967.

"L'Esercito e i Suoi Corpi," Ufficio Storico, Stato Maggiore dell'Esercito, Vol. 1. Rome: 1971.

Fermi, Laura, *Mussolini*. University of Chicago Press, 1941.

Flanner, Janet, "Come Down, Giuseppe!" *The New Yorker*, January 17, 1942.

Friedrich, Carl J., *American Experiences in Military Government in World War II*. Rinehart, 1948.

Gallo, Max, *Mussolini's Italy: Twenty Years of the Fascist Era*. Transl. by Charles Lam Markmann. MacMillan, 1973.

Gandar Dower, Kenneth Cecil, *Abyssinian Patchwork: An Anthology*. London: Frederick Muller, 1949.

Garland, Albert N., and Howard McGaw Smyth, *Sicily and the Surrender of Italy*. Assisted by Martin Blumenthal. Office of the Chief of Military History, Department of the Army, 1965.

I Gerarchi di Mussolini. Novara, Italy: Instituto Geografico de Agostini, 1973.

Germoni, Dante, *The Italian Fascist Party in Power*. University of Minnesota Press, 1954.

Gourlay, Jack, *Benito Musolini: A Biography*. Ed. by Ellie Kurtz. Thor Publications, 1966.

Grigg, John, *1943: The Victory That Never Was*. Hill and Wang, 1980.

Hart, B. H. Liddell, *History of the Second World War*. G. P. Putnam's Sons, 1971.

Heymann, C. David, *Ezra Pound: The Last Rower*. Viking, 1976.

Hibbert, Christopher, *Benito Mussolini*. London: The Reprint Society, 1962.

Katz, Robert, *Death in Rome*. MacMillan, 1967.

Kirkpatrick, Ivone, *Mussolini: A Study in Power*. Hawthorn Books, 1964.

La Guidara, Franco, *Ritorniamo sul Don fino all'Ultima Battaglia*. Rome: Edizioni Internationali, 1976.

Lazzero, Ricciotti, "Partono in Luglio i Soldati Italiani." *Storia Illustrata*. Milan: Mondadori, December 1967.

Leeds, Christopher, *Italy under Mussolini*. London: The Documentary History Series, Wayland, 1972.

Levi, Carlo, *Christ Stopped at Eboli*. Transl. by Frances Frenaye. Farrar Straus and Giroux, 1947.

Lewis, Norman, *Naples '44*. London: William Collins, 1978.

Lingelbach, Anna Lane, "An Inside View of Italy." *Current History*, January 1942.

Loffredo, Renato, *Cheren*. Milan: Longanesi, 1973.

Lombardi, Martina, and Marilea Somaré, *La Villeggiatura*. Milan: Longanesi, 1981.

Lombroso, Sylvia, *No Time for Silence*. Transl. by Adrienne W. Foulke. Roy Publishers, 1945.

MacGregor-Hastie, Roy, *The Day of the Lion*. Coward-McCann, 1963.

Mack Smith, Denis:
    L'Italia del 20° Secolo, 1925-1934. Milan: Rizzoli Editori, 1977.
    L'Italia del 20° Secolo, 1935-1942. Milan: Rizzoli Editori, 1977.
    Italy: A Modern History. University of Michigan Press, 1969.
    Mussolini's Roman Empire. Viking, 1976.

Massock, Richard G., *Italy from Within*. MacMillan, 1943.

Matthews, Herbert L., *The Fruits of Fascism*. Harcourt Brace, 1943.

Maugeri, Franco, *From the Ashes of Disgrace*. Ed. by Victor Rosen. Reynal & Hitchcock, 1948.

Michaelis, Meir, *Mussolini and the Jews*. London: The Institute of Jewish Affairs, 1978.

Monelli, Paolo, *Mussolini*. Vanguard, 1954.

Mosley, Leonard, *Haile Selassie: The Conquering Lion*. Prentice-Hall, 1964.

Mussolini, Benito, *Memoirs: 1942-1943*. Ed. by Raymond Klibansky, transl. by Frances Lobb. Howard Fertig, 1975.

Mussolini, Rachele, with Albert Zarca, *Mussolini: An Intimate Biography by His Widow*. William Morrow, 1974.

Murphy, Robert, *Diplomat among Warriors*. Greenwood Press, 1964.

Noether, Emiliana, "Mussolini and d'Annunzio: A Strange Friendship." *Cesare Barbieri Courier*. The Cesare Barbieri Center of Italian Studies, Trinity College, 1980.

Nolte, Ernst, *Three Faces of Fascism*. Holt, Rinehart and Winston, 1966.

Origo, Iris, *War in Val D'Orcia: A Diary*. Edinburgh: The Traveller's Library, 1951.

Packard, Reynolds and Eleanor, *Balcony Empire: Fascist Italy at War*. Oxford University Press, 1942.

Parrish, Thomas, ed., *The Simon and Schuster Encyclopedia of World War II*. Simon and Schuster, 1978.

Passingham, M. B., "Italy's Challengers." *Wings*, Vol. 6, Part 77. London: Orbis, 1978.

Petacco, Arrigo:
    La Seconda Guerra Mondiale. Rome: Armando Curcio Editore, no date.
    Storia del Fascismo, Vols. 1 and 2. Rome: Armando Curcio Editore, no date.

Pisano, Giorgio, *Storia della Guerra Civile, 1943-1945*, 3 vols. Milan: Properieta Literraria, 1965.

Playfair, I. S. O., et al., *The Mediterranean and Middle East*. 6 vols. London: Her Majesty's Stationery Office, 1966.

Potts, Thomas, "L'Operazione Cinzano." *Aerospace Historian*, March 1981.

Rhodes, Anthony, *Propaganda, The Art of Persuasion: World War II*. Ed. by Victor Margolin. Chelsea House Publishers, 1976.

Ricci, Corrado, and Christopher F. Shores, *La Guerra Aerea nella Africa Orientale, 1940-1941*. Ed. by Ufficio Storico, Stato Maggiore Aeronautica, Rome. Modena, Italy: S.T.E.M.-Mucchi, 1980.

Rommel, Erwin, *The Rommel Papers*. Ed. by B. H. Liddell Hart. Harcourt Brace, 1953.

Saitta, Armando, *Del Fascismo alla Resistenza*. Florence: La Nuova Italia, 1961.

Salvatorelli, Luigi, and Giovanni Mira, *Storia d'Italia nel Periodo Fascista*. Torino, Italy: Guilio Einaudi, 1964.

Salvemini, Gaetano, *The Origins of Fascism in Italy*. Ed. by Roberto Vivarelli. Harper & Row, 1973.

Santoro, Giuseppe, *L'Aeronautica Italiana nella Seconda Guerra Mondiale*. Vols. 1 and 2. Rome: Edizioni Esse, 1957.

Seaton, Albert, *The Russo-German War: 1941-1945*. Praeger Publishers, 1971.

Segrè, Claudio G.:
    "Douhet in Italy: Prophet without Honor?" *Aerospace Historian*, June 1979.
    "Fascism as Fiefdoms: Balbo, Mussolini and the Totalitarian State." *Cesare Barbieri Courier*. The Cesare Barbieri Center of Italian Studies, Trinity College, 1980.

Shaw, John, and the Editors of Time-Life Books, *Red Army Resurgent* (World War II series). Time-Life Books, 1979.

Shepard, Eric, *A Short History of the British Army*. London: Constable, 1950.

Shirer, William L., *The Rise and Fall of the Third Reich*. Simon and Schuster, 1960.

Skorzeny, Otto, *Meine Kommandounternehmen*. Munich: Limes Verlag, 1976.

Snyder, Louis L., *The War: A Concise History, 1939-1945*. Julian Messner, 1960.

Stern, Mario Rigoni, *The Sergeant in the Snow*. Transl. by Archibald Colquhoun. London: MacGibbon & Kee, 1954.

Sykes, Christopher, *Orde Wingate: A Biography*. World Publishing, 1959.

Tannenbaum, Edward R., *The Fascist Experience: Italian Society and Culture, 1922-1945*. Basic Books, 1972.

Thompson, Jonathan W., *Italian Civil and Military Aircraft: 1930-1945*. Aero Publishers, 1963.

Toland, John, *Adolf Hitler*. Doubleday, 1976.

Tompkins, Peter, *Italy Betrayed*. Simon and Schuster, 1966.

Vita di Mussolini. Edizioni di "Novissma," 1965.

Webster, Richard A., *The Cross and the Fasces*. Stanford University Press, 1960.

Zangrandi, Ruggero, *Il Lungo Viaggio Attraverso il Fascismo*. Milan: Feltrinelli, 1962.

PICTURE CREDITS

Credits from left to right are separated by semicolons, from top to bottom by dashes.

ACKNOWLEDGMENTS

For help given in the preparation of this book, the editors wish to express their gratitude to Nino Arena, Rome; William P. Bird, Reston, Virginia; Colonel Oreste Bovio, Ufficio Storico, Stato Maggiore Esercito, Rome; Countess Maria Fede Caproni, Museo Aeronautico Caproni di Taliedo, Rome; General Flavio Danieli, Italian Air Force (Ret.), Rome; Charles F. Delzell, Nashville, Tennessee; Brigadier General Vittoriano Giachini, Air and Defense Attaché, Italian Embassy, Washington, D.C.; Giordano Bruno Guerri, Milan; Donald S. Lopez, Chairman, Aeronautics Department, National Air & Space Museum, Washington, D.C.; Maurizio Pagliano, Milan; Senator Giorgio Pisanò, Milan; Eugene C. Provenzano, Rochester, New York; Colonel Cesare Pucci, Military Attaché, Italian Embassy, Washington, D.C.; Riccardo Sarti, Italian Aerospace Industries, Arlington, Virginia; Captain Achille Zanoni, Naval Attaché, Italian Embassy, Washington, D.C.

The index for this book was prepared by Nicholas J. Anthony.

INDEX

Numerals in italics indicate an illustration of the subject mentioned.

A

Addis Ababa, 32, 92, 97, 99-101, 143
Aduwa, 20, 30, 32
Africa campaigns. *See* East Africa campaign; North Africa campaign
Agordat, 91, 96
Agricultural production, 11
Agrigento, *181*
Air raids, 155-156, *172-173*, 174, *176-179*
Airborne operations: Allied, 159-160; German, 105, 164; Italian, *70-89*, 105
Aircraft: armament and bombloads, 72, 76, 79-80, *82*, 83-84, 86; cargo-transport, 80, *81*; production, 27, 72-86
Aircraft types: Ansaldo C-3, *70-71*; Cant Z.501 Seagull, *78-79*; Cant Z.506B Heron, 78, *79*; Cant Z.511, 78; Cant Z.1007 Kingfisher, *84-85*; Fiat BR.20 Stork, *82-83*, 84; Fiat CR.42 Falcon, 72, *74-75*, *81*, 91, *116*; Fiat G.50 Arrow, *76*; Fiat G.55 Centaur, *76*; Imam Ro.43 floatplane, *78*; Macchi MC.200 Thunderbolt, *76*, *77*; Macchi MC.202 Lightning, *76*, *77*; Macchi MC.205 Greyhound, *76*; Martin B-26 Marauder, *172-173*; Me-110, *76*; P-40 Warhawk, *77*; P.108B, *72*, *103*; SM.79 Sparrowhawk, *73*, *86-89*; SM.82 Kangaroo, *80-81*
Albania, invasion of, *38*, 39, 62-63, 65
Alfieri, Dino, 63
Allied invasion, *142*, 143, 146, 154, 159-161, 167-170, 174, *175*, 196
Amba Alagi, 99
Ambrosio, Vittorio, 140-141, *143*, 155
Antiaircraft defenses, 64
Aosta, Duke of, 91, *92*, 94-97, 99-101
Aprilia, *10-11*
Ardeatine Caves massacre, 168
Askaris. *See* Italy, Army of
Asmara, 91-92, 97, *98*
Athens, 63
Atrocities by Germans, *168*, 174, 179, 188, *189*, *194-195*
Audisio, Walter ("Colonel Valerio"), 171
Austria, independence of, *19*, 28-30, 35

B

Badoglio, Pietro: in Ethiopia, 32, 101; flight of, 161, 166; government exercised by, 139, 156, 166-167, 169; on military readiness, 22, 39, 59; and Mussolini appointments, 57; Soviet recognition of, 168-169; and surrender and cobelligerency, 158-160
Bagnolini, 41
Baionetta, 160
Balbo, Italo, 25, 27, 36, *37*, 54, 132
Balearic Islands, 33, 141
Balkans region, 163
Bardia, 64
Bartolommeo Colleoni, 52
Bastianini, Giuseppe, 142
Beda Littoria, 132
Belaia, 94
Belgium, bases in, *74-75*, 83
Berbera, 91, 95
Berberi, Pietro, *45*
Bianchi, Michele, 26
Bismarck, Otto von, II, 141
Black market, 135-136, 167, 179, *183*
Bologna, *188*, *190-191*, 196, *200-201*
Bolzano, *162-163*
Bonetti, Mario, 97
Bonomi, Ivanoe, 169

Bottai, Giuseppe, 54, 57, 68, 133, 139
Brambilla-Carminati, Giulia, 68
Brenner Pass, 35, 40-41, 69
Brig's Peak, 96
Brindisi, 160-161, 166
Britain, Battle of, *82-83*
British Army, 64, 90-97, 104-105
British Broadcasting Corporation, 137
Broadcasting, control of, 137
Buffarini-Guidi, Guido, 68, 133
Bug River, 102, 120
Burye, 97-98

C

Calabria, 52
Calypso, 41
Cameron Ridge, 96
Camouflage, *81*, *84-85*
Campbell, Ronald Hugh, 158
Canterbury, Archbishop of, 27
Capalbio, 57
Cape Bon, 88, 143
Cape Spada, Battle of, 52-53
Casablanca, 134
Cassibile, 159
Cassino, *175*, 192
Castellano, Giuseppe, 158-159
Casualties: Army, 64, 97-98, *130-131*, 139, 162, 167; civilian, 64, 156, 161-164, 168, 180; German, 168, *192*; Jews, 161-164; Navy, 161
Catholic Church, relations with, 8, *14-15*
Caucasus region, 120, 138
Cavallero, Ugo, 58, 68-69, 105, 139-140
Censorship, 65-66, 104
Chamberlain, Neville, 35, *82*
Cheesman, Robert E., 90
Churchill, Winston, 8, 27, 41, 133, 158, 188
Cianetti, Tullio, 166
Ciano, Galeazzo, *37*, 104; on Africa campaign, 53, 64; and Albania, 38; and Cinema City, 12; and colonies, 91; and Czechoslovakia, 38; financial enterprises, 68, 137; and France, attack on, 22, 25, 41; and German alliance, 38-39, 139; and Greece invasion, 62; loyalty questioned, 68; and Malta, 105; Mussolini evaluated by, 56; and Mussolini's removal, 139, 155-156, 165-166; on Petacci's influence, 68; political career, 36; removal by Mussolini, 140; on riots, 65; trial and execution, 165, *166*
Cinema City (Cinecittà), *12*, *13*, 65
Clothing shortages, *112*, 135, *136*
Cobelligerent status, 158-160, 166-167
Collaborators, *198-199*
Colonies, acquisition of, 30, 32, 108
Communists, gains by, 139-140
Como, 171
Conte Biancamano, *19*
Conte di Cavour, 64
Cornell, Julien, 157
Corriere della Sera, 165
Cuneo, 188, *191*
Cunningham, Alan, 93-95, 97, 99
Czechoslovakia, 35, 38, 40

D

Daladier, Édouard, 35
Dambacha, 98
D'Annunzio, Gabriele, *36*
De Bono, Emilio, 25-26, 30, 32, *36*, 166
Debra Markos, 98-99
Denmark, 41
Deserters, 95, 98, 162, *186-187*
De Simone, Carlo, 94-95, 98-99
De Vecchi, Cesare Maria, 25, 36
Diredawa, 95, 97
Dnieper River, 102, 120, *123*

Dniester River, 120
Dollfuss, Engelbert, 30
Don River, *118-119*, 120, 125, *127*, 128, 131, 139
Donets basin, 120, 126
Dongo, 171
Dongolaas Gorge, 95-96
Duilio, 64
Durazzo, *38*, 62

E

East Africa campaign, 90-92, *map* 93, 94-101
Eboli, *184-185*
Economy, deterioration of, 23-24, 32-33, 39, 61, 65, 104, 108, *109-115*, 134-136, 167
Eden, Anthony, 31, 99
Egypt, drive on, 62, 97, 104-105, 132
Eisenhower, Dwight D., 159-160
El Alamein, Battle of, 132, 134
El Wak, 93-94
Elena, Queen of Italy, 33
Eliot, T. S., 157
Empire Guillemot, *88-89*
Eritrea, 30, 90-91, *map* 93, 95-97
Essen, 33
Ethiopia, campaigns in, 18, *19-21*, 30-31, 59, 72, 90-92, *map* 93, 95, 97-101, 108, 143
Exile system, 67, 68

F

Facta, Luigi, 25
Farida, Luisa, *199*
Farinacci, Roberto, 36, *37*, 58-59, 69, 135, 139, 141, 155
Fascist Party: decline in popularity, 65, 155; dissension in, 68, 139; excesses of officials, 137-138; executions by, 165-166; founding, 24-25; and Mussolini's removal, 155-156; research, resistance to, 61; restoration of, 165; revolt against, 139-141, 180; terrorism by, 26, 66, 143, 165; treason trials, *166*; weaknesses in, 53-54
Fascist Youth, *16-17*, 26, *106-107*, *112-113*, *136*
Favignana Island, 67
Feltre, 155, 164
Fermi, Enrico, 60
Ferrara, 60
Florence, 62, *172-173*, *196-197*
Flying bomb, 86
Food supplies and shortages, 61, 65, 104, *114-115*, 134-135, 167, 179-180, *182-183*
Fort Dologorodoc, 96
Fort Emmanuel, 98
France, attack on, *22-23*, *24*, 40-41
Franco, Francisco, 33, 58
François-Poncet, André, 23
Freemasons, 146, *148*
Frost, Robert, 157
Frusci, Luigi, 91, 95-97
Fuel shortages, 61, 108-109, 111, 134-135

G

Gaeta, 160
Galimberti, Tancredi, 188
Gallabat, 91
Gardiner, William T., 160
Gargano, 165
Garibaldi, Giuseppe, 69
Gasparri, Pietro, 14, *15*
Gaudenzi, Pietro, *45*
Gebel el Akhdar, 69
Genoa, 64-65, 196
Germany: alliance with Italy, *1*, 8, 23, 34, 38-41, 154-155; military aid from, 39-41, 155
Germany, Army of: airborne operations, 105; atrocities by, 167, *168*, 174, 179, 188, *189*, *194-195*; casualties, 168, *192*; occupation

and exploitation by, 69, 143, 146, 160-162, 164-165, 167-168, 173, *174*, 179, *189*, 190-197; operations controlled by, 155, 158, 160-161; prisoners lost, 104, 143, 196-197; surrender in Italy, 170-171. *See also* Hitler, Adolf

Gibraltar, 61, 141
Gideon Force, 93, 97-98
Giovanni delle Bande Nere, 52
Gojjam Province, 97
Gold Coast troops. *See* British Army
Gold-collection campaign, *33*
Gondar, 95, 99
Göring, Hermann, *140*, 170
Gorla, Giuseppe, 55, 140
Gothic Line, 169
Gottardi, Luciano, *166*
Graft, 60, 68-69
Gran Sasso d'Italia, 164
Grandi, Dino, 36, *37*, 133, 139, 155-156
Graziani, Rodolfo, 53, 58, 64, 102
Greece, invasion of, 62, *63*, 68-69, 102, 143
Guariglia, Raffaele, 159
Gulf of Suez, 97

H

Haile Selassie, 31-32, 90, 92-93, *95*, 99-101
Hailu, Ras, 98-99
Hammarskjöld, Dag, 157
Harar, 95
Hassell, Ulrich von, 28, 41
Havock, 52
Hemingway, Ernest, 157
Himmler, Heinrich, 133-134, 136, 143, 161
Hitler, Adolf: and Africa campaign, 102, 104-105, 134; assassination attempt on, 170; and Austria, 28-30, 35; conscription decreed by, 31; and Czechoslovakia, 35, 38, 40; and Egypt, 132; France, campaign against, 40-41; and Greece, 63, 69, 102; and Italian capitulation, 154-155, 158, 160; and Italy as ally, 40-41, 134; and Italy, occupation of, 143, *174*; and Malta, 105; Mussolini evaluated by, 38-39; Mussolini, influence on, 38-41, 63-64, 66, 102, 141-142, 155, 161, 165, 170; Mussolini, meetings with, 28, 33, *34*, 35, 40-41, 62, 102, 138, *140*, 141-143, 155, 169-170; Mussolini, mutual emulation, 27-28, 34-36; Mussolini rescued by, 164-165; physical decline, 141; and Poland, 38-39; and resistance forces, 168, 192; and Soviet Union invasion, 101-102, 104, 120, 138-139, 142; and Sudetenland, 35, 40. *See also* Germany; Germany, Army of

Hoare, Samuel, 158
Humbert, Crown Prince, 169

I

Ibis, 160
Illustrious, 64
Imports, reliance on, 108-109, 112, 134-136
Indian troops. *See* British Army
Industrial production, 61-62, 65
Inflation, 65, 134-136
Informers, use of, 65, 67-68
Innsbruck, 35
Isbuschenski steppe, *124-125*
Italian Social Republic. *See* Salò Republic
Italy, Air Force of: aircraft strength and losses, 39, 59, *72-89*, 90, 92, 95; combat effectiveness, 58, 72, 154; interservice rivalry, 61; modernization program, 27, 70-72; operations by, 53, *72-89*, 91; radio and radar, lack of, 74; rescue missions, 78; training programs, *80-81*. *See also* Balbo, Italo
Italy, Army of, *100-101*; airborne operations,

80-81, 105; armored operations, 92; artillery assaults, 94; artillery strength, 99; bicycle troops, *38*; Black Shirt units, 59; casualties, 64, 97-98, *130-131*, 139, 162, 167; cavalry operations, *118-119*, 120, *124-125*; chaplains, *14-15*; as cobelligerent, *169*; combat effectiveness, 1, 22-23, 38-39, 41, 58-59, 62-63, 90-91, 99-102, 139, 154; command structure, 59; demolitions by, 94, 96; deserters, 95, 98, 162, *186-187*; engineer operations, 94, *122*; German treatment of, 139, 141-142, 150, 162; interservice rivalry, 61; mining operations, 96; modernization program, 27, *28-29*, 38; morale status, 59, 68, 93, 95, 98, 154; poison-gas use, 31-32; prisoners captured by, *127*; prisoners lost, 64, 97, 134, 139, 143, *162-163*; ski troops, *128*; supply operations and captures, 59, 61-64, 92, 102, 104, 120, 122, *126-127*, 128, 131, 139, 141; training programs, 17, *19*, 26, 59; troop strength, 90, 93, 96, 98-99; weapons and equipment, *19*, *28-29*, 58-59, 64, 91-92, 95, 97, 101-102, 120, 128, *129*, 131, 139
Italy, Navy of: casualties, 161; combat effectiveness, 59, 61, 154; interservice rivalry, 61; modernization program, 27; oil and equipment shortages, 61; operations by, 41, 52-53, 97, 105; radar, lack of, 61; surrender, 161; training programs, 61; warship strength and losses, 53, 59, 64, 97, 161
Italy. *See* Fascist Party; Mussolini, Benito

J

Jambare Mangasha, 93
Japan, alliance with, 104
Jelib, 94
Jews, persecution of, 34-35, *60*, 66, 146, 157, 161
Jijiga, 95
Jodl, Alfred, 160
Juba River, 94
Judicial system, 66-68
Jumbo, 94

K

Kalamos River, 62
Kappler, Herbert, 161
Kassala, 91
Kenya, 90-91, *map 93*
Keren, 92, 95-97
Kesselring, Albert, 105, 155, 161
Khartoum, 90, 97
Kismayu, 94

L

La Maddalena Island, 164
La Spezia, *70-71*, 164
La Stampa, 136
Lake Bracciano, 164
Lake Como, 171
Lake Garda, 165
Lake Tana, 97
Lateran Accords (1929), 8, 14-15, 46
League of Nations, 32, 108
Leros Island, 52
Levi, Carlo, 68
Libya campaign, *53*, 64, 102, 104
Life, 157
Lipari Islands, 66
Little Saint Bernard Pass, 41
Littorio, 64
Loffredo, Renato, 96
Luce, Clare Boothe, 157
Luftwaffe, operations by, 68, 104-105, 161
L'Unità, 139-140

M

MacLeish, Archibald, 157
Makale, 32
Malaparte, Curzio, 68
Maletti, Pietro, 64
Malta, 64, 104-105
Manchester Guardian, 8
Marconi, Guglielmo, 61
Marinelli, Giovanni, *166*
Marzabotta, 195
Massawa, 30, 91-92, 97, 99
Massock, Richard, 63, 65
Matsuoka, Yosuke, *104*
Maugeri, Franco, 52-53, 59, 61, 64, 137, 160
Mayne, Ashton G., 99
Menaggio, 171
Menton, *24*, 41
Mera River, 33
Mersa Matruh, 53
Messe, Giovanni, 102, 120
Milan, 33, 61, 64-65, *114-115*, 140, *167, 176-177, 180-181, 183*, 196, *199*
Military aid programs, 59
Military government, 166
Military indoctrination, *16-17*
Modena, *198*
Mogadishu, 94-95
Monte Cassino, 167
Monte Lungo, *169*
Montgomery, Bernard L., 159
Morale status, 40, 58-59, 64-65, 68, 93, 95, 98, 133-134, 154
Moscow, drive on, 104
Mount Etna, 26
Mount Vesuvius, *77*
Mussolini, Benito, *42-48, 100-101*; administrative routine, *54*, 55, 57-58; and Africa campaigns, 64, 105, 132-134, *135*, 138, 141; and air power, 53, 59; on air raids, 65; and Albania invasion, 38-39; and Allied invasion, 143; and armed-forces modernization, 26-27, 38, 53-54, 58; and Austria, 28-30, 35; and Balearic Islands, 141; and Battle of Britain, 83; and black market, 135; and Catholic Church, 8, 14, *15*, 46; and Christmas, 104; and Cinema City, 12, *13*; conceit, 26, 44, 55; and Czechoslovakia, 35, 38, 40; and Denmark, 41; early career, 23-24, 44; and Ethiopia, 18, 30-31, 90-91, 99, 108, 143; evaluations of, 8, 27, 38-39, 56; expansionist program, 18-19, 30-33, 38, 41; family and private life, *42-51, 103, 137*, 171; in Fascist Party founding, 24-25; flight and execution, 170-171; and France, attack on, 22-23, 40-41; and German support, 38-41, 91, 154-155; German surveillance of, 68, 133-134, 136, 143; and Gibraltar, 141; governments formed by, 25-26, *27*, 36, 139-140, 146, 150, 152, 165-167, 188; graft, attitude toward, 68; and Greece invasion, 62-63, 102; Hitler's evaluation of, 8, 23; Hitler's emulation of, 27-28, 34-36; Hitler's influence on, 38-41, 63-64, 66, 102, 141-142, 155, 161, 165, 170; Hitler, meetings with, 28, 33, *34*, 35, 40-41, 62, 102, 138, *140*, 141-143, 155, 169-170; Hitler's rescue of, 164-165; on imports, 108; and Japanese alliance, 104; Jews, persecution of, 34-35, 60, 161; and judicial system, 66; loyalty to, *1*, 6-21, 26, 28, 35, 63, *142*; and Malta, 105; and material shortages, 61; and military air programs, 59; morale, stress on, 58; news manipulation by, 55-56, 104, 137-138, 143; and Norway, 41; and Pantelleria, 143; physical decline, 133, 141, 165; and Poland, 39-40; political miscalculations, 23, 30; political and social reforms by, 8, 11, 14, 24-27; posturing by, 11, *18-19*, 28, *45*, 132-

133, *167;* as Prime Minister, 11, 25, *47;* public-works projects, *9-13,* 61-62; and rationing, 65; removal, 139-143, 146, 154-158, *170,* 171, 174, 180, *184-185,* 188, 198; and resistance forces, 192; and Roosevelt's death, 170; and Salò Republic, 165-166, 170, 188; and sanctions, 108; and secret weapons, 61; and Soviet Union invasion, 101-102, 120, 138-139, 141; and Spanish Civil War, 33, 58; subordinates, relations with, 36, 54, 57-59; successors considered, 139; as supreme commander, 53, 61, 155-156; surrender attempt, 170-171; on technology, 61; and United Kingdom, 31; United States, war on, 104; war aims, 53-54, 91, 101; war record, *44;* women, relations with, 44, 48-49, 51, 56-57, 116, 137-138
Mussolini, Bruno, *46,* 102, *103,* 171
Mussolini, Edda, *103,* 166
Mussolini, Rachele, *33, 46-47,* 165, 171
Mussolini, Vittorio, 44, *103,* 170
Muti, Ettore, 36, *37*

N
Naples, 59, 64-65, 167, *168, 170,* 174, *178-179, 183*
Nasi, Guglielmo, 91, 98-99
News, control of, 55-56, 104, 137-138, 143
Nice, 41
Nigerian troops. *See* British Army
Normandy campaign, 158
North Africa campaign, 53, 62, 64, 68-69, 75-77, 80, 97, 102, 104-105, 132-134, 138, 141, 143
Norway, 41

O
Oil shortages, 61, 108-109, 111, 134-135
Oran, 134
Osborne, D'Arcy, 158
Ostia, *42-43*
OVRA, 66, 135, 155

P
Packard, Eleanor and Reynolds, 59, 62, 135-136
Pantelleria, 143
Pareschi, Carlo, *166*
Partisan groups. *See* Resistance forces
Paul II, Pope, 55
Pavese, Cesare, 68
Pavolini, Alessandro, 166
Pescara, 161
Pesenti, Gustavo, 94
Petacci, Clara, *51,* 56-57, 68, 133, 137-138, 165, 171, 198
Petacci, Marcello, 68
Petacci, Myriam, 138
Pétain, Philippe, 41
Pilferage, 167
Pirandello, Luigi, 112
Pisa, *103*
Pius XI, Pope, 34-35
Pius XII, Pope, 155-156, 161
Piva, Gustavo, 138
Platt, William, 91, 95-97
Poison gas: defense against, *31;* use, 31-32
Poland, 38-40
Police forces and measures, 65-66
Political indoctrination, *16-17, 26*
Political parties, 168-169, 196-198
Poltava, *122*
Pomezia, 9
Pontine Marshes, *9,* 11
Ponza Island, 164
Poole Harbour, 90
Pound, Ezra, *157*

Pratica del Mare, 164
Pricolo, Francesco, 58
Propaganda campaigns, *57,* 58-59, *60,* 63, 65-66, 90, 108, 136-137, *138, 144-153,* 157
Public-works projects, *9-13,* 61-62
Puntoni, Paolo, 156

R
Radar, lack of, 61, 74
Raeder, Erich, 105
Rapallo, *157*
Rastenburg, 102, 138-139, 164
Rationing, 65, 104, 111, *114-115,* 134-136
Recreation facilities, 65, *138*
Recruiting campaigns, *150-152*
Reggio di Calabria, 159
Resistance forces: casualties, 188, 196; formation, 67, 139, 188; operations by, 167, 169-171, *188, 190-193,* 195, *196-201;* political parties in, 168-169, *191,* 196; strength, 167, 169, 190, 195; supply system, 190
Rhodesian troops. *See* British Army
Ribbentrop, Joachim von, 38, 40, 170
Riccardi, Arturo, 57
Riccione, *48,* 133
Ridgway, Matthew B., 159-160
Rionero Sannitico, 188
Riots, 65-66, *180-181*
Ritchie, Neil, 105
Roma, 161
Rome, 6-8, *12, 18-19, 20-21, 28-29,* 40, 65, 68, *104, 106-107, 110-111, 114-115, 136, 138,* 155-156, 159-161, 169, *174,* 180, *199*
Rommel, Erwin, 69, 102, 104-105, 132, 161
Roosevelt, Franklin D., 23, 170
Rosselli, Carlo, 68
Royal Air Force, 63-65, 91, 95, 97, 99, 104
Royal Navy, 41, 52-53, 77, 88, 95, 104
Rumania, 61

S
Salerno, 161
Salò Republic, 165-167, 170, 188
Salvage drives, 33, 112-113
Salzburg, 39, *140,* 141-143
Sanchil, 96
Sanctions invoked, 32, 108
Sandford, Daniel, 93, 95
Sardinia, 143
Sarfatti, Margherita, 26, *50,* 51
Schuster, Cardinal, 170
Scorza, Carlo, 143, 156
Sebastiani, Osvaldo, 69
Senise, Carmine, 58, 133, 140-141, 143
Serafimovich, 126
Serena, Adelchi, 68
Shipping losses, *99,* 104, 141
Sicily campaign, *142,* 143, 154, 160, 174
Sidi Barrani, 64
Siena, 31
Skorzeny, Otto, 164
Slim, William, 91
Smith, Walter Bedell, 159
Somaliland, 30, 41, 90-91, *map* 93, 94
South African troops. *See* British Army
South Tyrol region, 165
Soviet Union: and Badoglio government, 168-169; invasion of, *100-101,* 102, 104, *118-131,* 138-139, 141
Spain, civil war in, 33, 58, *72*
Speer, Albert, 39
Stalingrad campaign, 120, 138-139
Starace, Achille, 36, *37,* 59, 68
Steffens, Lincoln, 27
Stevens, Edmund, 98
Strait of Messina tunnel, 62
Strikes, 140-141, 143, 169, 174

Strong, Kenneth D., 159
Student, Kurt, 105
Sudan campaign, 90-91, *map* 93
Sudetenland, 35, 40
Suez Canal, 31-32, 53, 61, 92, 132
Surrender proceedings, 158-160, 162, 170-171, 174
Sydney, 52

T
Tanganyika, 91
Taranto, 64, 161
Tassinari, Giuseppe, 68
Taylor, Maxwell D., 160
Terminillo, *48*
Terrorism campaigns, *26,* 66, 143, 165
Tiengo, Carlo, 140
Tobruk, 64, 77, 104-105, *135*
Togliatti, Palmiro, 169
Togni, Renato, 92
Toselli Pass, 99
Transportation system, 65, *109-111*
Treason trials, 157, *166*
Trento, 64
Trieste, *194-195*
Tripoli, 52, 104, 132
Tunis, 143
Tunisia campaign, 41, 134, 141, 143
Turin, 61, 64, *116,* 140, 174, 180, *197*

U
Ukraine campaign, 102, *120, 123*
Um Iddla, 92
Uman, 102
Unemployment, 65
United Kingdom: air operations against, *74-75, 82-83;* naval talks with Germany, 31; relations with, 40; shipping losses, *88-89*
United States, 104, 158

V
Valenti, Osvaldi, *199*
Valerio, Colonel (Walter Audisio), 171
Velletri, 27
Venezia Giulia, 165
Venice, *31,* 174, 196, *197*
Ventotene Island, 164
Verona, *100-101,* 165
Victor Emmanuel III, *19;* and attack on France, 41; and cobelligerency, 166-167; and Ethiopia, 32; flight and abdication, *160,* 161, 166, 169; hostility toward, 146, 156; and Jews, persecution of, 34; and Mussolini's removal, 133, 154, 156-158, 174, 188; relations with Mussolini, 25; and surrender proceedings, 158
Vidussoni, Aldo, 143
Villa Rosa, *142*
Visconti-Prasca, Sebastiano, 57, 62-63
Voice of America, 137
Voroshilovgrad, 138

W
Wages, control of, 65, 135
Wal Wal, 31
Wingate, Orde, 93, 95, 97-101
Wolff, Karl, 170
Women: in industry, 108, *116-117;* in resistance forces, 167
Woodbridge, *83*
Work force, shortages in, 108

Y
Yonte, 94
Youth, indoctrination of, *16-17, 26*

Z
Zulu, 77